For Dad

CONTENTS

INTRODUCTION

The story begins on 23rd April 2003, a gentle Mancunian spring evening.

After being humbled 3-1, and given a footballing lesson *par excellence* from a majestic Zinedine Zidane inspired Real Madrid at the *Bernabéu* in the European Cup quarter-final first leg. Manchester United's battling, but ultimately doomed attempts to pull back the deficit had ended in despair at Old Trafford. Nevertheless a wonderfully flowing match finished 4-3 for the home side. Yet the everlasting memory was not David Beckham's thunderously hit free kick, nor Luis Figo's mesmeric sleight of foot. It was a substitution that occurred in the sixty-seventh minute, when 66,000 people at Old Trafford rose to movingly applaud the magnificent Brazilian Ronaldo off the field.

Suddenly it became clear that within the genes of these two great clubs there exists a very special mutual respect; one that has stretched across generations. For despite Ronaldo's sensational hat-trick that sent them crashing from the European Cup, the United supporters still found it in their hearts to acknowledge the sheer brilliance of this sharp-shooting *Madrileño*.

Even the Madrid directors present shook their heads in astonishment at this marvellous tribute from the United crowd. Watching on proudly were two old warriors of Manchester United and Real Madrid; men whose lives had been interwoven with the grand histories of these two legendary footballing institutions. Bobby Charlton and Alfredo Di Stefano. But where did this bond of friendship come from? To understand you have to go back to the very birth of the competition which made both clubs famous, for this is the tale of two cities.

THE BLOND ARROW

Don Santiago Bernabéu was a man driven by an all consuming vision. He envisaged a footballing Camelot carved out of white marble, reaching high into the Madrid heavens. Blessed with the vision and wealth to create such beauty, Bernabéu sought out knights of sufficient quality to defend its walls. The call went forth and an open cheque book lured the best of the best. Soon the white knights began to gather under the Madrileño's banner. And yet, despite such riches, Bernabéu sought that little extra - the spark to flame the fire and ignite an inferno. Rumour reached him of a footballer blessed with a remarkable talent in the relative backwaters of the Colombian league. Argentine born Alfredo Di Stefano...

In 1948 a mass players strike in Argentina forced the cream of the country's talent to ply their talents elsewhere. It was a bitter dispute which ripped the Argentine game apart and saw an exodus of talent. The peso-rich Millonarios of Colombia, owned by a cartel of rich local businessmen, took advantage offering tax free wages. Foremost on Millonarios' wish list was emergent River Plate superstar Alfredo Di Stefano. A young man wise beyond his years and worldly enough to understand his own value, Alfredo did not lack the slightest belief in his inestimable talent - Di Stefano always demanded top dollar and got it.

Born 4th July 1926, to Southern Italian parents, originally from Capri, his family owned a small farm in Barracas on the outskirts of Buenos Aires. Legend has it that the heavy workload placed on Alfredo's young shoulders attributed to his legendary stamina. Talent spotted by River at fifteen, Di Stefano made his professional début a year on and so began a tale set to be written into the annals of footballing legend.

Here was a staggeringly talented player whose gifts were so immense that few on first viewing them, believed their eyes. To give Di Stefano a position seemed preposterous, for his movement across the pitch meant it akin to attempting to catch the wind. Blinding ball control, ferocious speed and acceleration together with tactical awareness and the ability to find team-mates with passes so perfect they arrived with their name carved upon them - this was Di Stefano.

A hugely impressive forty-nine goals in sixty-nine appearances for *La Banda Roja (the Red Stripe)* followed. Once the strike broke out, the twenty-three year old Di Stefano bade farewell to boyhood dreams and chased the dollar. Di Stefano drove a hard bargain and took huge advantage of the Colombian's desire for a dream team. Not daring to lose him, Di Stefano quickly became the club's heartbeat. He was expensive but worth it. For five years the Argentine earned fortunes in Millonarios' colours. Such talent, though, could not go unnoticed forever and an impressive showing in a club tournament played at Real Madrid's *Chamartin* stadium first brought him to the attention of Real's ambitious President. Alfredo Di Stefano scored twice in a jaw-dropping performance as the Colombians thrashed the home side 4-2. Sensing the need for a general to lead his troops on the field, Bernabéu acted fast.

Don Santiago sent his fixer Raimondo Saporta to convince Di Stefano that his future lay in Madrid. Armed with a suitcase full of money and the promise of footballing immortality in the imperial white shirt, Saporta arrived in Bogotá and swiftly sought out Di Stefano. Unbeknown to Saporta there was another equally desperate emissary who sought Di Stefano's services who had been present at the very same tournament where the Argentine had glittered - FC Barcelona's legendary former player and coach, and now chief scout, Pepe Samiter.

Barca despised Real Madrid, Santiago Bernabéu and everything they stood for. Representatives of FC Barcelona arrived in Colombia determined to land their target and put one over General Franco's favourite plaything. Catalonia had suffered intolerably under the wrath of Franco's jackboot nationalism; their flag and native language was banned and people paid the price for a brave but ultimate disastrous stand against him in the civil war. To rip Di Stefano from Real's grasp at the last would have been a sweet victory.

A transfer wrangle now took place with both sides offering treasures but neither able to land Di Stefano's signature. For who owned him? Whilst Barcelona reached an agreement with River Plate, Real cut a deal with Millonarios. *FIFA* stepped in to claim that Barca had won the race, only for Spain's Ministry of Sport, General Jose Moscardó, a leading figure in the Franco regime, to suddenly introduce a new rule banning foreign players in Spain.

The timing could not be ignored – the Catalans would not be allowed such riches. Behind closed doors a plan was hatched. Another biased ruling from the plotting Moscardó would be declared. Di Stefano was to be exempted from this ban if he should play alternate seasons in Barcelona and Madrid. A chaotic period ensued with each side finding legal loopholes to prevent the other succeeding before finally, under orders from Moscardó, the Spanish FA acted in offering Solomon like advice to solve an intolerable stand-off. Alfredo Di Stefano would play two seasons apiece with each.

Moscardó felt he had good reason to make the Catalans suffer, his soul remained forever scarred from events that occurred amid the savagery of the civil war. Even though the bullets had ceased to fire he remained a man still seething with those whom had cause him untold grief.

During the 1936 seventy-day siege of Alcázar in Southern

Spain in which Nationalist forces, commanded by Moscardó, held out against overwhelming Republican numbers, a tragic scenario occurred for the General. One that was every Father's nightmare. Day after day, the then Colonel sent out daily radio reports: "Sin novedad en el Alcázar" - "Nothing new at the Alcázar" - a defiance which served to lift the spirits of Franco's supporters and inflame Republican forces who had launched and lost hundreds of lives on the assault of the town.

Then, on 23rd July, the attackers struck lucky with the capture of Moscardó's sixteen-year old son Luis. In a conflict that saw unspeakable atrocities performed by both sides, what followed was just another barbaric act in a country that had gone mad. A Republican political officer telephoned Moscardó in the besieged town to inform him that unless he surrendered Alcázar, Luis would be executed by firing squad. Suddenly the line went quiet before Moscardó came on and asked to speak to his son?

Legend has it that he said, "Luis, commend your soul to God and die like a patriot."

"I can do that Father," answered the boy before he signed off with a passionate scream of "Long live Spain!" Shortly after, in reprisal for an air raid, Luis Moscardó was shot dead. Finally, when the siege of Alcázar was lifted, Colonel Moscardó was purported to have greeted the relief force's commander with the poignant words,

"I have lost my son but saved the garrison." Then, standing stiffly to attention, he reported, "No change to report in Alcázar.'"

For this sacrifice Moscardó was promoted to General and the fate of his kin and the defence of Alcázar became a famous symbol of Francoist Spain. Knowing the invaluable power of propaganda, Franco authorised Moscardó to wear a special black cloak of mourning over his army uniform. At the war's end, the General was rewarded by the regime for his grievous loss with a position as head of the Government Sports Ministry. There he would continue to show undying loyalty to Franco.

Left with no option but agree to Moscardó's ruling, the warring parties reluctantly went along and Alfredo Di Stefano headed for the mountains of Catalonia to begin his Spanish adventure. He played a series of three pre-season friendly matches and in each Di Stefano was wretched. The Argentine looked heavy-legged, disinterested. His ball control was atrocious, shooting appalling and his passing would have shamed a blind man - Barca officials were raging.

Who the hell had they bought? Whispers began to emerge that Barcelona had been sold a dud. The Catalans raged - this man was a fraud, an impostor. It was swiftly agreed Di Stefano was not of sufficient quality to play for the great FC Barcelona. Let him go. Let the *Madrileños* clear up their own mess. Madrid were contacted and told the Argentine was to be released early. Good riddance. With unholy haste a new deal was drawn up and overnight Alfredo Di Stefano travelled south to become a Real Madrid player.

Two weeks later, on 25th October 1953, the Argentine made his *Chamartin* début for the *Madrileños* against Barcelona, scoring twice in a 5-0 rout. Di Stefano had arrived at his spiritual home! Thousands of white handkerchiefs were waved in tribute to the man as if he was Spanish royalty – it was a grand performance. When lightning bolts collide the jagged streaks create energy few can imagine; a goal for the Argentine in the first minute signalled the start of an unforgettable, historic slaughter of their greatest rivals. His touch was that of a great actor who knows a spellbound audience could not take their eyes off him. Wreaking havoc, he appeared a class apart even in such sumptuous company.

The Catalans had been played like a guitar for Di Stefano had already been sold the Madrid dream by the golden charms of Raimondo Saporta. What occurred in Catalonia was simply a ruse to free him from Barca's right of contract. So began a glorious period for Real Madrid's knights in white satin and there were none more special than the one who became known as, *Saeta Rubia* - the *Blond Arrow* - the incomparable Alfredo Di Stefano.

★

For the son of an Albacete lawyer, Santiago Bernabéu, football had been a lifelong passion. In 1909 he arrived at Madrid as a promising fourteen-year-old centre-forward to play for their youth team. His death in 1978 ended an astonishing sixty-nine year old love affair with the *Madrileños*.

The acquisition of the remarkable Di Stefano was to prove prescient, for 1955 saw the birth of the European Champions Cup and a manically enthusiastic Bernabéu was amongst the first to wholeheartedly support the novel competition. However to compete was never going to be sufficient for Don Santiago. They had to win it.

The competition was essential in providing a stage for his football club and to show the world that Real Madrid were a team of miracles: made up of magicians and conjurers, footballing artists from all corners of the globe. They represented not just a city but an ideal - one that appealed to all who believed in the beauty of a game that still held the power to take the breath away.

Then the "Grand Old Man" as he later became fondly tagged by an adoring Madrid public, would again up the stakes for he intended to build not just a team but a footballing dynasty that would dominate at home and abroad for a generation. This was a man who would never rest until Real Madrid ruled the world.

Santiago Bernabéu had first come to Real's aid at its lowest ebb back in 1943. It was a city ravaged by the atrocities of a civil war, devastated with three savage years of incessant bombings and senseless slaughter. Bernabéu's first act on becoming Real President was to plan for a new stadium. He needed funds and in order to raise the necessary capital Bernabéu issued shares to supporters. It would be their stadium, their team. One love, a shared passion. Madrid's pride and joy and he, Don Santiago, would reside over the fiefdom. Millions of much needed funds were raised to help in the rebuilding of the bomb shattered *Chamartin*. Bernabéu never forgot this extraordinary act of generosity by the people of Madrid and he was later to recall, *"There was a smile in every stone."*

And so in September 1944 local parish priest, Father Jose Maria Murat, blessed the sacred grounds on which the new *Chamartin* would rise. Stood alongside a beaming and proud Bernabéu, Father Murat was invited to dig the first pieces of dirt from the ground to begin the excavation. From this moment an empire the likes of which football had never known began. By 1955 the ground would be renamed in Don Santiago's honour. The *Estadio Bernabéu* would stand as a lasting monument to one man's stunning vision. A stadium that originally held only 16,000 would in only a short time reach an astonishing 130,000 capacity.

Real had not won the league title since 1933. In 1949, on a fateful afternoon at Oviedo, only a last day win saved the *Madrileños* from the ultimate humiliation of relegation. But times were changing and the season in which Alfredo Di Stefano signed saw the championship banner soar high once more over Madrid for the first time in twenty-one years and only the third in their history. Di Stefano was sensational, scoring an astonishing twenty-seven goals in just thirty appearances that season and a further twenty-six the following season when Real retained the title.

A great side was emerging; in goal Juan Alonso was unspectacular but steady, the one position in this team of all stars which such attributes were allowed. The captain Miguel Muñoz was a classy, assured defender with outstanding technique and heart to match. Alongside him the terrifying figure of Manuel Marquitos. In another line of work Marquitos would probably feature on a *Dead or Alive* poster but in many ways he was equally as important to Real as the *Blond Arrow himself*. As was the clever, skilful but tenacious Jose Zarraga. All three formed a formidable barrier for any to break down. The *Madrileño* rallying call *"No Pasara"* – *"they shall not pass"* was taken to the extreme by the ruthless, cold blooded Marquitos and his compadres.

Content the rearguard was in safe hands, those upfront were charged with illuminating the landscape and providing the artistic swishes to the Madrid canvas that exploded upon opposing defences like a blinding white supernova. Bought from Racing Santander at Di Stefano's recommendation, to race like a fierce gust of wind down the Madrid left wing, was Francisco Gento. Christened with a variety of nicknames by the enchanted Real followers, there was none more apt than Manchester United defender Bill Foulkes' description of Gento as *El Motorcycle*. He was ably abetted by the Argentine goal machine Hector Rial, another signed by Bernabéu on the *Blond Arrow's* recommendation. Di Stefano had stated quite bluntly to his President: *"I need someone capable of passing the ball back to me."* Rial was a forward whose finishing ability and positional play was uncanny. He provided the perfect foil for Madrid's undisputed leader. A king without a crown but a king no less. A marriage made in football heaven, the rhythmic clapping of the Madrid crowd would electrify the Argentine's soul and Di Stefano would soar.

UNCHARTED WATERS

Real Madrid's epic romance with the European Cup began on 8th September 1955. Drawn away to play Servette FC of Switzerland in the first round, they came away with a hard fought 2-0 after the strangest of visits at half-time from a most unexpected source. An insipid first half showing by the *Madrileños* had left Di Stefano, already an imposing character, in a terrible mood. Whilst sat alone bemoaning his *compadres'* inability to string two passes together, into the dressing room walked Raimondo Saporta with an exalted guest. The then 17 year-old Spanish Prince, (now King) Juan Carlos. Based in Switzerland at a finishing school, the Prince had taken the afternoon off to come and see his countrymen. Immediately all the players stood up before his regal presence - all except one. Not one for ass kissing and too annoyed with events on the pitch, a sullen Di Stefano remained seated. It was instead Prince Juan Carlos who acknowledged Alfredo by walking over and offering his hand. Only then did Di Stefano rise. The starstruck Prince turned to face the disbelieving Real players and exclaimed the now legendary comment,

"Ese chico ahora es el rey!" - *"Now this guy really is a king!"*

His day made, the Prince turned to leave but not before declaring to the Argentine: *"Saeta, los emigrantes esperan una victoria."* *"Blond Arrow, the Spanish immigrants are hoping for a win,"* to which Di Stefano simply smiled and nodded. Impressed by the young man's demeanour and respect for his royal self, Madrid's number nine would make the Prince's wish his command.

The second half saw a much improved Real and, not wishing to let the future monarch or indeed their own King Alfredo down, they scored twice with goals from Miguel Muñoz and a last minute strike from Hector Rial. The second leg at the *Estadio Bernabéu* saw no mercy spared as Real Madrid cut loose in emphatic fashion to win 5-0 and leave the depressingly defensive Swiss still refusing to attack when five down. Scoring twice Di Stefano had left an early calling card on a tournament which in time he would come to dominate and all but own.

KNIGHT IN WHITE SATIN

Happy to gaze fondly in the mirror at their own reflections and suffering worrying delusions of invincible grandeur, Real Madrid sauntered into the European Cup quarter-finals. There they would almost come flying off the rails in unforgettable fashion. Paired against the tough and talented Yugoslav champions of Partizan Belgrade, the ugly face of post-cold war politics reared its head.

Not daring to risk the possibility of losing to Communists, General Franco contacted Bernabéu and insisted they withdraw from the European Cup. Real Madrid had unfortunately become an important symbol of Franco's Fascist regime. For a while it appeared that the Madrileño's first attempt at conquering the continent would end in an embarrassing shambles. However Bernabéu still had one card left to play...

He was a man who could charm birds from the trees. The President sent word and his fixer Raimondo Saporta went to work with considerable wit and intelligence on the Generalissimo. Saporta argued that it was in Franco's best interests to let Real Madrid play the Yugoslavs, for were they not a magnificent team? Football was the cheap drug the masses craved, it crossed previously impassable borders, changed minds and shifted attitudes. What price in propaganda terms the pride of Spain humbling Tito's finest? All would reflect well back on Franco, allowing him to bask in the glory of Di Stefano and his wonderful orchestra of footballing artists.

And so on *Christmas Day, 1955* (surely a sly joke played on

Partizan Belgrade by Santiago Bernabéu to let these communists experience some rare seasonal spirit) they finally clashed. Just to ensure Franco did not have a change of heart, the Partizan players were smuggled into Spain through a side gate at Madrid airport bypassing passport control and customs.

Their reward for such secrecy came when Real Madrid took apart their Eastern European opponents 4-0. It was a victory capped on seventy minutes when Alfredo Di Stefano picked up a pass from Miguel Muñoz to streak clear before firing low past Partizan goalkeeper Stojanovic to complete the rout. Earlier efforts, two from reserve winger Castano and the other from Francisco Gento, had left the Yugoslavs wondering what had hit them.

Partizan had begun the game on the attack and had two early goals from their dangerous centre-forward Bora Milutinovic strangely disallowed. Disgruntled, the visitors lost heart and must have felt that whatever they did, it was not going, or more succinctly, it would not be allowed to be their day. At the time Di Stefano's fourth goal was considered simply icing on the cake for the *Madrileños* as a place in the semi-finals appeared sealed already. However events in the return in Belgrade would leave all associated with Madrid a little humbled and promising never again to underestimate a fellow champion.

The plane carrying Real Madrid to Yugoslavia landed at Tito airport in the midst of a blinding snowstorm and with temperatures ten degrees below zero. Matters hardly improved when the game began in conditions beyond belief. As a raging blizzard swept across the pitch, Partizan ripped into the Spanish aristocrats. Madrid goalkeeper Alonso recalls standing beneath his crossbar when a snarling drive from Partizan's Bora Milutinovic smashed angrily against it causing the snow which had settled since kick-off to cover him from head to toe!

Eager to avenge their humiliation in the *Bernabéu* the Yugoslavs attacked with zeal. With the terraces packed full of comrade soldiers roaring on their team and the Real players slipping and sliding on the treacherous surface, their ball skills rendered useless in such pitiable conditions, they fell behind in the thirteenth minute. Hector Rial was swiftly handed the opportunity to equalise from the penalty spot and put the tie out of reach but the Argentine wafted his shot hopelessly over the crossbar. Di Stefano shot his fellow countryman a look of murderous disgust.

Spurred on, the home team continued to pin back Madrid and as their supporters chided the struggling *Madrileños* with endless hails of snowballs (an unofficial cold war?) a second goal arrived from striker Milutinovic who, unlike Rial, mastered the surface and slashed his penalty high past a diving Alonso. Suddenly bedlam had come to Belgrade!

Sensing a historic moment Partizan blazed forward and Milutinovic upped the stakes ever higher when he crashed home a third for the Slavs to leave the Madrid players arguing amongst themselves and on the verge of utter humiliation. The last kick of the match almost saw Milutinovic complete a magnificent hat trick, only to see his close range effort beat Alonso but cruelly stick in the slush that had built up on the goal line. Madrid survived but only through huge good fortune and last ditch defending from their battered defence - notably Marquitos who at times fended off this Belgrade offensive almost single-handedly.

The *Madrileños* departed the Balkans lucky, bruised but still alive and in the European Cup semi-finals. But it had been oh so close. Even today the dramatic events of Belgrade are etched in the rich tapestry of Real Madrid's European history. Forever remembered as *The Snow Game* – it was a match they would never forget.

The semi saw Real pitched against the classy professionals of AC Milan. The Italians had splashed out a world record £72,000 for the awesome attacking prowess of the exceptional Uruguayan forward Juan Schiaffino and if any team was equipped to knock out the Spanish it was the *Rossoneri*. The first leg at the *Bernabéu* saw an enthralling encounter with the Italians twice roaring back to equalise.

With the score at 2-2 Milan fought furiously and with great skill against the *Madrileños*. Schiaffino in particular handed out heart attacks to the Madrid crowd, his delicate touch, rich in finesse and laced with a deadly eye for goal, posed a constant threat. However Real possessed that rare ability to ease through the gears when necessary and two late strikes from Rial and Di Stefano saw the *Bernabéu* rise once more in tribute to their side.

Milan: Not a place to give out gifts, Real Madrid played with rare conservatism on a rock hard *San Siro* pitch to ease themselves past their opponents. An early away goal put away clinically by Madrid winger Jocieto put paid to AC's challenge and despite two Del Monte penalties in a swiftly emptying stadium, Real remained composed. Come the final whistle the white shirts celebrated booking a place in the inaugural European Cup final.

It was to be fitting that the finale would be held in Paris for the notion of a European Champions Cup was first mooted by the editor of French sports magazine *L'Equipe* – Parisian Gabriel Hanot. Through nothing but dogged resilience and sheer bloody mindedness, Hanot saw his dream of the continent's mightiest teams coming together in a single tournament. Among Hanot's most committed allies was Santiago Bernabéu and it was felt only fair that his club should be part of such a grand occasion.

That their opponents would be French was perhaps the biggest surprise. Rheims had amongst their ranks a player deeply coveted by Bernabéu. The son of an immigrant Polish miner, Raymonde Kopa was a devastating winger, mainly on the right side but equally capable of causing havoc on the left or through the centre. Already other elite European clubs were planning to swoop for the dynamic Frenchman, convincing the Real president that he had to act fast. The mouth-watering prospect of Kopa rampaging down one wing and Gento the other meant that once more Bernabéu summoned his right hand man Raimondo Saporta. Armed with a blank cheque and the romance and glory of the white shirt, Saporta travelled to

France. With both teams set to play in the final, serious doubts were raised on the timing of such a deal. A serious conflict of interest had arisen but the irresistible pull of Real Madrid and a mind boggling transfer fee of 52 million francs sealed the unlikely coup for the Spaniards. A three-year contract was signed by Kopa, yet another audacious coup by this kingmaker and fixer *extraordinaire*.

After losing out in the league to the fiercely combative Athletic Bilbao the Madrileños were under intense pressure to beat Rheims. The Basques had left Madrid trailing after a storming finish to win the championship, meaning only a victory in Paris would enable Real to qualify for the following season's European Cup competition. 38,000 packed the *Parc Des Princes*, the vast majority desperate to see Rheims put these strutting Spaniards in their place.

The signing of Kopa was being seen in France as a grossly unfair tactic meant to undermine the French beforehand. His loyalty was questioned; how could he possibly perform at his maximum and help destroy the hand that now fed him? Pouring more fuel onto the fire, Kopa had even made a guest appearance the previous week for Real in a 4-2 victory against Brazilian club Vasco De Gama at the *Bernabéu*.

Any doubts regarding the Frenchman's intent appeared misguided as the early stages saw Kopa run the Madrid defence ragged. Exploding in front of their own people, Rheims roared forward. Their exquisite one-touch passing cut Real to pieces and in just ten minutes they had built up a two-goal lead - first through midfielder Michel Leblond before an awful mistake by Juan Alonso was pounced upon and smashed into the net by forward Jean Templin as the goalkeeper watched on in despair. The Spanish were reeling, their famous swagger invisible, the composure absent. Disaster loomed, Bernabéu's master plan strangled at birth.

Suddenly Alfredo Di Stefano decided enough and puffing out his chest the *Blond Arrow* went to work. He single-handedly dragged Real back into the contest. On fourteen minutes he picked up the ball and raced into the Rheims area before lashing a shot goalwards to halve the deficit. Madrid were awake. As if struck by electricity they returned to life, Gento and Rial reacting to their talisman's promptings and devilishly astute passes. A much deserved leveller came before half-time when Rial met Gento's cross to flash a header past Rheims' goalkeeper Jacquet at his near post.

Yet just when it seemed normal service had been resumed and the Spaniards would run away with the contest, their valiant opponents regained sufficient poise to hit back. On the hour a free kick from Kopa found the head of French attacking midfielder Michel Hidalgo, who beat a flailing Alonso to make the score 3-2, and send the *Parc Des Princes* into raptures. This was not in the Real Madrid script and they poured forward in need of yet another equaliser. On sixty-seven minutes their prayers were answered when salvation arrived from a most unlikely source, Manuel Marquitos stabbing home from six yards on one of his rare forays forward.

With white shirts moving like ghostly images amongst the courageous but now badly toiling French, their passes slick, movement hellish and pace incredulous, it appeared just a matter of time before Rheims were handed a knock-out blow. It came eleven minutes from time when the *Madrileños* concocted an opportunity for Hector Rial to slot home from eight yards and surely win the European Cup?

As the seconds counted down, one last almighty scare awaited Real Madrid, for as the referee stood with whistle in mouth ready to blow, a desperate Leblond shot crashed against the Spaniards' crossbar. But it was Madrid's trophy and President Don Santiago Bernabéu watched with tears in his eyes as Captain Miguel Muñoz, amid a mad huddle of blinding flashlights and cameras, lifted the European Cup aloft. To show his appreciation General Franco handed Santiago Bernabéu the freedom of Madrid. Not that the President needed such a decree! And so began a glorious era for the *Madrileños*. Across Europe there appeared none capable of living with this white storm. With Di Stefano at its very heart, the walls to the *Bernabéu* appeared impregnable.

On 1st November 1956, Real Madrid began the defence of their newly won crown beating the skilful Austrian champions Rapid Vienna 4-2 in a thrilling contest at the *Bernabéu*. A two goal advantage was thought more than sufficient to take over to Vienna, however on a night of blazing incident and before an Austrian crowd baying for Madrid blood, a most unlikely hat trick from Rapid's veteran defender, thirty-three year old Ernst Happel, handed them a 3-0 half-time lead to stun the *Madrileños* and leave them on the verge of humiliating elimination.

It was a breathless showing by the unfancied home side who had caught Madrid unaware and a little too sure of themselves. For the magnificent Happel it had been a personal triumph, his two free kicks and a penalty leaving Real on their knees. For the visitors it was an embarrassment, none more than to their red faced President who was so disgusted with his team that he stormed down to the dressing room to confront them. What Santiago Bernabéu said that day in Vienna was actually recorded on tape and has entered Real Madrid legend.

Bernabéu removed a ridiculously expensive cigar from his mouth and grinded it into the floor with his heel. As the players stared forlornly at their boots, humbled and a little bit wary of their fuming El Presidente, Don Santiago let rip:

"No one is getting away from here this easily. We have not come here on holiday and I want to see more balls out on that field. I don't know if you understand, but you have got the Real Madrid shield on your shirts and I have seen thousands of Spaniards who have come to support us. People who work their hearts out in the factories to earn a living. You can't let them down like this."

The second half saw a Real Madrid rally and a lone Di Stefano goal ended the overall tie at 5-5. A little pride, if not victory, had been restored. To settle matters a play-off would be required and it is here that once again President Bernabéu worked his magic. He summoned Raimondo Saporta and sent him to do business with his Austrian opponents. Rather than a neutral venue where the financial benefit would suit neither club, Saporta argued the case for the game to be played at the *Bernabéu!* The incentive for the Austrians was a fifty percent cut of a guaranteed sell out. After two monumental encounters against the *Madrileños* the Rapid officials felt sufficiently confident to take up Don Raimondo's generous offer. The outcome almost inevitably saw them go out 2-0. Sadly and rather shamefully the Austrians preferred the lure of Spanish pesetas to the opportunity of glory. But Saporta proved once again his business acumen was equal to anything the white knights ever produced on a football pitch.

Following the harrowing experience of Vienna lessons had been learned and the quarter-final against French champions Nice caused the *Madrileños* few problems. A 6-2 aggregate hammering saw Real Madrid one step away from a second successive final appearance. Confidence was high – Bernabéu had demanded no more slip ups. He paid the best, demanded the best and with such came the power and the glory.

However, far away in the northern English city of Manchester something was brewing that would soon give the President sleepless nights. Two weeks previous to Real Madrid putting paid to the French, their great domestic rivals and Spanish champions Athletic Bilbao had encountered a team that would come to be immortalised for all time as the *Busby Babes*. United were coming.

THE BABES TAKE FLIGHT

On 11th March 1941 air raid sirens screamed out over the city of Manchester. Dancing shafts of light illuminated the night sky searching for invaders. The ferocious crackle of anti-aircraft fire roared up at an invisible but deadly foe. The decision had been taken by German High Command to destroy the munitions factories in Trafford Park. For three hours the bombs rained down as throughout the evening fierce battles raged to stem the fires that blazed across the city. Leaping flames emblazoned against a red horizon - Manchester was on fire. An unexpected victim of the carnage was the home of Manchester United Football Club. A stray incendiary device fell, setting it alight. Behind one goal an entire grandstand lay gutted, whilst the rest of the terraces were reduced to rubble. Come the war's end Old Trafford cut a pitiful sight. It appeared only divine intervention could revive this ailing; seemingly dying club.

Four and a half years later, on 22nd October 1945, a man arrived by train at Victoria station, clutching a suitcase, wearing a trilby hat and smoking burnt-down cigarettes. Company Sergeant-Major Matt Busby was home from the war and had come to Manchester.

In the early summer of 1956 and with an average age of just over twenty, Manchester United had become First Division champions. These were interesting times. A board meeting held beneath the newly rebuilt stand at Old Trafford heralded profound implications for all concerned. The damaged wreaked by Hermann Goring's Luftwaffe was mended and after being revamped, the whiff of fresh paint still hung in the air. United had the feeling of a club reborn.

Despite the nonsensical stance of the Football League arguing against United's desire to partake in the European Cup, Matt Busby was determined his club would compete. He persuaded the board to accept the invitation by saying it would bring in extra cash to pay for the new floodlights and help with an expanding wage bill. Also, it would produce competition and more games for the huge numbers of young players on United's books. In typically unassuming manner Busby's powerful argument could not be dismissed and the *Babes* were set to take flight.

From the burnt out wreckage of a skeletal stadium Busby's astute management had guided Manchester United to the pinnacle of English football. The post-war predicament of a bombed ground and huge debt was overcome with remarkable resilience and stewardship. But the United manager did not do this alone, his assistant Jimmy Murphy would stand alongside him for three decades.

Busby first came across this fiercely proud Welshman in Southern Italy during 1943. He stood with great interest to watch the firebrand Murphy extol the virtues of how football should be played to a group of awestruck soldiers. Matt Busby recognised a kindred spirit and by war's end Murphy agreed to join Busby in Manchester. Jimmy remembered those troubled days: "*When the war broke out I went from the Far East to the desert with the Eighth army for four and a half years. So I saw the worst of it. Terrible things. When the Germans were finally driven out of North Africa I ended up in a rest camp in Italy There I met Matt and he asked me to go with him to Old Trafford to look after the kids and be his right hand man.*"

Something magical had occurred in this northern outpost. A dash of angel dust amongst the Mancunian smog and smoke led to the creation of a team which would become immortalised as the *Busby Babes*. They emerged to add Technicolor to a grey, drab, murky city. Their youth side, which had won the FA

Youth Cup five times on the trot, was plundered for talent – like ripe apples plucked from a tree, Murphy would hand his prizes over to his manager.

In 1956 the time arose to lift the roots and go for broke. Like stars appearing in the night sky they emerged; dazzling players blessed with poise, technique and raw power. Jimmy taught them the basics; pass and move, give it to a red shirt and look for angles. It was such a simple game but when played correctly an object of beauty.

For finally in England, the last bastion of kick and rush, the stunning reality of Hungary's 6-3 master class at Wembley on November 25th 1953 was dawning. The Magyars ended forever the myth of supposed English invincibility. The Hungarians new-age tactical approach left England appearing like impostors in a game they had invented and these lessons were taken on board by those such as Jimmy Murphy, who realised the sport he and Busby had known was changing beyond all comprehension.

If United were to stand any hope of competing they had to produce footballers capable of living with the continent's elite. The rewards for such vision were swift and spectacular as never in Football League history had a club gambled so much on those so young. The 1955–56 First Division title was won and with it entry into the heady, unworldly heights of the European Cup.

When asked by reporters how he and Jimmy Murphy set about creating a football team, Busby would always reply: *"Imagine a sculptor turning a slab of stone into an elephant. He simply knocks off the bits that don't look like an elephant."* The reality was hard work; endless hours spent on a training pitch perfecting the skill that would be required to take on Di Stefano, Gento *et al.* And foremost amongst United's works of art was a young giant called Duncan Edwards.

Wolves and England Captain Billy Wright said of him, *"Compared to Duncan we are all Pygmies."* Never in professional football had Matt Busby and Jimmy Murphy witnessed such talent in one so young. Prodigious never did Edwards justice; stolen, almost kidnapped, from the grasping arms of his hometown club Wolverhampton Wanderers and their manager Stan Cullis (at the time United's main rivals), the Dudley giant had been destined for greatness in Wolves' old gold shirt. However word reached Busby from an old wartime friend Joe Mercer that he had it on good understanding that Duncan was a United supporter. This was enough to instigate a mad rush by Busby and Murphy to the prodigy's home town. There they camped outside the youngster's house. Together they convinced Edwards there was only one stage worthy of his talent.

On 4th April 1953, aged just 16 and a half, Duncan Edwards made his Manchester United début. Although beaten out of sight by Cardiff City 4-1, there was little doubt that in Edwards United had unearthed something quite remarkable. Not one for superlatives, when it came to Duncan Edwards Busby relented, *"Duncan is the finest player of his age I have seen. Yet although he has soared up among the stars, his feet are still on the ground."*

Later, Jimmy Murphy loved to relate the tale of when he was Welsh manager and they were facing England at Ninian Park. In a pre-match team talk Murphy set about boosting his players' confidence with a rousing devaluation of their opponents. He went through each of the team rubbishing their supposed talents.

"He's only got one leg, can't head it, no bottle, couldn't tackle a fish supper." When Jimmy Murphy had finished his clinical disembowelment of the *Three Lions* a lone voice amongst the Welsh footballers spoke up. *"Hey boss, you forgot about Edwards? What about Duncan Edwards?"*

"Stay away from him son," said Murphy, *"he will bloody murder you!"*

Manchester United did not just enter the European Cup, they came bursting through the door with all the ferocity of a forest fire at their backs. On 11th September 1956 they travelled to play Belgium champions RSC Anderlecht in the first qualifying round. The arrival of the English champions had electrified the Belgium capital and the game was advertised locally as *Le Grand Match International en Nocturne*. Played at the wonderfully picturesque Astrid stadium, so different then to the antiquated English grounds they were used to, United, in front of 35,000 spectators, produced a gritty, mature performance to win 2-0. However events hardly ran smooth early on when Mark Jones conceded a penalty which fell to Belgium international Captain Jeff Mermans to convert. Mermans was the golden boy of Belgian football, a devastating forward whose nickname *the Bomber* was well earned. However on this occasion he bombed out when his spot kick smashed against the post and bounced clear.

It was a let off for the visitors who almost immediately took advantage when Dennis Viollet broke away to score a fine individual goal. The game developed with Anderlecht attacking throughout and United playing on the break. Fifteen minutes from time they doubled their lead with a typically thunderous header from Tommy Taylor to seal the result. The Football League criticism that Manchester United's and more singularly Matt Busby's decision to partake in the European Cup would affect their performances in the league was proved to be, like most comments from Alan Hardaker's mouth, total nonsense as Busby's side blitzed a tough Sheffield Wednesday the following Saturday, goals from Johnny Berry, Tommy Taylor, Dennis Viollet and Billy Whelan delighting an Old Trafford crowd and more than proving Busby's point.

However it was in the second leg that the Babes truly took flight on a never to be forgotten evening at Maine Road, on Wednesday 26th September 1956. Forced to share Manchester City's Maine Road ground due to the Old Trafford floodlights still being in the process of being erected, United illuminated their neighbour's home by hitting an astonishing ten goals past the poor, unsuspecting Belgians. Duncan Edwards was the only change from Brussels coming in for Jackie Blanchflower. Yet on a pitch flooded with pools of water, the *Babes* ran riot; their football lightning fast, electric, bewildering. The ball was not so much passed around the Anderlecht shirts but struck like a pinball.

The goal scoring list read like movie credits; Dennis Viollet scored four, Tommy Taylor three, Liam Whelan a brace and Johnny Berry made the total double figures. Despite Taylor's hat-trick and Viollet's four haul, the undoubted star of the evening, the one who tortured the Anderlecht defenders to create the vast majority of the goals, was United left-winger David Pegg. It was the type of night when everything Pegg attempted came off as he effortlessly switched wings causing equal havoc on each. Indeed such was his contribution, the final moments were spent with his grateful team-mates trying desperately to gift him a much deserved goal, only for the ball, seemingly tired of hitting the Belgian net, refusing to comply.

This savage mauling reverberated across Europe for Anderlecht were no easy touch. This was an outstanding team and Jeff Mermans spoke afterwards of his total shock. Still reeling at what had befallen them, Mermans claimed, *"We have played against the best teams of Hungary and Russia and no one has ever beaten us like that, no one."* An exuberant Matt Busby failed to hide his excitement at seeing his young side play in such fashion. *"It was the finest exhibition of teamwork from any side I have ever seen, club or international. It was near perfection."*

The following month, on 17th October 1956, the European campaign continued when the champions of Germany, Borussia Dortmund, came to Manchester. A huge Maine Road crowd of 76,598 witnessed a blistering first half showing from Busby's youngsters as they continued in the same vein of form which had blown away Anderlecht. A 3-0 interval lead was established as the golden satin shirts of the Germans found themselves being handed a hiding that threatened to rival that served out to the Belgians. Two goals from Dennis Viollet, a striker of such clinical precision that his partnership with the powerful Tommy Taylor tore apart the Borussia rearguard preceded a third from German defender Bursmuller who, after being hassled and harried by

David Pegg, contrived to put the ball in his own net. Only the bravery and heroics of Dortmund goalkeeper Kwiakowski, wearing a green jersey borrowed off fellow countryman Bert Trautmann, had kept the score line down to just three.

Half-time arrived and deafening cheers rang out from the Maine Road terraces in appreciation of yet another superb Manchester United performance. It appeared to many United supporters that this European Cup held no fears, however such thoughts would change, for in the second period Borussia responded to deliver the home side a priceless lesson.

Perhaps buoyed and a touch cocky thinking the job was done, United eased off and soon found themselves on the back foot. The first half bravura faded as the Germans came roaring back to snatch two late goals. Defensive errors crept in. Captain Roger Byrne, rather than kicking clear, tried to chest the ball down and was robbed by quick thinking left-winger Helmut Kapitulski, who slammed the loose ball past a helpless Wood. Then Dortmund's best player Alfred Preissler, who terrorised the United defence in the final twenty minutes, grabbed a vital second and the home crowd were reeling – Borussia had been gifted a real fighting chance to finish off United on home soil. Afterwards a baited Roger Byrne unusually bit at pressman who asked him if he thought his error would prove crucial, *"Yes it was a silly mistake,"* snapped the captain, *"*b*ut don't you lot ever make bloody mistakes?"*

Suddenly and without warning Manchester had been awoken to the trepidations of the European Cup. Amid the glamorous names and unfamiliar faces, the dangers of the unknown had surfaced and the *Busby Babes*, far from looking a certainty for the quarter-finals, now faced a battle for survival in far off Dortmund.

On 21st November 1956 at the Rota Erde stadium, Manchester United were forced to defend for their lives against a ninety-minute onslaught from the German champions. On a dreadful bone hard surface resembling an ice rink and watched by 44,450 spectators, including 7,000 British servicemen stationed in the Ruhr valley, United were constantly pinned back.

The home side came at them in waves and the manner in which Dortmund created an abundance of chances, only to invent entirely new ways to miss them, had their fans agonising throughout. Their wonderfully gifted captain Preissler, wearing an unfortunate hairnet, was an ever-present thorn in the visitor's defence, as he appeared to skate over the ground. To compound United's problems the container holding the rubber studs that would have replaced their normal ones had mysteriously disappeared on the day of the match. Whether German mischief-making or simple carelessness was to blame, it represented big problems for trainer Tom Curry as he struggled to find replacements. Thus the United players were forced to take to the field wearing wholly unsuitable studs on a pitch that felt more concrete than grass!

Somehow United, with huge good fortune, great heart and no lack of defensive know-how, held on. It was a performance of such guts and grim determination that it surprised even their manager, who had feared the worst after the Germans' late flurry of goals in England. A stupendous goalkeeping performance from a tracksuit bottomed Ray Wood, including two world class saves in the opening minute from point blank range, proved critical while a wonderful captain's performance from Roger Byrne as he marshalled his ill-shod troops around the penalty area, more than made up for his first leg error. Centre-half Mark Jones was immense, as was a towering Duncan Edwards, breaking up countless attacks and refusing to bow down as United buckled and rocked but never broke. With the astonishing Edwards crashing into tackles and showing great calm and presence when on the ball, United stood their ground. As the game strove to a dramatic climax, even the German fans began to applaud this young English lion of a player.

In the dying moments Dortmund saw a penalty appeal waived aside when Bill Foulkes clearly handled inside his own penalty area. It was a lucky break for the Mancunians and as the stadium roared its disapproval the game ended and a fortunate

United were through. It had been a severe struggle. Afterwards Dortmund's captain Preissler was generous in defeat as he praised his English opponents, predicting,

"In England Manchester swamped us with incredible football. In Germany they fought like tigers. They will win the European Cup."

THE BATTLE OF LA CATEDA

The 1956-57 season saw this Manchester United team, reared from the crèche by Matt Busby and Jimmy Murphy, fighting to attain a previously unthinkable treble. It was deemed impossible, it seemed madness to even suggest it could be achieved. For United's opponents in the European Cup Quarter-finals were crack Spanish champions Athletic Bilbao. Few gave the Red Devils hope against such vaunted opposition - a team that on home soil had ripped the title from the imperial grasp of the great Real Madrid. But in fifties Manchester, with the Busby Babes lighting up a city still recovering from the pummelling it received at the hands of Hitler's bombs, there was something in the air. Away at Bilbao for the first leg if United could somehow stay in the tie, then back home all bets would be off...

That previous season, deep in northern Spain, the defiant Basques had taken to the streets in frenzied celebration as, against all odds, their team of hearts, Athletic Bilbao, had pipped General Franco's favourites Real Madrid to claim the Spanish championship. Unprecedented scenes of delight erupted throughout their homeland. It was a fierce outburst of pride from a place that had suffered unspeakable crimes during the wretched civil war. The carnage and horror of the civil war was forever etched in the souls of every Basque and to understand their mindset at the time it is perhaps fair to travel back and try to explain the reasons why.

On 6th April 1937 the pretty hillside town of Guernica was chosen at random to be wiped off the map. General Franco's unholy alliance with Adolf Hitler allowed the Nazis ample opportunities to fine tune their war machine in preparation for the forthcoming world storm. On a beautiful late spring afternoon the people of Guernica stood milling around their town square. It was market day and many were preparing to pack up their stalls after a day's work. The surrounding streets were filled swiftly with traders heading home. Others stayed to chat or swap gossip over a bottle of wine. For a moment the ghastly horrors of the civil war that raged around them felt far away. It was to prove a sad, brief respite for high above in the church tower came the frightful wailing of the air raid sirens.

Approaching from the south appeared a lone aircraft. The locals had become accustomed to sporadic attacks by the Nationalist air force, at worse the pilot would jettison a small load then retreat out of harm's way. But not that day in Guernica – for this was different. As inhabitants watched in terror the plane daubed on both wings with a Nazi swastika dropped three bombs into the town centre then performed a victory roll. The Germans had come out to play.

Suddenly from high beyond the clouds the sky filled with Stuka dive bombers swooping down to let fly a hellish outpouring of raking machine gun fire. Operation Rugen was under way. Blind fear gripped the terrified Basques as the ground exploded with the splatter of bullets and shrapnel. Shells dropped by the thousands as a huge fleet of Luftwaffe Junkers unloaded a deadly arsenal of incendiary bombs.

The stukas dived low, cutting down hordes of civilians as they raced in vain for cover. With typical Nazi efficiency Guernica was razed to the ground. Craters emerged as a second wave appeared to join in the massacre. Seemingly not content with the devastation already caused, they continued before the

Germans finally departed leaving behind unbearable scenes of human suffering.

What was left behind resembled Dante's Inferno: charred bodies were strewn for as far as the eye could see. Dark billowing smoke engulfed the town as flames leapt from burning buildings into the early evening Basque sky. The fires were seen twenty miles away in the village of Lequieto. Volunteers from Bilbao rushed to Guernica only to be forced back by a raging firestorm. Everywhere the dead lay scattered as the survivors looked for family before collecting their charred and mutilated corpses in wheelbarrows.

The numbers killed are still disputed but the fact remained on that fateful day, hell upon earth descended on Guernica.

Franco had conquered the region and brought it to heel but he was never able to dampen the Basques' unquenchable thirst for freedom and revenge. It was a passion evident in Bilbao's refusal to allow non-Basques to wear their shirt. Their most prized asset was the man-mountain central defender Jesus Garay. Without equal in Spain, it was Garay more than any who was responsible for the title being paraded in the *San Mames* stadium.

Winning the league placed Bilbao into the European cup and the draw against the feted youngsters of Manchester United hardly filled the mighty Basques with dread. Rumours had reached Bilbao of these much talked of *Busby Babes* but this was a side who had taken on and destroyed the might of Real Madrid and Barcelona. What fears could a handful of boys from Manchester hold?

Yet the ultra professional Basques were not about to take any chances. The Sunday before they took on United in the first leg they played a remarkable nine reserves in a 2-0 defeat at Barcelona. With the possibility of a semi-final or final showdown against Real Madrid for their European crown – a god-given opportunity to spear Franco in the full glare of a watching world – meant they could ill-afford to slip up against United. The Basques viewed United as a difficult challenge but hardly an insurmountable task.

Monday 15th January 1957. On a frosty Mancunian morning the plane ferrying Manchester United to Spain for their quarter-final first leg against Athletic Bilbao found itself immersed in a ferocious snowstorm. The Dakota shuddered violently, rocking from side to side as the air turbulence threatened to tumble the troubled aircraft from the skies. On board the atmosphere was one of impending doom and, as the plane approached Basque territory, the United party cut a frightful sight. The Dakota nosed onwards towards the Spanish mainland and from within the party could see the dark foreboding, mountainous cliffs that etched out into the sea. Finally the intrepid travellers spied their destination where events would hardly improve.

Since taking off at Ringway airport Duncan Edwards had been horribly airsick. He sat alone: green, apprehensive and silent. Defender Bill Foulkes earned the wrath of his shivering team-mates by falling asleep with his gangling legs resting on the heater and unknowingly switching it off. When woken from slumber Foulkes faced an inquest resembling a mid-air lynching. Finally, after twenty minutes of sheer torture and to everyone's great relief, Captain Charles Riley began the descent. As the Dakota dipped its wings the views from the portholes were of hundreds of fishing boats covered in snow resting peacefully in Bilbao harbour. Making his wary path downwards, Riley struggled badly to locate any sign of the runway, but little did he know that the airport had been shut down due to the treacherous weather.

Only when a member of the British Consul spotted the plane circling was a call made and the runway swiftly re-opened, thus averting possible disaster. As chaos reigned on the ground, in the air it reached farcical proportions as Riley was reduced to tannoying his passengers to ask them if they could see anything of note?

Amid the turbulence, racing hearts and sweating brows,

Manchester United finally arrived with an almighty bump onto Basque soil. On landing a snarling, vicious sea of snow and ice engulfed the plane as it came to a fearful screeching halt. With the United players so familiar with holiday posters back in Manchester advertising "*Sunny España*" their first experience of Spain, as the Dakota's doors were wrenched open, was the remnants of forty-eight hours of sustained rainfall and a shut-down airport obliterated by a blistering snowstorm. More drama ensued on board as the tension of the rocky flight proved too much for seventy-five year old chairman Harold Hardman who suffered a minor stroke. Immediately on disembarking Hardman was rushed to hospital and missed the game, but recovered sufficiently to be allowed to return to Manchester.

On visiting the stadium and witnessing the pitch, a drenched quagmire of mud and snow, Matt Busby and Jimmy Murphy were convinced the game would be postponed. Busby despaired, caught between the lunacy of attempting to play football on a swamp or having points deducted by the Football League for not returning in time to play on Saturday. He urged against any postponement, if necessary his *Red Devils* would have to play in Wellington boots to ensure their ridiculously tight schedule was adhered to. On meeting with German referee Albert Deutsch the United management and Bilbao officials agreed for the game to go ahead.

Busby was fearful, for Athletic were a class apart from anything their lads had ever faced. They had lost only one home match in three years. He knew the real battle for the European Cup would begin in the shadow of the Basque mountains, in the *Estadio San Mames* - named after a Christian who was thrown to the lions by the Romans. The heavens smiled on the fortunate *Mames* as the lions refused to eat him and he was later canonised. Now in *Mames'* sacred footsteps United hoped for similar luck. United's worries over Duncan Edwards' illness eased when the player declared himself available for selection. Never would Edwards' inspirational presence and all round prowess be needed more than in the intimidatory blood curdling atmosphere of *La Cateda* where the Basques came to devour their opponents.

And so in driving rain and amid lashing snow of almost Arctic proportions and with 45,000 screaming, fanatical Basque supporters yelling for their Mancunian scalps, all seemingly wearing traditional black berets and armed with the same coloured umbrellas, the game began. Almost immediately United went close to taking the lead when Dennis Viollet worked himself an opening before letting fly, only to see his shot stick in the mud on the Bilbao goal line with the goalkeeper Carmelo beaten.

Wasting little time the fortunate Carmelo booted the ball back down pitch where United defender Mark Jones, struggling in the wretched conditions, lost possession. As Jones desperately chased back Athletic striker Artiche showed blinding pace to explode forward and smash a low effort past a diving Ray Wood – it was the beginning of a nightmare first half for the visitors in which Bilbao ripped them to pieces. An audience baying for Mancunian blood saw their appetites sated twice more in that opening period as the rapier-like Artiche and his equally dangerous partner in crime Ignacio Uribe indulged themselves, causing mayhem in the Mancunian defence. Clever, incisive football played at breakneck pace proved far too good for Busby's side and they were 3-0 down at half-time with the hosts threatening many more.

As battles all over the field were being lost it appeared that only Tommy Taylor, in a monumental duel with Jesus Garay, was holding his own. Christened 'The Smiling Executioner' by *Daily Herald* journalist George Follows, Taylor had fought and scrapped for every ball, not always winning, in fact many times being hacked, kicked and even punched by Garay for his trouble, yet the Barnsley-born Taylor, the lad signed by Matt Busby for £29,999, had given as good as he got.

It was an ashen-faced United manager who spoke to his forlorn players in the dressing room at half-time. Busby and Murphy's fears regarding the outstanding quality of the Basques had proved correct throughout an opening period when at times the contest resembled men against boys. Busby assured them in measured tones that Athletic were not supermen and if they just played their game, chances would present themselves. Jimmy Murphy reminded them of who they were representing, of the people back in Manchester sat waiting desperately for news of their progress.

It was the perfect double act and Murphy was not nicknamed 'The Preacher' for nothing. Every morning back in England before training the Welshman would attend mass but when they needed fire and brimstone on the training pitch, players would feel the lash of Murphy's acid tongue with a language hardly ever heard in the hushed halls of the Vatican!

The second half saw Manchester United come out blazing with Duncan Edwards, Murphy's favourite adopted son, to the fore. Edwards ploughed through the Basque mud, urging his team-mates forward and for the first time in the tie United played like the devils on their shirt. They hit back three minutes after the break when the tenacious Taylor momentarily escaped his shadow Garay to finish off Dennis Viollet's pass and rekindle Mancunian hopes. Then, as the Basques rocked, Viollet swooped in typical manner to add a second from close range as he flicked out a foot and diverted the ball past Carmelo making it 3-2. Ignoring Busby and Murphy's frantic touchline pleas to consolidate, United continued to sweep forward in search of a sensational equaliser.

The game became stretched and Bilbao hit back from a corner when their left-winger Merodio crashed home a fourth for Athletic. Then, as a fraught United defence looked on in despair, Arteche shot past Wood from six yards to restore their three goal lead. Bilbao were rampant once more and again Busby's words had gone unheeded. At 5-2 this quarter-final appeared over, United were all but done.

Five minutes remained when Manchester United's unassuming, quiet, yet beguiling Irishman Liam Whelan carved himself a notch in the short, tragic but glorious history of the *Busby Babes*.

Whelan, a devout Roman Catholic whose faith remained important to him above everything else, came from Dublin. He was a young man who could count many priests amongst his closest friends and who once told off United apprentice Nobby Stiles for swearing in a five a side game. This was the same Liam Whelan who, in 1954, was observed by the Brazilian world cup squad playing in a youth tournament in Switzerland who enquired about taking him home, so impressed were they with his touch and technique. Recommended by legendary scout Billy Behan to United whilst playing for League of Ireland's Home Farm, the gangling but utterly sublime Whelan was amongst Busby's most precious jewels. At first sight an unlikely, awkward footballer, on the ball Liam *"Billy"* Whelan came alive with a wonderful poise, balance and eye for goal.

Now, receiving a pass in his silky stride from Duncan Edwards, the tall, wiry figure of Whelan headed with silent intent towards the Basque penalty area. On the sidelines with nerves exhausted and hearts racing Busby and the entire United bench were screaming at him to pass to an unmarked Tommy Taylor, only for Whelan, ankle-deep in mud, to take a different path. Suddenly, as if he could read his player's mind, Busby whispered within earshot of Jimmy Murphy, "Go on Bill hit it". Taking aim, Whelan spotted an opening and let fly a swerving shot that flew past Carmelo into the top corner. It was a lifeline, one grasped by the boy from Dublin who, with a moment of instinctive brilliance, had dragged his club back into the European Cup. At 5-3 the game ended, both sides reasonably satisfied and knowing all was still to play for when battle resumed in Manchester.

Yet perhaps a bigger task now faced the Mancunian party – the journey home...

A lack of foresight on behalf of the aircrew meant the Dakota had been left stranded in Bilbao airport throughout the blizzard, almost certainly stranding United in Spain. With an important league match the following Saturday against Sheffield Wednesday, Busby could ill afford the possibility of returning late and being docked points by a still bitter and vindictive League administrator Alan Hardaker. "*A competition made up of wogs and dagoes*" had been Hardaker's contemptuous assessment of the European Cup. He insisted that "*Manchester United should have nothing to do with the European Cup.*" This was a man silently seething at United's refusal to bow down to his demand not to compete in the competition. Moreover, he was determined to wreak revenge on Busby who had taken on and humiliated him by refusing to be bullied as Chelsea had the season before.

For now United just had to get home and all hands were drafted in by Busby to ensure the plane was made airworthy. Left with little option he later recalled, "*I could well imagine the repercussions if we failed to turn up at Hillsborough.*" With Captain Charles Riley taking charge, players, coaching staff, journalists and supporters helped to shovel snow and ice off the wings. There exists a photograph taken by hero of the hour Liam Whelan of the team posing with huge grins beneath the plane's fuselage with spades and shovels in hands. It was to prove a haunting epitaph.

Finally, after four hours of toil, permission was received for take off and the plane taking the *Busby Babes* home rose rather half-heartedly into the snow speckled Basque sky. The flight was not to be without further strife and incident for on approaching a refuelling spot in Jersey they encountered a severe gale, one which saw the Dakota dip frighteningly below a cliff. Then, as the pilot opened up his throttle with the runway in sight, they shot over and bounced ominously upon the ground to land with a nerve-shattering thump. After a harrowing journey United finally made it back, the fraught perils of early air travel experienced at first hand. There had been lessons to be learned, but tragically in time not taken on board.

TOMMY'S WAR

Manchester. A city where Marks joined Spencer to make a penny bazaar, where pride and passion came from the soul not from a birthright. Jew and Gentile; Irish, Italian and Welsh, Catholic and Protestant, all living in harmony. Drinking, cussing, laughing and arguing. John Lennon would later sing of imagining such a dream. It was a city hardly rich in diamonds and pearls but open and welcoming to all. No more than to the Basque. At least off the pitch, for come one, come all, bring your best and keep your worst but don't ever dare take Mancunians for granted. Welcome to Manchester...

The Return: Wednesday 6th February 1957. The City of Manchester awaited with nervous anticipation the return of the Basques. Again, with Old Trafford not quite ready to hold evening midweek matches, Maine Road would host United's potential last stand in the European Cup. The build up was intense, the pressure unyielding – expectations rose for a miraculous recovery beyond footballing reason.

People in factories and pubs, on buses and in shops talked of little else. In an effort to take his players away from this stifling atmosphere Matt Busby retreated to his favourite refuge – Blackpool's Norbreck hotel. There, at the seaside, he and Murphy planned the great escape. They were left with two options - all out attack and pray beyond the Mancunian skies that God in heaven would declare it to be their night under the glare of Maine Road's floodlights.

The Athletic Bilbao coach, fifty-seven year old silver

haired, former Barcelona manager Ferdinand Daucik, landed in England declaring it was almost insulting to suggest they could be eliminated. *"No team on the planet can beat the Basque nation by three goals!"* the Czech insisted. Daucik had bought into the Basque mentality with all the intensity of a religious conversion and the delusions of grandeur, undoubtedly brought about by his time spent in Bilbao, meant he seriously believed such comments.

A relaxed Bilbao captain Agustin Gainza happily posed for photographers making a 0-0 sign with his fingers. When asked if he felt United still had a chance he simply smiled – as if to suggest it was some silly joke. Amid the Athletic party there existed a rather unhealthy air of over-confidence, a feeling that the job had already been done.

The evening before the tie the Bilbao players undertook a Ballet-style training session on the Maine Road pitch. The City ground staff watched nonplussed as Athletic went through a series of subtle and delicate body stretching exercises. This was totally alien to anything they had ever witnessed. English pressmen looking on from the stand sniggered at these supposed fierce Basque warriors. Such continental preparation was met with scorn and sarcasm – one scribe penned that, "A slight smell of perfume lingered disconcertingly on the field!"

Cometh the hour and no matter what Daucik claimed, hope sprung eternal in the hearts and minds of 70,000 Mancunians as they crammed into Maine Road, waiting for the second leg to begin. The passion that rose into the dark night from those Moss Side terraces soared loudly into the Manchester sky and could be heard over twenty miles away. People across the city described it as distant thunder. There was a red storm brewing in the rainy city.

The mood, though apprehensive, remained one of quiet confidence. That United possessed the calibre to score three goals was never doubted. But could they keep a clean sheet against the swift counter-attacking Basques? At 7.20 the waiting ended as Roger Byrne and Jesus Garay led out their respective teams to a deafening roar. Under the dreamy glare of the Maine Road floodlights and a barrage of flashing cameras the two captains shook hands in the centre circle.

A pretty, raven-haired señorita, dressed in traditional Basque costume, presented a blushing Byrne with a monumental bouquet of flowers. The Beswick Prize Band was on hand to perform the two national anthems. As the teams lined up on the touchline, a hush fell across the grandstands as the Spanish version began before "God Save the Queen" was sung with great gusto. Once finished, the band marched off and the crowd erupted again. These pleasantries completed, the teams took up their positions and battle was set to begin.

Tommy Taylor started the game by rolling the ball to Bill Whelan and all hell broke loose in Manchester – the action began at a frantic pace and never relented. On the sidelines Matt Busby stalked, clutching tight to a cigarette, watching on anxiously as his *Babes* roared forward in search of a miracle. Taylor and Jesus Garay had resumed their personal duel with blood-curdling relish. This was a clash of giants in heart and stature. On ten minutes United looked to have grabbed an early breakthrough, only for the German referee, Albert Deusch to disallow it as, latching onto a Tommy Taylor knock down, Dennis Viollet slid the ball home only for supporters' cheers to be caught in their throats as the linesman flagged offside.

Bilbao broke - their forwards Gainza and Arteche swift and deadly. The latter was so close to getting off a shot after a short back pass by Bill Foulkes only for Ray Wood to come rushing out and save the day. Throughout the first half United pressed but Bilbao held firm. Tempers frayed, niggled and at times exploded as the tension from the terraces found itself seeping onto the pitch.

Inspired by Duncan Edwards, the home side kept going. Working in unison with Eddie Colman, United's number six commanded the midfield. Under orders from Busby to remain in his own half for the time being, Edwards followed his manager's instructions to the letter. At one stage when racing toward the halfway line he simply put the brakes on, his arms wind milling, trying to prevent himself stepping an inch into Basque territory!

Chances came. A clever ball inside the Athletic full-back Canito by Eddie Colman saw Johnny Berry go flying through. Looking up the popular Brummie spotted Taylor as ever guarded by the giant Garay. This option closed, Berry found instead Dennis Viollet, who from six yards drove the ball past Carmelo to ignite Maine Road. Again they proved false hopes as, to the horror of the crowd, Herr Deutsch once more ruled offside. In tandem with his linesman the German at that moment was in serious danger of being lynched by irate Mancunians as they bayed for his head. Much as United drove on, there was little pattern or fluidity but it was still exhilarating, all or nothing football with both teams refusing to give an inch, as Busby's words from the touchline to settle down were lost amid the wall of noise inside the stadium.

It was carnage and confusion and amid it all a match took place. Finally let off the leash by Busby, Duncan Edwards set off on a barnstorming run into the Basque half. Roared on by the crowd and shrugging off tackles from Mauri and Etura as if swatting flies, he let go a flashing drive that almost ripped a hole in Jesus Garay's midriff – the Basque defender was by this time almost a one man rearguard as he sweated blood to keep United out.

Four minutes of the first period remained when Edwards ventured once more into Basque territory. Now given freedom to roam he wreaked mayhem – receiving the ball Big Dunc let fly from the edge of Bilbao's penalty area. It was a ferocious low drive that Carmelo failed to hold. For once, luck shone on the home side as ghosting in came Dennis Viollet to smash home and unleash a Mancunian roar that split the heavens! Born in nearby Fallowfield, a goal-kick away from Maine Road, Viollet found himself swamped by ecstatic team-mates for his lifeline.

Half-time came and the home players were applauded wildly for the huge effort all the way down the tunnel – Manchester

United were within a goal of a Parisian play-off. In the relative tranquillity of the dressing room Busby stressed the importance of remaining calm amid the hysteria that surrounded them. As ever Jimmy Murphy stood by his side, praising and urging more. Across the corridor, the Basques sat in stunned shock. Jesus Garay nursed his war wounds caused by Tommy Taylor. Never in his illustrious career had he encountered one such as Taylor. Even the ball playing artists of Real Madrid and Barcelona had not troubled him like the United centre-forward. Daucik implored his men to remain strong for such was the immense energy being spent by United that they surely had to run out of steam and then they would catch them out.

From the re-start disaster came close for United when an over-anxious Eddie Colman was caught by Bilbao's winger Arteche, who bore down on him, took the ball and ran clear on Ray Wood. Time appeared to stand still as Arteche went round the goalkeeper and shot goal wards, only to see from nowhere United Captain Roger Byrne return to hack the ball clear. As Maine Road heaved a huge sigh of relief, an infuriated Byrne sought out Colman and handed the apologetic Salfordian a very public berating.

An hour had passed of this pulsating contest and United were still like a red rash all over Bilbao but failing to convert opportunities when they arose. Taylor again hit the woodwork with a thumping header, Johnny Berry hit the outside of an upright and suddenly only twenty minutes remained. Athletic goalkeeper Carmelo was performing heroically; he was brave, agile and seemingly attracted like a magnet to the ball as it flew endlessly across his area.

Amongst the crowd were many local priests given free tickets by Manchester United, possibly hoping for a heavenly helping hand. As time sped on all favours were being called in. On went David Pegg tearing away down the left hand touchline. Turning and twisting, desperate to give himself an inch, Pegg sent a cross into the penalty area where, arriving like an express train was the magnificent Tommy Taylor. By this stage of an enthralling contest Taylor had run the legs off Jesus Garay. The pride of the Basques was all but on his knees. Roaring free of his flailing Bilbao shackles *The Smiling Executioner* took the ball in his stride and flashed a splendid shot low past Carmelo into his far corner. Manchester exploded!

An evening that had threatened to tug at the heartstrings had become something quite extraordinary. Manchester United had fought, scrapped and clawed their way back into the European Cup. The Basques were bleeding and ripe for the taking. Sensing no need for the Paris play-off, United went in search of a killer third. The Athletic coach Daucik could barely watch as his beleaguered defence were close to collapse. Five minutes remained and Maine Road had become something almost unworldly: 70,000 people produced a volume of noise deafening to the ear and chilling to the bone.

Playing like a man possessed, Taylor powered past an exhausted Athletic full-back Canito. On he charged into the penalty area. With the crowd screaming for their hero to let fly, Taylor instead kept his calm and played the ball to an unmarked Johnny Berry in a better position. At full speed Berry hit a scorching drive that roared into the top corner past Carmelo to win the tie and cause unadulterated madness to engulf Maine Road as one the Athletic players fell to the turf, their resistance broken and shattered.

On the touchline Busby and Murphy danced a jig of delight. Amongst spectators there were tears of joy and relief; their voices hoarse beyond all call of duty for they had given as equally as the team. There was to be a last-second scare when Bill Foulkes under hit a back pass to signal a frantic race between Ray Wood and Gainza which the United goalkeeper won by an inch. Finally, a night laced with drama and emotion came to a close. At their first attempt Manchester United had qualified for the European Cup semi-finals.

The final whistle saw wonderful scenes of sportsmanship displayed by the beaten Bilbao players. Great dignity was shown, none more so than by Jesus Garay who sought out Tommy

Taylor and shared a quiet word with him before warmly embracing his young tormentor. That evening at the post-match banquet in the Midland Hotel, ecstatic crowds gathered at the main door to cheer the players in. Though devastated at losing the opportunity to take on Real Madrid further on in the competition, the Basques proved generous in defeat. Fine words were spoken by the visitors.

Ferdinand Daucik praised not only the United team but the efforts of the crowd! *"In all my years in football I have never encountered noise like it,"* he admitted. Daucik's pre-game comments returned to haunt him in a manner he could surely not even have dreamed of when Athletic scored that fifth goal on home soil. Jesus Garay insisted he be allowed to say a few words in the after-dinner speeches regarding Tommy Taylor. Garay toasted the United player before stating, *"Taylor is the finest centre-forward that I have ever played against."* The Basques went home beaten but unbowed, as for United, Real Madrid awaited in the semi-finals. A story yet to unfold.

The date on which this memorable football match occurred, 6th February would in a short time grow to have a terrible poignancy for all concerned with Manchester United. For twelve months to the day eight players would perish at the end of that infernal Munich runway. Including tragically Tommy Taylor – it was news that broke the heart of one Jesus Garay.

LOS CHICOS

Manchester United manager Matt Busby and his assistant Jimmy Murphy had fashioned and developed an exciting young team that had already taken British football by storm and was threatening to do so in Europe. A first tilt at the European Cup had already seen them demolish an outstanding Anderlecht 10-0 and put paid to formidable Spanish champions Athletic Bilbao. A semi-final pairing against holders Real Madrid awaited and the Madrileño's were under no illusions that these Busby Babes posed a huge threat to their much heralded crown. The masters against the pupils. A battle royale was expected against the great Real Madrid and so it proved...

It was the startling events of Wednesday 6th February 1957, on a never to be forgotten Mancunian evening that caused serious questions to be raised in Madrid. Just how good was this English team? On boarding the plane home to Bilbao, Basque captain Agustin Gainza could still not believe what had become of his team and the sheer ferocity and pace of his opponents, "United played with such passion we were simply overwhelmed."

Manchester United had laid down a marker that could not be ignored. Madrid had been warned. Yet whilst there would be huge respect for United, they were hardly shaking with fear in the Spanish capital despite all the Mancunians flowering wealth of talent. True they possessed the astonishing, barnstorming Duncan Edwards, the deft touch and trickery of Eddie Colman and the aerial prowess and raw power of Tommy Taylor and much more, so much more. Yet they did not have amid their ranks a player rated by Matt Busby as the greatest of them all.

In Nice, on March 14th 1957, Matt Busby, accompanied by the Northern England press pack, sat in a crowd who watched in awe as Alfredo Di Stefano inspired Real Madrid to win 3-2 and stake a semi-final spot against his team. What Busby saw on that long gone evening on the French Mediterranean coast captivated his footballing soul.

Two goals from Di Stefano, who on that night for the first time in a Madrid shirt began to operate in a roving role, saw the reigning champions through 6-2 on aggregate. Taking it upon himself, Di Stefano had gone against his coach Jose Villalonga's instructions to stay up front and instead switched to a position which, given his awesome ability to dominate a football match, suited him to perfection.

With grace and artistry dripping from every pore, Di Stefano was magnificent; a king amongst Spanish princes. The twenty-nine year old with a balding pate and eyes that filled with disdain anytime a *Madrileño* failed to attain his highest standards, was considered by many arrogant and aloof. He was short tempered and the worst of losers but without doubt, in Matt Busby's opinion, a most glorious footballer.

On returning to Manchester Busby was moved to write, "*I have just witnessed Alfredo the Great! In a lifetime of football I have never seen a better player, he is simply unique.*" Worryingly for the United coaching staff, Busby never spoke of opposing players in such glowing terms but such was his admiration of Madrid's *Blond Arrow* he could not help himself. Indeed, when the two men finally met, Di Stefano thanked Busby for his kind words and asked him if he would consider becoming his publicity agent!

On their fearsomely fast winger Francisco Gento, Busby told the defender who would be handed the awesome task of marking him, Bill Foulkes, that Gento, "*was the fastest thing he had ever seen!*" An already apprehensive Foulkes did not appreciate such flowery comments from his manager. When questioned by the players Busby told them simply, "Just play the best you can lads."

Almost as if wary of telling them just what he had witnessed in Nice, Bobby Charlton remembers having the worrying notion of whooping, savage wild-west Indians approaching fast from the other side of the hill, that they could hear but not yet see, with the *Blond Arrow* leading from the front.

Matt Busby thought long and hard about how to contain Madrid in the *Bernabéu*, specifically the threat of Alfredo Di Stefano, for he knew that given an inch on his own stage in front of an adoring partisan home crowd, Di Stefano would destroy them. This semi-final was regarded as the biggest game in the short history of the European Cup with the Red Devils viewed as Real's main rivals for the foreseeable future. The Bernabéu was the perfect stage for a man who craved and demanded adulation not just from spectators but the opposition and it was an opportunity that Di Stefano's ego would not let pass.

For at times strange forces appeared at work in the *Bernabéu* whenever Di Stefano took possession. As if lit by sudden bursts of hidden electricity, Francisco Gento would ignite and find the ball landing at his feet from a wondrous Di Stefano pass. Gento would fly to be joined by equally sleight of foot *compadres*, the newly acquired Raimondo Kopa, Hector Rial and local boy Enrique Mateos.

Alfredo Di Stefano was well aware of his priceless worth to Madrid's ambition in creating a footballing dynasty to last for a generation. An expensive fact President Don Santiago knew only too well as he made out cheques amounting to a king's ransom for his most valuable asset. In attempting to stem the deadly rapier strikes of Di Stefano, the United manager came up with an unlikely solution. He detailed his ball playing, highly intelligent twenty-four year old Irish central defender Jackie Blanchflower and snake hips Eddie Colman to keep the great man quiet.

Busby briefed Colman not to leave Di Stefano's side, *"Follow that man to the ends of the earth!"* were his manager's words. It was an unenviable task but one which the Salford born Colman would endeavour to carry out. For those ninety minutes in the *Bernabéu* he would be Di Stefano's shadow.

Born in Archie Street, Salford, the real life Coronation Street, Eddie Colman was perhaps the most loved of the *Babes*. He was one of their own, a natural happy-go-lucky, mischievous and charming character with an easy, friendly manner and enough devil to excite the Old Trafford regulars. Eddie had few equals in England as he teased and tormented First Division defenders. Trusted by Busby to stay disciplined, Eddie Colman's unerring ability to twist and turn at great speed also played a significant part in his manager's thinking. In using Colman, who would undoubtedly find himself dragged all over the pitch by Di Stefano, Busby could then keep together his back four.

However Colman was reassured by his manager that he would not be alone in this awesome task as once the Argentine crossed the halfway line he would be helped by Jackie Blanchflower. Originally coming to United as an inside forward, Jackie had quickly realised with rivals such as Bobby Charlton, Dennis Viollet and Liam Whelan battling for two positions, opportunities would be limited. After converting himself into a centre half, Blanchflower was capped by Northern Ireland and new doors opened in his Old Trafford career. An ability to read the game, intercept rather than tackle and a cute eye for a damning pass saw the Belfast born youngster flourish. Between this pairing of a Salfordian and an Irishman, Busby and Murphy hoped to limit the destructive capacities of Di Stefano.

The United player many perceived was best suited to man-mark Di Stefano was the remarkable twenty-year old Duncan Edwards. Already an English international and surely a future captain of the national side. Blessed with an unfair abundance of all round talent Edwards was powerful, ferocious in the tackle, inspirational, could play off either foot with equal brilliance, was towering in the air and had seemingly indomitable spirit. It said it all that whenever United were struggling in a game, the Old Trafford terraces would shout in supplication "Just Give It

To Dunc!"

If Alfredo Di Stefano was the most precious of Real Madrid's brightest lights then Duncan Edwards was United's heart and soul. Busby felt that in the white hot atmosphere of the *Estadio Bernabéu*, Edwards' unique prowess would never be needed more as United prepared to withstand what was certain to be a white storm descending upon them.

The anxious Scot was all too aware that even if, by some miracle, they managed to keep the lid on Di Stefano, the calibre of players such as the thundering Frenchman Raimondo Kopa, the Spanish bolt of lightning masquerading as a footballer Francisco 'Paco' Gento or the Argentine hit man centre-forward Hector Rial would surely strike. All were more than capable in their own right of ending Manchester United's fledgling European adventure in the blink of an eye.

United would have to perform like never before to survive a beating in the *Bernabéu*. They could not go in all guns blazing, charging about with typical aplomb to the sound of the cannons, to do so risked obliteration at the hands of these Spanish magicians. Instead they would tread carefully on foreign soil, for Busby knew Madrid was not just unknown territory but potentially lethal also.

Expectations in Manchester after what had been achieved against the much lauded Athletic Bilbao had reached fever pitch. There were not many supporters who felt Real Madrid, though grand in name and stature, would halt what for them was simply a triumphal procession to a first European Cup success. It all felt inevitable.

Sporadic clips of *Pathé* newsreel footage was all most had witnessed of Real Madrid. Though spectacular, angelic even, these knights in white satin flashing across the cinema screen were balletic, undoubtedly beautiful and left a lasting impression but surely they would be no match for Matt's boys? This was a team built in Busby's own image, playing blistering, open attacking football; one touch, pass and move. Like the nascent rock 'n'roll beat that accompanied their staccato play, they electrified any and every ground they played at and now that their beat had crossed onto the continent, most of Europe was aware of these flashing Mancunian dervishes. United were gunning for Real Madrid's European crown. It was all just a matter of time. Santiago Bernabéu's prophesy of an all conquering club had come to fruition much sooner than even a man of his vision could possibly have envisaged. The flowering years of the European Cup saw Real blow away all opposition. No side on the continent had appeared capable of living with Di Stefano and his orchestra of stars. Until now...

Leading up to the first leg the Spanish press and public devoured every fact and news story about this remarkable, exciting young team who dared to challenge the mighty *Madrileños* and they waited with baited breath United's arrival on Spanish soil. Accustomed to other managers fawning in admiration over the brilliance of Real and seemingly beaten before they even took to the field, Matt Busby's confidence that he believed "*United were a better team*" and that "*Real Madrid will need at least three goals to take back to Manchester*" caused many to become apprehensive of just what exactly was coming their way. While Busby was bullish in public, privately he felt that the Spaniards would have just too much guile and know how for his talented but still raw team.

The weekend before Real warmed up by routing Los Palmas 5-1 away. A majestic Alfredo Di Stefano helped himself to four and appeared primed and ready for the English champions. Making the grim error of taking the lead, Los Palmas swiftly found themselves buried in an avalanche of *Madrileño* goals.

A thousand miles away in Manchester, United were involved in a hard fought 0-0 draw against their closest title rivals Tottenham Hotspur at Old Trafford. Busby's team were minus two of their star players, left-winger David Pegg and Duncan Edwards were both away on international duty but come the final whistle a relieved Busby was able to announce a fully fit squad to take on Madrid the following Thursday.

And so on Monday 8th April 1957, the plane carrying

Manchester United soared off the runway at Ringway airport to take them to the biggest game in their history. Leaving behind a murky Mancunian drizzle, they landed in blazing sunshine at Madrid airport and were greeted by hundreds of Real supporters, so eager to see these much talked about Los Chicos, with their own eyes.

A barrage of flashbulbs exploded in their eyes as the players, resplendent in their MUFC blazers, walked down the gangway. Immediately they were besieged by over-eager autograph hunters – the clamour coming from equal numbers of lady admirers as well as football supporters.

The Babes cut a swagger with English flannel and grey trilbies dipped acutely over their eyes to give them the impression of 1920's Chicago hoodlums. Chaos ensued but it was all remarkably good natured as a mad huddle surrounded the charismatic visitors. Manchester United had come to Madrid. This sophisticated, wealthy European city a world away from murky post-war Manchester but on the football pitch they would start equal.

United centre-forward Tommy Taylor appeared among the most popular players after his epic collision with Jesus Garay of Athletic Bilbao in the previous round. He and Taylor had fought an epic personal duel over the two legs with the United striker finally coming out on top and the Yorkshireman's reputation had soared across Europe as a result and nowhere more than in Madrid.

However in Real's ranks there lurked equal devilment with defenders and midfielders of the calibre of Manuel Marquitos, captain Miguel Muñoz and Jose Maria Zarraga. Whilst all technically sublime they verged on the fanatical in the heat of battle and were prepared to give no mercy. They had been well briefed on the talents of this particular Englishman and would be ready. There were none more brutal than the dark haired, steely eyed, twenty-seven year old Marquitos. Blood-curdling when roused, Marquitos had already made it known that he would not go the way of Garay. He and his studs prepared to make their mark on this European Cup semi-final and in particular Tommy Taylor.

Busby was taking no chances. United took twenty-two players to Madrid, a reserve for every position. He also was given assurance from the manager of the plush five-star Fenix Hotel in the city's heart where United would reside that only English style food would be served to his party. Busby also insisted that only bottled water was to be drunk, thus avoiding the dread of all Brits abroad, the infamous Spanish tummy.

United's arrival heralded a press frenzy the likes of which Madrid had rarely witnessed – the media scrum seemed more fitting for the arrival of a top Hollywood movie star than a visiting football team. Whenever the players set foot out of the hotel they were immediately mobbed. Ever present around the Fenix were the ticket touts demanding a thousand pesetas for a hundred peseta ticket – the prices might have seemed outrageous but with 250,000 ticket applications already made to the club and with receipts said to be worth a world record £55,000, they did brisk business.

On match day Madrid awoke to feelings of fear and exhilaration. Never before had their *Madrileños* faced such a deadly foe. The previous evening Real had allowed United to train on the *Bernabéu* pitch. But fully aware that the Spanish would undoubtedly have spies watching their every move Busby kept the sessions simple and gave nothing away.

Situated in one of the more lavish palatial quarters of Madrid, the *Chamartin* district, the Estadio *Bernabéu* soared high into the heavens. Built from white concrete it was a majestic, awe-inspiring sporting cathedral fit for the footballing gods. As the game drew near thousand gathered outside the stadium, many without tickets while others attempted to rush the barriers, only to be forced back by mounted police. For a while chaos ensued before order was restored and in they came, over 130,000 spectators demanding a rout.

For hours before kick-off the terraces were packed. The expectation was high that the home team would put these

English upstarts in their rightful place. The visitors would not be without support in the stadium with five chartered aircraft full of United supporters having travelled over to cheer their boys on. Whether they would be heard in such a vast arena when up against such fanatical backing was debatable.

Easter drew close in the Spanish capital, the traditional beginning of the bullfighting season nearby at the *Monumental* plaza. But Madrid had only one slaughter on their minds, to gore Manchester United's European hopes. For like a red flag to a bull the Babes had antagonised these self-anointed kings of European football.

Shortly before kick off United received a visit from Madrid officials who were carrying photographs of the eleven *Madrileños* they were set to face. After handing them to Matt Busby they in turn asked for pictures of those in red shirts taking the field. A non-plussed United manager politely explained that such a custom was unheard of in England, but they had his word that Manchester United would not be including any ringers! Trying hard not to lose his calm as the visitors insinuated all was not as it should be, Busby finally let fly at this unwanted presence in the sanctuary of the dressing room. He informed them that all the passports were safely locked up in the hotel vault, but that if Real wished he would happily show them to whoever after the match.

However the sullen Spaniards were insistent and not wanting to cause an international incident, Busby instead decided to leave and he headed off for a quiet chat with assistant Jimmy Murphy and to check out the playing surface. Incredibly, due to the rising tide of hysteria that had gripped the *Bernabéu*, the only place they could hear each other speak was in the centre-circle. There the two men, in the heart of Madrid's great stadium, discussed just how they would topple this giant from its imperial perch.

CLUTCHING AT RAINBOWS

In the mid afternoon of Thursday 11th April 1957, Real Madrid and Manchester United stepped out into the Spanish sunshine to do battle. The arrival of the two teams was greeted by a magical shower of white roses thrown from the highest bastions of this magnificent stadium. The United players looked on in astonishment as this cascade of flowers floated down onto the pitch. The Real captain, Miguel Muñoz, applauded his supporters for their remarkable display – it was a truly epic and moving spectacle.

Flashbulbs glittered across the terrace like a million fireflies as the Bernabéu exploded in a glorious, deafening symphony of rockets and cheering. A huge posse of photographers scuttled like ants across the turf as both sides posed for their team photos. It was to be an afternoon they would talk about in Madrid for generations to come...

The small party of travelling British Journalists luckily enough to be present could not believe the luxurious comfort of the *Bernabéu* press box. There, waiters dressed in immaculate white jackets attended to all their needs. Even the Madrid supporters sat below them were obliging as they passed up to the disbelieving, hard-bitten hacks pigskin bladders filled with red wine.

Dutch referee Leo Horn, easily Europe's most famous official, had been a war hero who fought with great courage for his country's resistance. However an eternally much crueller fate befell his brother Edgar, tragically murdered by the Nazis in a concentration camp. At the war's end Horn returned to refereeing and the fact he was also a black belt in Judo meant his no nonsense approach on the pitch was respected by players of all sides.

So it began.

For an hour Manchester United fought tooth and nail to stem an endless array of *Madrileño* attacks. Many times they were simply penned back into their own penalty area, unable to break out. However United held firm, unyielding. On the wings left-back Roger Byrne was having considerable success against Ramonde Kopa. Byrne's intelligence and pace curtailed the Frenchman's usual rampaging assaults.

However on the other side, right-back Bill Foulkes was in the midst of a living nightmare against the flying machine Francisco Gento. Time and again Gento would feint to go one way then change direction, switching instantaneously to over drive with a blistering turn of speed that left Foulkes gasping for breath in the Spaniard's wake. He was left clutching at rainbows.

With Alfredo Di Stefano's every step shadowed by Eddie Colman, the *Blond Arrow* found his aim stunted and touch unsure. The great man became increasingly rattled as Colman followed his every move, a red shadow etched onto a white knight. Whenever it appeared Alfredo's blistering acceleration would take him clear of his Salfordian nemesis, Jackie Blanchflower intercepted to tighten the noose further and upset Di Stefano's regal state of mind further.

Finally the scowling Di Stefano's patience snapped and he launched a sickening lunge on Blanchflower that scythed him down and should have seen the Argentine dismissed. The foul was committed only yards away from the referee and Leo Horn appeared to have no option but to dismiss him, but how do you send off the leading man in his own personal theatre? Probably not wishing to face a local hate mob after the match, Horn for once failed in his duty and allowed the Argentine to stay on the field.

But this undeserved slice of luck did not save Di Stefano

from the wrath of an outraged Bill Foulkes who, seeing his friend Blanchflower almost decapitated, grabbed him by the shirt and was threatening to do much worse before being wrestled away by team-mates.

Occasionally creaking and at times sliced wide open, the *Babes* by some miracle kept the marauding *Madrileños* at bay. Matt Busby's tactical ploy to keep Di Stefano on a short leash was holding, just, for there were occasions that even with such close attention Madrid's number nine found space and time to engineer a pass or have an attempt at goal. In the rare moments United managed to venture over the half-way line their swashbuckling centre-forward Tommy Taylor found himself victim to a succession of murderous tackles and challenges that verged on assault.

Aware of the dangers posed by the English centre-forward, the villainous Marquitos hacked and slashed both on the ball and off. He was ably abetted by partners in crime Muñoz and Zarraga, who thought nothing of kicking poor Tommy up in the air for the mere fun of it. And yet Taylor, brave beyond all cause of duty, would not be intimidated and shortly before half-time, following a cross by David Pegg, he missed by a hair's breadth with a header when it would have been easier to score. United taking the lead would have been daylight robbery such was Madrid's dominance. Nevertheless, the first period ended with the home crowd whistling their frustrations. This was not in the script; they came demanding English blood and all they had seen so far was a peerless display of grit and determination by the visitors.

But ninety minutes was an awful long time to test your mettle against wizards and magicians. One master stroke from Di Stefano's baton and all hell could yet be let loose upon them. Hard work and discipline were worthy attributes but there remained much work to achieve before returning home with satisfaction to Manchester.

With an hour gone the European champions, so relentless in their pursuit of an opening goal, finally unlocked the red vault and it was Francisco Gento who went powering through with all guns blazing. Teasing and jinking poor Bill Foulkes to distraction, Gento tore away and without even glancing up delivered a superb cross onto the head of Hector Rial, who powered a fierce stooping header from close blank range past a helpless Ray Wood – the *Bernabéu* erupted!

Across the huge terraces that stretched upwards, thousands of white handkerchiefs were waved in delight. Madrid was on fire, the deadlock broken. Now, thought the home supporters, it was just a matter of how many. With the crowd baying for blood Real moved in for the kill. After enduring a frustrating match Alfredo Di Stefano finally rid himself of a badly tiring Eddie Colman. Attached like a limpet throughout, with seventeen minutes remaining Colman's chains fell away and he broke free! With fearful speed and purpose, like a man wrongly jailed and now determined to right an injustice, Di Stefano roared past a ragged bevy of bedraggled red shirts to race dangerously clear into the visitor's half.

Leading the chase to catch him was the immaculate United captain Roger Byrne, but Di Stefano was in no mood to be caught, and with heavenly precision he executed a perfect chip over Ray Wood that landed perfectly under the crossbar to double Real's lead. Two goals down and the roof was caving in on Matt Busby courageous young team. They now faced the serious prospect of being massacred.

The *Madrileños* roared their approval – the crowd were buoyant, expectant, demanding more. "Olé" rang across this grand stadium. Every Madrid touch was cheered to the rafters. It was fiesta time as they taunted their exhausted opponents with keep ball. Never had Busby's team experienced this level of football, played with such infinite precision and touch. Theirs was a technique unmatched, a mastery bewitching. This was a foreign game for many of the United players. Outclassed and out-thought their truly outstanding players such as Duncan Edwards, David Pegg and Liam Whelan were now realising that they remained mere pupils compared to the masters from

Madrid.

From the touchline Busby urged his players on and, showing incredible spirit, the *Babes* rallied. Suddenly from appearing down and out the red shirts surged forward. United's typical pass and move and swift interchanging had Madrid on the back foot. David Pegg was making life horribly uncomfortable for the defender Jose Becerril. Time and again Pegg led Becerril a merry dance. United pressed on and with just eight minutes remaining Tommy Taylor escaped the clutches of his hatchet men to head a Liam Whelan cross past Alonso into the net. An unexpected lifeline had been grasped by the *Red Devils*. Back in Manchester hope sprung eternal in packed households and workplaces as radios crackled with the glad tidings. It had become a battle royal. United had somehow dragged themselves back into a contest that in reality should have been over. As the ball crossed the line a silence fell across the *Bernabéu*, an anxiety not noticeable since the opening stages had returned. Taylor found himself mobbed by team-mates as Dennis Viollet and Johnny Berry leapt on top of the United striker, it was game on.

Yet instead of settling for a 2-1 deficit United continued to go forward in search of an equaliser. They came so close to achieving it when Viollet took aim and smashed a low drive onto the Madrid post. Then Tommy was sent sprawling in the area by Marquitos in what appeared a definite penalty, only for the referee to ignore their claims. Never had Real experienced such pressure on home soil. Typically brash and cocky the *Busby Babes* attacked. Meanwhile on the touchline a proud manager watched his team play out a footballing version of Russian roulette as they fought to level.

As the clock wound down and with time almost up they were to pay a heavy price for such youthful belligerence. A brilliant interchange between Gento and Rial let through the brilliant Mateos to fire in off the post past a diving Wood to seal a much deserved 3-1 victory for Madrid. Mateos stood to attention, slowly raising his arms to the heavens and remained in this pose for what felt an eternity to receive the adulation of a goal crazy crowd.

It was heartbreak for United and left them a mountain to climb when only seconds beforehand it resembled only a steep hill. Come the final whistle, the home players and supporters celebrated as if they had won the European Cup itself. This victory meant that much and it was with great fervour and no little relief that Di Stefano and his team gathered in the centre-circle to take the acclaim of an adoring *Bernabéu* audience.

In the United dressing room their trainer Tom Curry heaped praised on the players, *"You all deserve gold medals as big as frying pans,"* he declared. Busby singled out the exhausted Bill Foulkes, *"No other defender in England could have played Gento better,"* he told him. All at Real Madrid knew that although a fine victory had been achieved this semi-final was not yet won.

Athletic Bilbao had assumed their work was done after taking a two-goal lead to England and they received a 3-0 drubbing and were crushed in spirit at the manner of their humiliating defeat. The Bilbao players spoke of a crowd roar that resembled a plane taking off. Of a raw passion that resonated down from the terraces onto the pitch, causing the United players to lift their game to unparalleled heights. Of a magic in the Mancunian air, that there was something special in that northern city. Murky and grey, hidden by smoke and fog and rain sodden maybe but every so often illuminated by a startling red dash capable of lifting hearts and achieving footballing miracles.

It was known as Manchester United.

As was their wont, Real Madrid served up a sumptuous post match banquet for the English visitors. This was a club not just teeming with class on the pitch but also off it. Every United player and member of the coaching staff was presented with a gold watch in lasting memory of their memorable encounter at the *Bernabéu*. One United footballer particularly taken with this special memento was Duncan Edwards. All were in high spirits, many toasts were raised in what was a wonderful display of generosity by the Madrid hosts. Even Tommy Taylor, who had found himself battered throughout the match by Real defenders, now enjoyed many a drink, laugh and joke with his tormentors. His killer line, *"Let's see what happens in Manchester"* causing Marquitos and his *compadres* a few sleepless nights before battle recommenced at Old Trafford.

Don Santiago Bernabéu made a heartfelt speech pledging the importance of friendship between these two great clubs. One man particularly taken by Bernabéu's words was Matt Busby. He was overwhelmed by Madrid's impeccable staging of the occasion and made himself a promise that Manchester United must emulate and even attempt to better what had taken place on that special night.

As the evening wore on Busby found himself cornered by two Madrid players. One was alleged to have said to him: *"Please come and manage us! With you at our helm we would win every trophy in the world!"* The United manager, though flattered and wondering if Don Santiago was behind this friendly mugging, replied with an honesty and class that left his Spanish inquisitors disappointed but still smiling. *"Listen my dear friends, if you were to give me Di Stefano, United would win every trophy in the world!"*

The following day's headlines in the *Daily Herald* screamed out: **MURDER IN MADRID!** The *Herald* reporter George Follows wrote: *"I have never witnessed such crude and violent tackling as that seen in the Madrid display."*

Follows singled out Marquitos as the main culprit whilst the general consensus amongst the British press was that the referee Leo Horn had been far too lenient with the home side. But it was not yet over and Busby knew that an early goal at Old Trafford and all bets would be off. Manchester United had survived to fight another day and with their ground ready to hold a European match under floodlights for the first time and 65,000 Mancunians roaring them on, the possibility of a miracle still existed.

The British press seemed to believe that these Spanish *"fancy dans"* would crumble and United would run riot. Insular to the point of ignorant, many English journalists still failed to grasp just what Busby's side was up against. With baited breath Manchester awaited the arrival of the *Madrileños*. There was a storm coming.

A white storm.

A PEDESTAL OF ONE

With a courtesy typical of the man, Matt Busby stood with pipe and trilby in hand at Ringway airport to welcome the great Real Madrid to Manchester. First to greet him was President Santiago Bernabéu. The two men shared a warm embrace with Bernabéu telling nearby reporters that, "it was wonderful to be in Manchester and to visit my great friend Matt Busby again." On spotting the United manager every Real Madrid player made a point of coming over to shake his hand. Despite a stormy first leg, a huge respect had already developed between the two clubs. One that would show itself many times throughout the years. However despite the blossoming friendly relationship only one team could progress and come kick off Manchester United and Real Madrid would go hell for leather to win the tie...

"Real Madrid will face hell at Old Trafford."

Roger Byrne

There was one signature more than any other who the legion of autograph hunters craved amongst the Real Madrid party. Alfredo Di Stefano found himself besieged by excited schoolboys and football supporters desperate to add the Blond Arrow to their collections. Hardly known for his patience, Di Stefano showed another side to his character as he stood smiling cutting a surprisingly obliging figure. Finally with all satisfied, Madrid's finest re-joined his compadres as they made their way to a waiting coach.

To escape the rising tension sweeping across Manchester,

Busby again took his team away to stay at the Norbreck hotel in Blackpool. There, on the wide open beaches, they would train and make final preparations for the imminent showdown against the *Madrileños*. United stood on the verge of creating history. With the league safely wrapped up and a place in the FA Cup final against Aston Villa assured, a unique footballing treble lay in their sights if they could overcome Real Madrid's two goal first leg advantage.

Yet a domestic fixture threatened to de-rail United's challenge. Following a 2-0 victory over Burnley at Old Trafford that Monday, United had now played four games in eight days. The title had been won that Saturday so, despite protests from Mr Hardaker, Busby was able to rest nine of his big guns for the second leg.

Worried at how United's left-winger David Pegg had ripped apart their full-back, Jose Becerril in the final twenty minutes at the Bernabéu, Madrid officials acted swiftly and loaned from Real Zaragoza the speedy Brazilian defender Manuel Torres. This was not so much breaking the rules as stretching them beyond their limits but it showed the level of concern about Pegg's pace and skill.

On being informed of this move, Busby felt aggrieved by what he considered gamesmanship and he let it be known privately that he was contemplating asking Preston North End if he could borrow Tom Finney for the evening! Whether Busby was truly serious remains debatable but the manner in which the visitors had hastily contracted Torres to just a six month loan meant that Real Madrid knew this semi-final was still to be won. Speaking years later Torres would say he earned more money during that short spell at the *Bernabéu* than in the whole of the rest of his career.

Come match day and Manchester was awash with excitement. An April morning tinged with the early signs of summer, bright sunshine and a brisk wind. It was a good day to be alive, especially when Real Madrid were in town. Tickets had gone on sale the previous Easter Sunday and swiftly sold out. A huge sigh of relief was felt by many when it was declared Tommy Taylor had recovered from a thigh knock and was set to resume his duel against the Spaniards. From Manchester United's line up in the *Bernabéu* there would be only one change. An injury to forward Dennis Viollet had let in yet another *Busby Babe*, nineteen-year old Bobby Charlton, to be unleashed upon the *Madrileños*.

Charlton had watched the first leg from high in the stands and gazed down in wonder at these white streaks of lightning flashing across the pitch. There was none more imperious than Alfredo Di Stefano, who fascinated the young but fearful Geordie. For the *Blond Arrow* and his illustrious *compadres* appeared not just on a different plane to other teams but from another planet. And yet Matt Busby and Jimmy Murphy held great hopes for this latest of their *ripe apples*. Busby even saw something in the boy that reminded him of the great Di Stefano. A graceful playing style allied to superb power, speed and intelligence in one so young made Bobby a talent to behold. One who, alongside Duncan Edwards, Tommy Taylor, Eddie Colman and the rest of the *Babes,* could well take on Real Madrid and given time dominate not just English but European football for the next decade.

As for tactics to curtail Real Madrid's explosive wide men, Matt Busby and Jimmy Murphy discussed the possibility of an offside trap. However they were fully aware that the merest error would leave United susceptible to the fearsome acceleration of Kopa and Gento and they thought it best to leave well alone. Besides, to concentrate their players minds solely on Real's wingers may just edge the door open for the likes of the deadly Hector Rial and more worryingly, the terrifying Alfredo himself.

Instead, in a ploy of sound practice, the players were instructed to play their normal game. The age old rules applied, pass to a red shirt, keep the ball moving, do not lose possession or concentration, for Madrid were a side that would punish them severely. Chances would arise for United that would have to be taken, but they could ill afford to concede another goal.

Further controversy arose on the morning of the match when newspaper pictures showed the Old Trafford sprinklers at full force gushing onto the pitch. Under Matt Busby's orders the groundsman was told to flood the surface in order to make it difficult for Real's fleet-footed artisans. Horrified at such scenes, Madrid officials raced to the ground to demand they immediately be switched off, otherwise Real would refuse to play.

As pools of water gathered across the grass and with Busby not present it was left to United club secretary Walter Crickmer to face the irate Spaniards. On being informed by phone of their threat to go home, the United manager agreed to turn off the taps. The *Madrileños* were rattled, Busby's mind games had worked. Now it was down to his players. As kick off approached 65,000 made their way to Old Trafford, many expectant, some pensive. Across the swing bridge that bestrode the Ship Canal the red hordes swarmed. They knew well of the quality of this Madrid team but memories of that unforgettable night against Athletic Bilbao still shone bright. Their team had already put one magnificent Spanish team to the sword, so why not dream of miracles? But those Mancunians who knew their football recognised the size of the task. Overcoming a two goal deficit against Real Madrid would prove their greatest test.

On a balmy April evening at Old Trafford, *Madrileño* captain Miguel Muñoz led out the legendary Real Madrid. Alongside Muñoz strode Manchester United fronted by Roger Byrne - the heavenly white shirts of Real against the devil red of United. Though hardly statuesque when compared to the grandiose surroundings of the *Bernabéu*, for atmosphere and noise Old Trafford took some beating. It throbbed and heaved, the packed terraces roaring their support for the home team. Amongst the local masses there stood a small but raucous band of travelling Madrid fans holding a banner high with the words *HALA MADRID* etched upon it. Meanwhile on the touchline two Spanish *señoritas* dressed in traditional flamenco costume walked along, smiling and waving at the crowd, trying hard to ignore the wolf whistling and the many suggestions and invitations being hurled in their direction from an enthusiastic Mancunian audience.

The sight of a clearly wound up Duncan Edwards jumping up and down, full of nervous energy and raging once more for the game to start and have another crack at these alleged invincible Spaniards only helped to create a sense of hope amongst home supporters. The bitter memory of waging a losing fight against insurmountable waves of blurry white shadows, ghosts swarming around him in the *Bernabéu*, left Edwards frustrated and now on home soil it was expected he would be operating further forward. The opportunity to show his true worth and see United into the final dawned and if such was to occur Duncan Edwards would have to play the game of his young life.

United kicked off and seemingly forgetting their manager's instructions to start with caution, they roared onto the attack. Tommy Taylor renewed personal acquaintances with Manuel Marquitos as the two clashed early, this time Marquitos ending up in a heap. Straight away the Madrid players surrounded Taylor who pleaded innocence but it was clear the lad from Barnsley was not about to accept the treatment handed out to him in Madrid here on his own patch. A furious Marquitos rose giving Taylor a glance that suggested revenge would not be too long away.

From a Liam Whelan cross into the Madrid penalty area Alonso rushed out to punch the ball off Taylor's head. As United pinned back their esteemed visitors in the early stages, putting them under intense pressure, it appeared that Madrid could well go the same way as Bilbao. But with Marquitos and his *compadres* competing for every ball as if their lives depended on the outcome they held firm. Watching on Matt Busby and Jimmy Murphy appeared transfixed. Desperate for an early breakthrough but one wary eye always on the Madrid counter-attack.

Then it happened, a loose ball from a United shirt was latched onto by Francisco Gento whose fiendish acceleration saw him hurtle clear into the home half, before finally being brought to earth by a last ditch Roger Byrne tackle. This lightning burst by Gento brought a collective gasp from the crowd, his sheer speed off the mark causing disbelief.

Madrid were on the move. Rial's incisive through pass found Di Stefano on the edge of the box who turned and cracked a fierce drive which Wood was forced to tip over the bar. Real came again and with United retreating Gento exploded into the penalty area, but when he pulled the trigger he found himself caught by a thunderous Edwards challenge. Busby watched anxiously, eyes falling on one figure, forever expecting the worst. The *Blond Arrow* was biding his time, and then to the United manager's horror he made his move.

On twenty-three minutes disaster struck for the *Red Devils*. Di Stefano swooped onto the ball and his swift pass released Raymonde Kopa to shoot low past Wood from seven yards and give the visitors a three goal aggregate lead. Old Trafford was stunned, the two Spanish *señoritas* whom pre-match had so entertained the whistling expectant crowds, now danced alone on the touchline, watched by thousands of forlorn faces.

Madrid turned on the style, not simply passing the ball but cajoling and caressing it. Their arrogance and worrying ease suggested total confidence in being able to put United away whenever the mood required. Di Stefano was at their very heart, pulling the strings and conducting the orchestra – the *Madrileños* were putting on a show for their Mancunian hosts. Letting them know in no uncertain terms that the team who plied their sumptuous talents in the *Bernabéu* stood on a pedestal of one.

Shortly before half-time it was 2-0 when Gento careered down the wing before crossing for Hector Rial to smash home from close range past Wood and surely book Real Madrid's second consecutive European Cup final appearance. In later years records would show that Rial was actually forty years old that night, and not the stated thirty, as Madrid officials had been informed when they signed him. The realisation that United's dream was over lay etched on Matt Busby's face. His team, although still bravely battling away, had been outclassed by superior opponents. Sensing blood Real went in search of a killer third, to end United's challenge once and for all. Di Stefano demanded possession off his defenders and away he soared.

A rapier one-two with Rial before a pass inside to Gento, who skipped away from Bill Foulkes before returning the ball back to the grand Argentine. Alone he stood in the centre-circle, momentarily statuesque, as if to suggest *"Here I am. You have read the stories, seen the pictures and been told of the rumours."*

Half-time arrived like a fire engine at the scene of a raging blaze for the hosts. There was huge applause from the terraces for the efforts of their own team, but also the audacious, bravura display of these rampaging Spaniards and for Di Stefano specifically. The Mancunians had now seen in the flesh this wonder called Real Madrid and they realised that it was both terrifying and spellbinding. They came expecting something special and Di Stefano, Gento, Kopa and Rial had not let them down.

In the dressing room Busby praised his players for their determination and insisted they were still in the tie. He told them *"to keep playing, keep passing the ball and you will get your rewards."* Now four down on aggregate, he wished only for them to save the match, to give the *Madrileños* a reminder that come the following season Manchester United would again be the team to beat. Determined not to be humiliated and embarrassed on home turf, United re-appeared in the second half inspired.

Suddenly Madrid found themselves on the back foot as Eddie Colman, Liam Whelan and their first leg tormentor David Pegg began to stretch them from wide positions. White shirts lashed out to stem the red tide, now it was the Spaniards who were rattled, boots flying high. Marquitos, Muñoz and Zarraga took no prisoners, though even such a mean and combative trio of hatchet men found themselves unable to combat the colossus that was Duncan Edwards as he almost single-handedly wrestled back control of the contest from the *Madrileños*.

Time and again he powered across the halfway line, leaving in his wake tumbling bodies. With the crowd reaching fever pitch the roof almost came off on sixty-one minutes when the home side pulled one back. A flying David Pegg now treated the Madrid *ringer* Torres with the same contempt and ease in which he fired past Becerril in the first leg and raced forward. From a Pegg centre Tommy Taylor raced between two defenders and, under huge pressure, bundled a low shot onto the Madrid post. As groans engulfed the stadium the ball fell loose, and as Old Trafford held its collective breath, good fortune shone on Irishman Liam Whelan, who from three yards couldn't miss. Old Trafford erupted! Now three down on aggregate and with thirty minutes left to play echoes of Bilbao came flooding back into the minds of the home faithful. Manchester rocked, surely they could not do it again?

Real were frantic, their first half poise had vanished to be replaced by a grim determination and when necessary an utter ruthlessness to survive this Mancunian onslaught. As the crowd bayed for an equaliser, white shirts began falling to the turf with alarming regularity. Zarraga, though immense throughout, blotted his copybook when he collapsed in a heap after an alleged foul from Tommy Taylor who looked on in disgust at the Spaniard's play-acting. An outraged home support screamed in derision: all good feelings towards the foreigners had now disappeared as a *Madrileño* huddle surrounded the referee demanding Taylor's expulsion.

Tempers ran high. With the final to be played in the *Bernabéu,* the stakes for the Real Players were huge. Their desire not to succumb meant they felt all foul means were justified, but it hardly dignified their reputation. Howls continued from the terraces as the Spaniards lashed out at anything in red that dared to go by.

The clock for United seemed to be on fast forward, for

Madrid time almost froze. The battle raged – from fully twenty-five yards Edwards thundered in a shot, only to see Alonso save magnificently with a flying leap. Tempers flared once more when on a rare foray forward Rial attempted to stop Ray Wood taking a quick kick and was barged to the floor for his troubles by an angry United goalkeeper.

Five minutes remained when Real Madrid cracked again. It was the young lad so taken by Di Stefano in the first leg, Bobby Charlton, who levelled with a close range effort to set up a torrid climax to what had been a remarkable evening. Intent on just surviving the remaining moments, Real attempted to play keep-ball, but now thirsting for a monumental winner, United, inspired by the still rampaging Edwards, repeatedly won the ball back and continued attacking.

Though requiring two more goals the *Babes* refused to give up and when the Madrid players attempted to time waste, tempers flared on both sides. Again it was Pegg cutting in with the ball who clashed with Torres, who then in Oscar winning style collapsed as if shot by a sniper from the stand. Players from both sides crowded round the apparently assassinated player. The Spaniards intent on keeping him lying on the ground, whilst the United players tried to push Torres off the pitch and carry on the game.

Knowing time was short, home captain Roger Byrne was in no mood for such antics and took it upon himself to drag Torres back to his feet. However he swiftly found himself confronted by irate Madrid players who lifted their fallen *compadre* away to lay him back on the pitch.

Enter Duncan Edwards – angered by the cheating tactics of his opponents, he simply stormed through a host of *Madrileños* and picked up Torres, before placing him over the touchline. A melee followed before calm was restored and the final seconds were played out with United still going for glory at the final whistle. Honours ended even but the battle was won overall by a relieved and spent Real Madrid.

Saddened but proud, Matt Busby spoke in glowing terms

of his team in the bitter aftermath of defeat. "*Real Madrid beat Manchester United because a great experienced side will always triumph over a great, inexperienced side. Their average age was twenty-eight whilst ours was just twenty-one. I still believe my boys possess the potential to beat Real Madrid in a short time. If not next year then the one after. Manchester United are coming.*"

A sad note to an unforgettable match occurred when United supporters, still irate at the time wasting antics of the Spaniards in the desperate last twenty-minutes, hurled objects at the visitor's coach as it departed Old Trafford. Frustrations overflowed on a night when emotions and anger came to the fore.

As in Madrid, a wonderful banquet was held afterwards in which both teams put aside all animosity to enjoy a fine evening of toasts and goodwill speeches. Away from the dignitaries, opposing players mixed happily. Again Matt Busby was good naturedly harassed by Real stars to become their coach, much to the annoyance of the incumbent, an indignant Jose Villalonga!

However, later in the night when the party was in full swing, Don Santiago Bernabéu approached the United manager and told him, "*If you come to Spain I will make it heaven on earth for you. You will have untold riches you can only dream of.*"

Busby listened and promised the Real President he would write soon with his answer. Two weeks later a letter arrived on Bernabéu's desk from Matt Busby thanking him for the kind offer, "*But his heaven on earth existed right here in Manchester.*"

Don Santiago understood that due to the quality and age of their squad, Manchester United would pose the greatest threat to Real's European crown. Future investment in his own team was inevitable, including possible bids for United players to perhaps undermine the progress of what was occurring at Old Trafford with Bobby Charlton and Tommy Taylor just two of those being discussed by the Madrid hierarchy.

Whether they could ever be prised away from Busby's paternal grasp remained dubious but the sheer glamour and mystique of Madrid meant such moves could never be ruled out. For to imagine a United team in two years time with the likes of Duncan Edwards, Eddie Colman, Bobby Charlton, Tommy Taylor and Liam Whelan performing in Europe with a maturity that came through experience left the Madrid supremo almost shaking with dread.

In the afternoon sunshine at the *Bernabéu* on 30th May 1957, a delirious 130,000 home crowd roared with joy as Real Madrid retained their coveted crown with a convincing 2-0 victory over Fiorentina. The defensively-minded Italians came with little desire to attack and fought a negative rearguard action, which for seventy minutes frustrated the Madrid attackers. It resembled a street fight with the Italians determined to survive by any means.

Finally a stroke of luck for the Spaniards when referee Leo Horn, to the fury of the Italian defenders, deemed a trip by Fiorentina defender Ardico Magnini on Enrique Mateos a penalty, even though it appeared the linesman had already flagged him offside. Up stepped Alfredo Di Stefano to smash a well driven shot past *Viola* goalkeeper Guiliano Sarti. Forced for the first time in the contest to step forward in search of an equaliser, Fiorentina were caught on the break when a sublime through pass by Raimondo Kopa set Francisco Gento free. Off he soared, *El Motorcycle*, to beat Sarti with a delicate chip and win for Real Madrid a second consecutive European Cup. A fiesta mood descended on the *Bernabéu*.

So to the presentation, where to present Miguel Muñoz with the trophy was one of Real's most fanatical followers, General Franco. An uneasy sight even for many in Spain, Franco attached himself to *Madrileño* success like a flea to a dog. For their efforts an ecstatic Santiago Bernabéu paid each player a huge cash bonus. His dreams of a Madrid dynasty were already bearing fruit. The future looked white.

It was a relatively comfortable victory for the *Madrileños*. Paco Gento remarked after the match that the real final for him and his compadres were the two semi-final encounters against Manchester United. Gento, like his President, believed that come the following season United would again be the team to beat.

As for the *Red Devils* their season ended in deep disappointment when they went down 2-1 to Aston Villa in the FA Cup final, a game now etched in folklore for Villa's robust centre-forward Peter McParland's ferocious challenge on Ray Wood, that caused him to leave the pitch and Jackie Blanchflower take over in goal. Already 2-0 down, a late Tommy Taylor header gave United hope but in the end Wembley defeat left a sour taste in Mancunian mouths.

Yet even though the much talked-up treble had gone up in smoke, Matt Busby and Jimmy Murphy had every reason to feel optimistic for the 1957-58 season. Their ripe apples would be a year older and wiser, and the future for Manchester United promised, to quote Santiago Bernabéu's words when he attempted to whisk away Matt Busby to Madrid, *"untold riches."*

PRELUDE TO A REQUIEM: MUNICH

Manchester: Wednesday 14th January 1958: On a fog bound Mancunian evening, with Trafford Park's towering chimneys for once invisible, the Gypsy hid amongst the mist. A sorcerer from the Balkans intent on delivering a spell to end Manchester United's ambitions at the European Cup quarter-final stage. For the opening half Red Star's beguiling little play-maker Dragoslav Sekularac led the home side a merry dance. His touch and vision inspired. Busby's team reeled and went a goal behind. Come the interval Jimmy Murphy had a quiet word with United's number six and early in the second half the Gypsy bounced off Duncan Edwards and disappeared for the evening. Late strikes from Bobby Charlton and Eddie Colman saved the day and set up what was sure to be a fascination encounter behind the Iron Curtain in Belgrade. The last match...

Highbury Epitaph. Before departing for Belgrade, Manchester United travelled south to London to take on Arsenal in a game that would come to be remembered as one of the finest matches ever witnessed on English shores. A magnificent 5-4 victory was earned but only after a truly unforgettable contest which ended with the *Babes*, their all white strip with red trimmings caked in mud, being given a standing ovation at the finish.

Manchester United's heroes that day were undoubtedly two of their lesser lights. The nineteen-year old Welsh right-winger Kenny Morgans and Salford born eighteen-year old left-winger Albert Scanlon. Both had possibly their finest performances that day in a United shirt as they cut through the Gunners with magnificent pace and trickery. The goal fest began on ten minutes when Morgans sped past two chasing Arsenal defenders, before crossing perfectly for an onrushing Duncan Edwards to take the ball in his stride and smash gloriously past the diving Arsenal goalkeeper Jack Kelsey. On thirty-four minutes United doubled their lead, this time a devastating burst of pace from the lightning Scanlon who raced seventy-yards before feeding Bobby Charlton for a simple finish. Nine goals in ten games had seen Charlton preferred to Liam Whelan. But such was the competition for places at Old Trafford, one bad game and you would be out. On the stroke of half-time, the visitors were three up; Tommy Taylor finishing off a stunning move involving the brilliant, incisive play of Morgans and Scanlon. It was champagne football!

The *Babes* loved performing in the capital, their egos soothed by the press attention that built them up towards movie star heights. Here at London's biggest club they were providing scintillating entertainment, their touch and confidence grudgingly admired by the Arsenal die-hards in the raucous Clock End. United were truly "Top of the Bill" and their chutzpah showed that Manchester was not all cloth caps and rain. The *Red Devils* had captivated the Big Smoke.

The second half was a different story as the Gunners roared back with two goals in as many minutes from strikers Alec Herd and Jimmy Bloomfield. Suddenly, as the home supporters found their voice, an epic contest swayed back and forth. Sixty seconds later there was utter bedlam when Bloomfield grabbed his second and Arsenal's third with a brave diving header past Harry Gregg to complete a most unlikely comeback. Highbury exploded with joy. United were rocking now and Busby was livid. A squandered three goal lead did not bode well for events in Belgrade. Finding new gears, the visitors pushed on and five minutes later, from yet another Albert Scanlon cross, Dennis Viollet rose high to head past Kelsey making it 4-3.

The Arsenal players stood dumbfounded, all their hard work had come to nought and when, on seventy-seven minutes, Tommy Taylor scored his second and United's fifth from Kenny Morgans' superb assist it was surely game over at 5-3. One last time the home side found the strength to hit back when Arsenal's Welsh inside-right Derek Taspcott fired past Harry Gregg from a tight angle to cut the deficit once more. The final stages saw the Gunners lay siege to United's goal but the visitors, with generous portions of good luck, held out.

The final whistle saw the breathless crowd salute both sides as one. It was a scoreline that defied belief. Arsenal 4 Manchester United 5. There was no need for words to embellish the match itself – it was a glorious epitaph.

Saturday 1st February 1958: Londoners would never forget the day when the *Busby Babes* came south and rocked their city.

On the Saturday morning of the Arsenal game tragedy struck United when director George Whittaker was found dead of a heart attack in his room at the Lancaster Gate Hotel. Players were awoken from their slumber to become curious onlookers to this morbid scene as two policemen arrived to escort Whittaker's body from the building. The sad demise of a fellow director meant that they would now not be able to travel on the Belgrade flight in order to attend the funeral. With such a hand of fortune God clicks his fingers.

Shortly after 8am on a misty, rain-sodden Monday morning, British European Airways flight number *G-ALZU A857* soared off the end of a Manchester runway and headed south over the channel and deep into Germany. On board was the United team, though one familiar face was missing.

Jimmy Murphy had reluctantly been talked out of going by Matt Busby because of international duty in his position as Welsh team manager. Under Murphy's astute stewardship Wales now stood on the verge of qualification for the 1958 World Cup finals in Sweden. A play-off against Israel looked to have already been sealed after a 2-0 away win in Tel Aviv.

Barring disaster it was signed and sealed and Murphy argued that it was not essential for him to be in Cardiff for the second leg. For, although a proud Welshman, Murphy's heart bled United red. However Busby insisted he go, his reasoning being that Murphy would never forgive himself if by some strange quirk of fate Wales crashed out. The talk amongst the United party, press pack and invited guests was of the Arsenal victory, morale could not have been higher. A short stop at Munich for refuelling and they flew onwards for the final leg to Belgrade and Marshall Tito airport. The players passed the time playing cards and sleeping. In the background the constant drone of the Elizabethan's huge engines hummed away.

Finally they arrived behind the Iron Curtain, not so much a wall but a state of mind. Female soldiers shovelled the paths clear of snow. Army tanks were parked along the roadside. Their occupants sat abreast, smoking and watching - menacing. On being taken by coach to the Hotel *Metropole* which sat on the banks of the Danube, everywhere the players looked they saw evidence of poverty. People dressed in rags, queues so long they disappeared from view. A beautiful city strangled.

In the dressing room beforehand Matt Busby, in smart raincoat and sharp fitting trilby, was as composed as ever. He told his players, *"There are no terrors out there boys. We have beaten them once now do it again."* On a pitch with the last remnants of snow still visible but melting fast in the afternoon sunshine, spring seemed close, the game began.

Within ninety-seconds of the opening whistle drama occurred. A rampaging Tommy Taylor set up his striking partner Dennis Viollet, who shrugged off chasing Red Star defenders to fire past the legendary Yugoslav black shirted goalkeeper and ex-ballet star Vladimir Beara. Of Beara the great Russian stopper Lev Yashin once said, *"Beara was the finest goalkeeper of all time."*

With the home side stunned, the visitors went for an early kill. As Red Star buckled they should have gone two behind on fourteen minutes when Bobby Charlton finished delightfully from a Dennis Viollet header. To Red Star's huge relief the

Austrian referee Karl Kainer blew to signal an offside decision that left the visitors bewildered.

And yet still despite such good fortune Red Star struggled to hold the flashing red shirts that swarmed among them. Tempers frayed as winger Kenny Morgans found himself the victim of a knee high tackle from Red Star's volatile but sublime talisman Sekularac. With their supporters as anxious as their team, matters turned inexplicably worse for the Yugoslavs when the magnificent Charlton robbed the ball back off a defender before taking aim and hitting a glorious, rasping twenty-five drive low past the diving Beara.

Two minutes later, with Belgrade aghast, Bobby was gifted a second when Beara saved a typically explosive Duncan Edwards thunderbolt, only for a clumsy kick out to fall at his feet. Faced with an open goal the young Geordie took aim and shot home. With just thirty minutes gone and United playing like European champions elect, they looked to have already sealed a semi-final spot and possibly another showdown with their friends in Madrid. An astonishing 3-0 lead had been amassed as Busby's swaggering young colts staged a performance to rank alongside anything they had yet produced in the European Cup. The travelling English press pack who had been present at many of United's finest performances, were struggling for words of sufficient hyperbole to describe what was occurring here in the Belgrade sun and snow.

Whatever was said or threatened in the Red Star changing rooms at half-time had the desired effect for they returned a team transformed. Two minutes in their centre-forward Bora Kostic chanced his luck with a twenty-yard effort that sneaked past Harry Gregg into the far corner to ignite the stadium and rekindle Belgrade hopes.

To United's dismay and discomfort The Gypsy was back. Sekularac, blessed with the ability to create and dazzle, had disappeared during the first half, seemingly more intent on hacking down those in red shirts, but had now returned to lead the comeback. The Belgrade favourite caused mayhem, an artist painting pictures while masterminding the all-out assault on United's goal. His mesmeric flick set up striker Cokic who thundered a shot goalwards that screamed narrowly over the crossbar.

The visitors' cause was hardly helped by the constant barrage of snowballs launched by the spectators behind the goal at United's defenders and goalkeeper. The air filled with the playful if unwanted missiles, as with deadly intent the Belgrade crowd picked out their targets in red! With Busby's team being repeatedly penned in, their first half exhibition of attacking pass and move football appeared a distant dream as they fought out a desperate defensive action.

Such intense pressure finally told when Red Star were awarded a soft penalty, Herr Kainer again receiving the freedom of Belgrade for a decision that left all of a United persuasion baffled following.midfielder Lazar Tasic's theatrical fall over Bill Foulkes. As the *Crvena Zveda* held its collective breath, Tasic showed remarkable calm to thrash a precise spot kick high past Gregg. Suddenly United found themselves in big trouble and with an injured Duncan Edwards reduced to mere nuisance value and Harry Gregg lying hopeless on the turf, Red Star's Cokic somehow contrived to miss an open goal from five yards. The crowd went wild, Cokic punched the floor and behind the net hordes of supporters surged down from the terraces onto the running track, many tumbling and collapsing en masse. Dazed and staggering they were helped to their feet by Yugoslav soldiers.

Meanwhile on the pitch the siege went on. As the clock ticked down Sekularac's unerring talent to pick holes in the Mancunian rearguard was at times uncanny. Only by sheer dogged determination and willingness to throw their bodies into the line of fire were United surviving. Roger Byrne had been immense as had fellow defenders Bill Foulkes and centre-half Mark Jones, but there still remained time for all their good work to be undone.

His goal under siege, Harry Gregg ranted, raved and

performed heroics to keep the Belgrade forwards at bay. At one stage he came flying off his line to take the ball off Sekularac's toe on the edge of the penalty area. For a second the Irishman lay deathly still, much to the distress of Roger Byrne who, seeing what he thought blood on his goalkeeper's white shorts, feared he had been badly injured, only for Gregg to leap back up, the colouring being only the markings of the pitch – the Yugoslavs had painted the lines red instead of standard white because of the snow.

Two minutes remained when Red Star won a free kick just outside the penalty box. It was a dubious decision awarded against Harry Gregg as he dived at the feet of tricky Belgrade left-winger Branko Zebec, only then to slide outside the area on the treacherously slippy surface. Up came Kostic to let fly and see his shot deflect off Dennis Viollet's head, before slipping agonisingly through Gregg's fingers and into the United goal to level at 3-3, 5-4 on aggregate.

Red Star needed one more to take the tie to a replay on neutral territory. A limping, bedraggled United were all but done. From the touchline Matt Busby urged for a final monumental effort. One last time the *Gypsy* set off, alluring and deadly – Sekularac attacked, only to be stopped in his stride as Herr Kainer blew for full time.

An epic clash had ended with both sides exhausted. Dropping to their knees the home side received a magnificent ovation from their supporters, as did the much relieved visitors, the Yugoslavs recognising the class and sheer guts of the extraordinary *Busby Babes*.

It was to prove an unforgettable last stand for this doomed football team.

It was a joyous Matt Busby who celebrated along with his players into the early hours at a post-match party laid on wonderfully by Red Star. Replicas of Soviet Sputniks circled the Banquet room, speeches of good will were heard, endured mostly by the footballers and applauded by all. Presents were handed out as each visiting player received a tea pot and a bottle of gin!

Hostilities forgotten, bad tackles forgiven and for some those fortunate few, life-long friendships would be struck on both sides. Vast quantities of Yugoslavia's finest wine were downed, toasts made and songs sung. Captain Roger Byrne led a rousing version by his team-mates in tribute to their Yugoslav hosts, *"We'll meet again, don't know where, don't know when. But I know we'll meet again some sunny day."*

It was the last song sung before the party broke up.

Later, when the official duties had been performed, Byrne passed a scribbled note to Matt Busby asking permission for the players to be allowed a few hours grace. Aware he could trust them not to start World War Three, Busby agreed and to hushed cheers they made their plans. Most disappeared into the dark and intrigue of the Belgrade evening to enjoy the mysterious delights of Eastern European nightlife, where, away from prying eyes, they could let their hair down and truly celebrate reaching the semi-final. Others, such as Harry Gregg, Mark Jones, Tommy Taylor and David Pegg chose instead to remain behind at the hotel and play cards. Fuelled by the local beverages and suitcases stashed with essentials such as corned beef, biscuits and hard boiled eggs, they laughed at being able to play for astronomical stakes using the over inflated Yugoslav currency, cries of *"I'll bet you four thousand"* or *"raise you six thousand"* caused much laughter amongst young footballers oblivious to the dinar's true worth.

As a memorable evening drew to a close, outside the Belgrade sky was thick with snow falling like huge confetti onto the city. Soon for Manchester United it would be time to go home.

★

The next morning, it was a sorry looking hung-over group

of players, officials and reporters who gathered at *Marshall Tito* airport to board the plane that would take them home to Manchester, via refuelling at Munich. Bleary eyed but relieved, there was a last minute drama on leaving Belgrade when Johnny Berry's passport could not be found. Jokes of being sent to Siberia were aired before it finally appeared and he was allowed through customs.

At around 180 miles per hour the Elizabethan flight *G-ALZU A857* made its wary path over the Alps towards Germany. As they descended a huge blizzard swept across Munich airport. A short spell in the departure lounge followed whilst the aircraft was refuelled. A call then went out over the tannoy for all passengers to begin re-boarding.

At 2.30 pm the Elizabethan set off again down the runway. Slowly gathering speed and with the engines at full power it suddenly came to an ominous, shuddering halt, scaring all on board. Permission was sought from the air traffic control tower to try once more, only again to falter. Finally take-off was aborted and it was a worrying band of travellers who made their way back across the tarmac inside the building.

For the third time at 3.03pm flight *G-ALZU A857* accelerated down the Munich runway. At reaching a speed of 117 mph Captain James Thain noticed a surge in the boost control. The air indicator dropped dramatically and as the runway's end drew ever closer panic filled the cockpit. As the slush and sleet from the wheels hurled against the portholes the plane sped towards its tragic end. Back amongst the passengers many had their eyes shut. Fear was etched on faces as the reality that something had gone dreadfully wrong took hold. Frantically Thain tried to retract the undercarriage to get them airborne but the fuselage refused to lift. From that moment on they were out of control. There were sparks all around, it was a hellish rollercoaster.

The aircraft crashed into a nearby house slashing off its roof, then skidded into an empty army barracks. Forty yards away sat a fuel dump and part of the wing careered into it causing huge plumes of flames to shoot into the sky. Spinning round and round in ever maddening circles the hulking Elizabethan finally came to a sickening halt, quite literally ripped in two. A ghastly, twisted mess that threatened to explode at any time.

Amid the carnage, seven of the United players were killed outright; Roger Byrne, Tommy Taylor, David Pegg, Mark Jones, Geoff Bent, Eddie Colman and Liam Whelan. Dazed, confused and disbelieving survivors staggered through the wreckage. Bodies lay scattered, some burned beyond recognition. A shocking silence was broken only by a hissing noise emanating from the downed aircraft. Like a death knell.

Munich's black skies still filled with snow.

STRANGERS IN THE NIGHT

On Thursday, February 6th 1958 the plane carrying Manchester United back from Belgrade after a European Cup quarter-final crashed at Munich airport, killing 21 passengers including seven players. Captain Roger Byrne, Mark Jones, Eddie Colman, Tommy Taylor, Liam Whelan, David Pegg and Geoff Bent. Of the survivors left fighting for their lives in a Munich hospital, they included manager Matt Busby and the living breathing heart and soul of the now decimated Busby Babes, Duncan Edwards. Manchester was aghast in sorrow. Black drapes and wreaths and heartfelt epic poems to the fallen covered every house and shop windows. The coffins of the dead lay in state at the club gymnasium, looked over by two policemen whose only task appeared to be handing out tissues for the tears of weeping visitors. A city's heart lay broken...

"Everybody lost something at the end of that runway."
Matt Busby

Manchester United v Sheffield Wednesday
FA Cup Fifth Round – Wednesday 19th February 1958

A football club founded in Newton Heath in 1878 and all but wiped out on a German runway eighty years on, had reached the lowest point in its history. With a future uncertain and spirit broken it was a question of tossing a coin and calling either salvation or disaster.

For in time-honoured tradition, despite untold grief at the

loss of so many broken hearts and unhealed wounds, the show went on and just thirteen days after the catastrophic air crash Manchester United prepared to host Sheffield Wednesday in an FA Cup fifth round clash. With their flag flying at half mast over the ground as a mark of respect for the victims, those left behind prepared for a game that would go down in the folklore of Manchester United football club.

"Keep the flag flying Jimmy until I get back!" These were the impassioned comments of an ailing Matt Busby, still battling for his life in an oxygen tent in Germany to his assistant and friend Jimmy Murphy, who had flown over to the scene of the disaster. Busby lay gravely ill. The wall of his chest had been savagely crushed, severely endangering his lungs. What Murphy witnessed, heard and felt in Munich at the *Rechts de Isar* hospital almost broke him. His boys lay dead and dying, some injured so badly they would never play again, but it was the sight of one he deemed invincible, Duncan Edwards, that almost drove him to despair.

"What time is kick off Jimmy?" Big Dunc had blurted out in a state of semi-consciousness when Jimmy went to visit him. Suddenly Murphy realised that the gods had no favourites after all, that they gave and took as they pleased. For to take one so special as Duncan Edwards, to destroy everything he and Matt Busby had striven to create would test anyone's faith. A devout catholic, this firebrand Welshman from the Rhondda had seen his own life spared by an act of fate that would haunt him forever. Only Matt Busby's insistence that Murphy did not travel to Belgrade saved his life. Busby successfully convinced him it was his duty to remain behind in his other capacity of managing Wales. This meant that Murphy's normal seat next to the manager on the plane was taken by United trainer Bert Whalley, who was killed outright in the crash. But it was Busby's haunting words that gave Jimmy the necessary courage to carry on. *"Keep the flag flying Jimmy till I get back. Keep the flag flying, keep the flag…"*

Manchester was a city in mourning. Numb with shock,

shattered and in despair. In order to escape such a doom laden atmosphere the decimated United squad disembarked to their normal refuge of the Norbreck hotel. Its huge glass-fronted windows overlooked the rough waters of the Irish Sea. There Jimmy Murphy gazed at the far horizon and planned for an uncertain future. A welcome helping hand arrived when an old friend of Murphy's, former Manchester United goalkeeper Jack Crompton, left Luton Town to rejoin his former club as temporary assistant trainer taking the place of the much lamented Tom Curry.

And so to Wednesday 19th February 1958. Four hours before kick off bedlam reigned outside Old Trafford with thousands of supporters desperately on the lookout for tickets. It was an insatiable desire that could never be met and with passions running high, what should have been a solemn occasion threatened at times to spiral out of control with extra police drafted in to help keep the huge crowds in order.

The scenes were bizarre - most simply stood milling around, uncertain of what to do, say or feel while others looked to cash in. Ticket touts found rich pickings as they made a quick killing by demanding treble the face value. But in doing so they risked life and limb with some supporters regarding them as vultures picking the bones of their dead players. As emotions overflowed trouble inevitably flared around the ground with many touts given a good hiding and relieved of their tickets.

Such was the dire extent of United's plight, Jimmy Murphy found himself unable to name any semblance of a team when asked by the programme editor. Left with no option as the minutes slipped by, the programme went to press with the home team blank.

Since the grim reaper had ripped the heart out of the *Red Devils* Murphy had begged, borrowed, bought and stolen to ensure United remained in business on the pitch. He worked endlessly to bring in reinforcements for those whom had perished. Then there were the funerals to attend, each soul destroying, harrowing and causing Murphy untold heartache.

But amid all the deaths, tears and sadness it was essential that a sense of normality carried on.

At 5.30, two hours before the match began and with thousands still searching desperately for tickets, the decision was taken to lock the gates. This meant there would be no full house for, such was the chaos caused by the crowds, those with tickets could not get near the turnstiles. The official attendance was later given as 59,848, 7000 below capacity. Meanwhile, those lucky enough to be inside the stadium paid 4d for their match program – *The United Review*. On its front cover club Chairman Harold P Hardman penned the following:

"Although we mourn our dead and grieve for our wounded, we believe that great days are not done for us. The sympathy and encouragement of the football world and particularly of our supporters will justify and inspire us. The road back may be long and hard but with the memory of those who died at Munich, of their stirring achievements and wonderful sportsmanship ever with us, Manchester United will rise again."

For United supporters there followed the harsh reality of reading the team sheets. On the bottom of the centre pages the Sheffield Wednesday players were as listed: United's? A poignancy beyond mere words, just eleven empty spaces. To honour those who died many supporters came dressed in black overcoats whilst adorning red/white scarves around their wrist or necks. It was like a funeral without a burial service. The constant cheers of *'United'* thundering out from the packed terraces gave the impression of this being just another game. But then those who sang did so with tears streaming down their faces for a football club that had been brought to its knees.

A dreadful silence greeted the naming of Manchester United's team over the loudspeaker, broken only by sobbing or the screaming out loud of a dead player's name. In a voice shaking with emotion the tannoy announcer carried out his painful task, firstly asking for spectators to write in the names on the program sheet left blank. But few did, simply preferring to listen and weep. He continued:

"*Manchester United: Gregg, Foulkes, Greaves, Goodwin, Cope, Crowther, Webster, Taylor E, Dawson, Pearson, Brennan*"

Of those named only two were survivors of the plane crash; goalkeeper Harry Gregg and defender Bill Foulkes. Accompanied by Jimmy Murphy they had arrived back in England the previous Friday to be met by a barrage of pressmen and photographers as they stepped off the train. Neither player would comment on their horrific experience, instead it was Murphy who, to satisfy the constant questioning by reporters said, "*I am pleased we left our injured players and Matt Busby much better and it cheered us up on our long journey from Germany.*"

The reality was both men were in a state of bewilderment after the crash and in no mental state to partake in what was sure to be a traumatic occasion. But the monumental scale of United's dilemma meant that Jimmy Murphy was left with little option but to ask Gregg and Foulkes to help keep the red flag flying. The rest of the side was a hotchpotch concoction of promising youth and reserve players, allied with those who had been brought in to see the club through the eye of the storm.

Beyond that infamous Munich runway lay a new red dawn. A fearful place, one certain to be beset with trauma and worry. For those chosen to carry on, it would sadly be a case of drown or cover yourself in glory. Jimmy Murphy had few options with what he had left. Twenty-six year old Ian Greaves came in at left-back for captain Roger Byrne and his usual deputy Geoff Bent, both dead.

Greaves, now one of the most experienced players left alive at Old Trafford, recalled the horror and sadness of those terrible days for Manchester United: "*Having lost so many friends, it was hard to take; those first two or three weeks we were training and going to our friends' funerals, too. Geoff Bent, the left back, was my best friend. I should have been on that trip myself, but because of an injury situation Geoff went instead. But that was the thing about Munich – we all lost a best friend.*"

Reserve Freddie Goodwin played at right-half instead of Eddie Colman. Twenty-four year old former amateur footballer

Ronnie Cope was at centre-half for Mark Jones and Jackie Blanchflower, so seriously hurt that his career was over. The highly rated Colin Webster was on the right-wing for Johnny Berry who, like Blanchflower, was soon forced into injury-related retirement.

At centre-forward the prodigious battering ram Alex Dawson led the attack as he bravely attempted to follow in the footsteps of the late, much-lamented Tommy Taylor. Another talented reservist was Irishman Shay Brennan and potentially the best of the surviving United youngsters, along with Bobby Charlton was twenty-year old Mark Pearson. He filled in for the severely injured Dennis Viollet and the lost David Pegg. Alongside the home bred players were two newcomers. Blackpool's inside-forward Ernie Taylor and finally Aston Villa's hard tackling, twenty-three year old wing-half Stan Crowther signed only an hour and sixteen minutes before kick-off for £32,000.

Greaves again on United's late arrival: "*We were in the dressing-room and, at ten past seven Stan Crowther arrived in a taxi. We didn't know him – we just went out on the pitch and we didn't even know what he could do. We just got on with it. We had to. While you were playing, it just went from your mind, you were chasing a ball again and you didn't feel sorry for yourself any more. You were playing a game of football and not for your friends or the Munich disaster. Against Sheffield Wednesday, you just couldn't allow your mind to go.*"

Crowther was handed the ominous task of replacing Duncan Edwards, who at that time was still fighting for his life in a Munich ward, oblivious to the goodwill and prayers being said for his recovery. Having already played for Aston Villa in the FA Cup previously, Crowther received special dispensation from the Football Association to play for United in their darkest hour. It was a rare show of humanity from the authorities towards United and one which would not be repeated in the desperate weeks and months to follow.

At first Stan Crowther was dubious about the move to Manchester, claiming he was happily settled in the Midlands.

Tough and blond, he was not known for his sensitive side. Crowther resisted until the very end, only finally relenting to the sheer fervour of the crazy Welshman whose passion for Manchester United knew no bounds. Crowther was also wary that in turning Murphy down, he would have earned himself a lifelong enemy.

It was in Jimmy Murphy's pre-match speech before kick off that all the pain and anger stored up from the horrors of Munich was released and those present claimed it could have scorched the paint on the dressing room walls. *"Play hard for yourselves, for the players who are dead and for the great name of Manchester United."* Then he broke down and wept, unable to carry on. Murphy's assistant trainer Jack Crompton took over and simply told those now representing Manchester United, *"let's go lads."*

The appearance of Munich survivors Harry Gregg and Bill Foulkes as the first two United players out of the tunnel into full view of the crowd brought the atmosphere inside Old Trafford, which was already bordering close to boiling point, beyond the point of no return. The others followed, so many new faces in red shirts, these strangers in the night.

The referee Mr A. Bond from London called the two captains together, Bill Foulkes and Albert Quixall. Foulkes later recalled the moment, *"We shook hands and I looked at Albert and he looked at me and neither of us wanted to play. It was like what are we doing here?"* There followed a one minute silence in honour of those killed. The atmosphere was unnerving and unnatural, a communal grief. Even hard nose policemen, told by superiors to always maintain a stiff upper lip, were seen with tears rolling down their faces. Old Trafford has witnessed many dramatic nights since that have left unforgettable scenes of drama but none can come remotely close to matching what occurred on that fateful evening.

Earlier in the season Sheffield Wednesday had gone to Old Trafford and given The Babes an almighty fright before going down in a close fought match 2-1. On paper, all things considered, the visitors from across the Pennines had been handed a great opportunity to beat United and earn themselves a place in the FA Cup quarter-finals. Unfortunately for Sheffield Wednesday they were up against not just eleven players in red but a tidal wave of human emotion that ultimately overwhelmed them. Some spectators were halfway up the floodlight pylons, holding on for dear life with one hand whilst whirling their red scarves with the other. In a furious opening, Murphy's patched up Manchester United tore into the Yorkshiremen.

The visitors were a fine side, tough but fair and in no way deserving the intolerable pressure placed upon them as Manchester let loose all the sadness, anger and despair of the past fortnight upon their heads. It was a cruel twist of fate that left them the bad guys to those who had refused to go gently into the murderous Munich night, as Wednesday captain Albert Quixall, who signed for United the following September, would later say, *"We were playing more than just eleven players, we were playing 60,000 fans as well."*

With Stan Crowther crashing into tackles and Ernie Taylor the playmaker, constantly encouraging the youngsters around him, United played as if lives were at stake, and in a cruel manner out of their skins. In the stands sat next to Jimmy Murphy was Bobby Charlton. Driven from his family home in the north-east to be present as United attempted to fight back from the edge, Charlton had considered quitting the game. His mind was in turmoil after the crash but after much soul searching and speaking once more to Murphy he realised life and the club he so proudly represented, had to go on. Otherwise what meaning would those whose lives were lost have?

On fifteen minutes new signing Taylor so nearly became an instant Old Trafford legend when his fierce drive from twenty yards smashed against the Wednesday post. The noise from the crowd greeting the near miss was unworldly and deafening, what did this club have to do to get a break, had they not suffered enough? Still the blood red shirts pressed forward, on twenty-seven minutes the heavens cupped their ears as a goal arrived from a most unlikely source. Deputising as a left-winger, it was one of the new boys, twenty-year old Shay Brennan, who scored direct from a corner after goalkeeper Ryalls fumbled the ball on his goal line. The affable young Irishman had only been informed that morning that he would be playing and as his team-mates celebrated with him, Jimmy Murphy punched the air. Old Trafford exploded like never before and Shay Brennan became immortalised in Manchester United history.

As the game wore on it became blatantly obvious to neutrals that the Sheffield players were clearly not up to spoiling what was a cruel contest. Who would ever wish to cause upset at a wake? Throughout United's football was full of fire and heart; thrilling at times if sometimes lacking the quality the fans were used to. Murphy's scratch team gave everything but a lack of understanding and class was obvious in certain positions. Yet still they defied all logic by playing well above themselves. United hammered away endlessly at the Sheffield Wednesday goal, shots rained in but it wasn't until twenty minutes from time that they finally made another count, when once more the unlikely Shay Brennan seized onto a rebound from close-range to flash a shot past Ryalls. Five minutes from the end it was 3-0 when Alex Dawson, the son of a Grimsby trawlerman, capped an unforgettable night of drama by crashing a third low and hard into a besieged Ryall's net to confirm United's place in the FA Cup quarter-finals. They called it the 'Murphy Miracle' not that anyone at Old Trafford believed in miracles any more.

It had been a remarkable performance by Murphy's boys as they ran and fought like dervishes, the searing pain of Munich slightly easing, only to surface instantly once more in the cold light of the final whistle. At the finish most of the United youngsters were in tears with the overwhelming emotion of the evening taking a heavy toll. Back in the sacred surroundings of the dressing room, Jimmy Murphy addressed his team and told them how proud the lads who had died would have been of them. Then he broke down again, to be consoled by all. Both Harry Gregg and Bill Foulkes simply sat quietly remembering dead friends, their hearts and minds elsewhere, faces gaunt with the events of the past few weeks.

A *Pathè* news crew arrived armed with a bottle of bubbly to present to the players to celebrate a great victory, though when the pictures are viewed there are few smiles to be seen. Nevertheless it was perhaps the most important game in the club's history. This rag tag team of youth players, reserves and sequestered veterans had combined to ensure that Harold Hardman's evocative words *"Manchester United will rise again"* was made flesh. Most importantly, United had proved they were not yet willing to go gently into the night, the *Red Devils* had given themselves priceless breathing space and the veiled curtains that lay drawn across the city were opened ever so slightly to reveal the merest chink of light.

Just two days later the sky fell in on Manchester when Duncan Edwards lost his fight for life. He was the eighth player to perish in the crash. Sometimes words are simply insufficient. For those of a United persuasion it had become hard to breathe.

> *"Had we lost that match I think Manchester*
> *would have died from a broken heart."*
> Bobby Charlton

Duncan Edwards 1936-1958

BENVENUTO MILANO

It was an FA Cup run fuelled by emotion, masterminded and cajoled by Jimmy Murphy but mostly driven on by a desire not to look back. On Saturday 3rd May 1958, Manchester United and Bolton Wanderers stepped out into the Wembley sunlight to compete in the FA Cup final. United's appearance there was akin to getting blind drunk at a loved one's wake. They played on to numb the pain. Led by Murphy, this patched up team of hired hands, kids and survivors had, by some miracle, held itself together since Munich but were finally overcome by the biblical rain of tears that had all but drowned them since the crash.

Matt Busby was present but was still too physically weak to be able to assist Murphy. Instead, he sat silently throughout in a specially made wicker chair behind the United bench. His mind troubled, body far from healed and broken hearted at the loss of so many and so much. That Bolton triumphed 2-0 was hardly surprising for the Red Devils simply being there was victory itself. However, defeat to Wanderers and Nat Lofthouse's double, the notorious "shoulder charge" did not signal the season's end. There remained unfinished business...

The grief-stricken period which had engulfed United since the crash meant there still remained the small matter of AC Milan in the European Cup to play. For the winners a place in the final against Real Madrid awaited. Fate's hand complicit once more. Those of a red persuasion even dared to ask the tortuous question, "What if?" What if the Babes had lived? Edwards, Taylor, Colman and all, then United would possibly have started favourites against an immensely talented *Rossoneri* before playing Di Stefano's all conquering Real in Brussels, with the possibility to gain revenge for the previous season's semi-final defeat.

Of course the reality was few now cared and wished only for Jimmy Murphy's boys to avoid embarrassment and put to bed what had been and still remains the most diabolical year in the history of Manchester United football club. The city and the club needed time to mourn their dead and regroup. To fight again another day, another season. For recent events had proved, the remarkable game against Sheffield Wednesday so soon after the disaster and the scintillating and dramatic Wembley cup run that followed meant United were not going away.

The talk of air travel at Old Trafford was forever prevalent, no more so than amongst the survivors. Publicly they said little when asked, but privately all made it clear there was not a chance any would step foot on a plane for the immediate future. Aware of the feelings within United, chairman Harold Hardman stated before the semi-final draw, *"United do not have any plans to fly to any of the remaining European cup games."*

Harry Gregg, Bobby Charlton and Bill Foulkes spoke in fearful tones of once more boarding an aeroplane. Gregg was adamant, *"No way, I am not ready."* Foulkes admitted, *"To put it bluntly I don't want to fly. But what happened at Munich was so terrible to see. How shall I feel in time? I don't know."* Charlton still almost in shock simply added, *"I don't fancy it. Not one little bit."*

However UEFA acted to ensure such a scenario never occurred by agreeing to all but fix the draw. In an unprecedented move, the committee decided overwhelmingly that Manchester United would play the winners of the Borussia Dortmund – AC Milan quarter-final, rather than the more awkward cities to reach in Real Madrid and Budapest, thus allowing the Mancunians the possibility to travel by land and sea. Again, sympathy for United from their own FA was in short order as they insisted on taking Bobby Charlton from United for England's game against Scotland meaning he would miss both legs of the semi-final. It was a decision that shocked Jimmy Murphy but no longer surprised him, for he was becoming accustomed to being kicked when he was down.

Five days after the cup final on *Thursday 8th May 1958*, at Old Trafford in front of 45,000 Manchester United and AC Milan went head to head. Showing no mercy the Milanese began as if they intended to end the tie within the opening quarter. A makeshift home side was so outclassed that it appeared only a matter of time before the Italians went in front. Arguably Milan's greatest ever player, the alluring Uruguayan maestro, inside-forward Juan Schiaffino stole the show. So pale and slender, he dominated the ball as his snake-charming left-foot ripped the home defence apart at will. On twenty-four minutes the *Rossoneri* deservedly took the lead when Stan Crowther, a decent First Division player but out of his depth in such esteemed company, mishit a pass to defender Bill Foulkes. Reacting like a jackal ripping the throat off a fallen deer, Milan swooped and the lightning quick Norwegian international Per Bredesen found team-mate Schiaffino. With an artist's precision the Uruguayan placed his shot beyond Harry Gregg into the goal.

A turkey shoot threatened to ensue as the Italian champions pressed but duly squandered a host of opportunities to finish off United. An impassioned Jimmy Murphy raged on the touchline, infuriated and helpless as his side were toyed with. Playing in white, United were hardly angelic as they tore into tackles, some legal, others fraught with desperation in an attempt to repel Milan dominance.

Whipped into a fury at the sheer injustice and cruel circumstance of the last three months, the home crowd erupted in grim defiance. A wall of noise fell over the pitch. Milan rocked, the crescendo dampening their swagger. Harry Gregg hurtled into Schiaffino to leave him crumpled in a heap. Dazed and more than a little angered by the big Irishman's fierce challenge, the Uruguayan play-maker returned to the fray with a plaster above his cut eye.

With the recently signed Ernie Taylor beginning to dictate more of the ball, the decibel level went even higher. Five minutes before half-time the normally impeccable defender Cesare Maldini misdirected a back pass and watched in horror as United's Dennis Viollet intercepted. As Old Trafford held it's collective breath, he raced clear before dispatching with typical aplomb past goalkeeper Lorenzo Buffon to level. They had been outplayed and outmanoeuvred by AC Milan but with Murphy attempting to re-enact World War Two on the touchline, Manchester United were never outfought.

United returned after the interval in a blaze of fury and a second half blitz orchestrated by the guile of Ernie Taylor had the Italians hanging on. Welshman Colin Webster shot wildly over when it looked easier to score whilst Taylor himself saw a wickedly hit effort saved by Buffon. This scheming thirty-three year old ex- submariner had proved an inspired signing by Murphy and was swiftly earning himself cult status at Manchester United. Missing the first half promptings of Schiaffino, Milan fell back. The Uruguayan was a mere shadow of his true self following the collision with Harry Gregg. Knowing another goal was essential to have any hope for the second leg in Italy, United threw caution to the wind and with just eleven minutes remaining they received just reward.

Again it was the impressive Dennis Viollet creating trouble for Cesare Maldini as he outpaced the Italian to race clear into the penalty area. Struggling to keep up, Maldini cut across United's number ten, causing the two men to go down. As Old Trafford screamed for a penalty the Danish referee Leo Helge pointed to the spot and AC Milan to a man went mad! Maldini collapsed to the turf in mock grief, team-mates confronted and surrounded the referee, whilst officials raced from the stands to join in and demand Mr Helge reverse his decision. Finally, calmer heads prevailed and order was restored. Away from the madness United's penalty taker Ernie Taylor simply stood, watched and waited for his moment. Once Helge had forced all the irate Italian players back beyond the eighteen-yard line he motioned Taylor forward. With a stadium in uproar and teeming with emotion, up he came to lash the ball off the underside of the bar with such ferocity past Buffon that it almost broke the stanchion! Ernie Taylor's position in the annals of United folklore was secured.

Despite a cup run littered with bodies, burnt wreckage and scarred images of survivors, somehow United remained alive and had earned themselves a fighting chance of reaching the final when battle recommenced in the San Siro cauldron the following week.

Milan in the 1950s: A dynamic city of grace and style. Of sophistication, class and beauty. And a football team seething and determined to put right what they deemed to have been a severe injustice. On Wednesday 14th May 1958, a United side that had travelled overland to Italy were greeted with a hostility not seen in Milan since *Il Duce*, Benito Mussolini and his henchmen were executed and left to hang upside down in the city's *Piazzale Loretto*. For United it had been a tortuous journey; they left Manchester for London the previous Saturday where they stayed overnight. The Sunday saw them sail to Calais from Dover, then across Europe to arrive in Milan on the Monday. United stayed at the Hotel *Principe e Savoia* where they were lauded and treated with great respect by their Italian hosts.

However all that changed come the day of the match as 80,000 Milanese gathered at the San Siro with the mindset of a baying mob. In a blatant act of gamesmanship United's coach was refused entry at the stadium and the players only made it to the dressing rooms twenty minutes before kick off. The entrance of the two teams sparked a deafening display of flares and fireworks, some thrown directly at the visitors. The vitriol and animosity towards the Mancunians proved overwhelming and as they came into view rotten fruit, cups filled with urine and coins rained down upon their heads. Benvenuto Milano!

On the pitch matters were little different as German referee Albert Deutsch turned a blind eye to the scandalous off the ball antics of the home side. When Herr Deutsch dared give a decision in United's favour the entire Milan bench invaded the pitch to remonstrate! Four times this occurred as play was held up, much to Jimmy Murphy's disgust on the touchline. Carnage ensued. Shirts were tugged, elbows flew and punches thrown as United players were hacked down and spat at. Then there was overacting, when any Milan player was tackled, that would have shamed a circus clown. Alec Dawson was grabbed around the neck and almost choked, whilst Bill Foulkes was thrown over an advertising hoarding! The bile and vitriol even extended to the press box where English journalists found themselves the victims of supporters intent on doing them harm. Many feared being lynched if United actually scored!

As thunder rolled across grey Milanese skies, Manchester United were hammered 4-0 and dumped unceremoniously out of the European Cup. For amid all the thuggery and cheating AC Milan produced football that glittered. Juan Schiaffino, back on home turf, tortured the English. It was his precise, low strike from twelve yards past Harry Gregg that began the rout after just two minutes. Then, on thirty minutes, Herr Deutsch blew his whistle and stopped play for a minute's silence. The United players looked staggered for they had not been informed this would occur! At first the English contingency in the stadium presumed it was for the Munich victims, only later to be told it was in honour of an Italian FA official who had died earlier that week.

United held on grimly in the first half but shortly after the interval Milan scored again when a glorious Schiaffino chip beat Gregg, only for a defender to handball on the line. Up stepped *Il Barone,* the wonderfully sublime, blond Swedish attacking midfielder Nils Liedholm, to fire past Harry Gregg and open the floodgates. As the *Rossoneri* cut lose a badly outclassed and much intimidated United found themselves handed a thrashing. Further goals from Milan right-winger Giancarlo Danova twenty minutes from time and a last encore from the devilish Schiaffino put paid to Jimmy Murphy's brave but limited side. Ironically at the post-match banquet the Milan President gave a speech lauding the merits of sportsmanship. One can only imagine the thoughts of Murphy as he listened on!

And so the most horrific season in United's history ended. Murphy had worked miracles since the crash, but defeat at Wembley in the FA Cup final to Bolton and the massacre in the *San Siro* proved the road back from Munich would be long and arduous. In that miserable, early summer of 1958, Manchester United really did experience the worst of times.

CANONONCITO PUM

*It was a second coming not witnessed since the rock was dragged
clear and the resting place was found to be empty many Easters
past! The Major was all washed up, too fat and old. He had
fought his last battle and would gallop no more. His country in
flames, a brave revolution crushed mercilessly by an iron Soviet
fist, he had been reduced to the life of a footballing gypsy. Loved
by millions but left to roam without a club or a place to call home
- then came the call. An offer from a man who appreciated genius.
Who realised there was still so much to give from a player that once
enchanted and enthralled. A man who made 100,000 people at
Wembley Stadium gasp in wonder and England Captain Billy
Wright dance. He already had a Blond Arrow now he desired the
Major to fire the cannonballs.*
Puskás had come to Madrid...

In the summer of 1958 Ferenc Puskás boarded a plane for
Madrid to sign for the *Madrileños*. Thirty-one years old and
almost two stone overweight, he had every right to feel
pensive of the challenge ahead. Puskás had been handed a lifeline
from a most exalted source - the self-proclaimed Godfather and
President of Real Madrid, Don Santiago Bernabéu. Having
spent two years living out of a suitcase with his young family,
the legendary Magyar captain had struggled to find employment
with Europe's elite clubs wary of taking him on. The Communist
Hungarian authorities had taken a grim view of this former hero
of the Motherland and his decision not to return home. In a
spiteful act they withheld his registration and this, allied with an

ever expanding waistline, saw him in footballing purgatory.

There was one man though who looked beyond such minor hurdles for Santiago Bernabéu sensed that Puskás was a soul mate; a man like himself who saw no boundaries and was the perfect foil to play alongside the master Alfredo Di Stefano. It was at the *Bernabéu* in November 1956, when the exiled Honved team played out a 5-5 draw with their number ten outstanding in a galaxy of stars against a Madrid select XI, that Puskás first entered the President's thinking. He sent forth his right-hand man Raimondo Saporta to take care of any legal wrangling concerning the player's former Honved contract. Saporta's special charm and gift for knowing who could be dealt with saw the problem disappear and certain UEFA officials considerably richer in the process.

The *Blond Arrow* had recently led Real to their third successive European Cup triumph with a hard earned 3-2 victory over AC Milan. The semi-final conquerors of a decimated post-Munich Manchester United were finally despatched in extra time, but only after a fascinating battle in the *Heysel* stadium, Brussels. A tie that ended at 2-2 in normal time, with all the goals coming in the last half hour, was finally settled after 107 minutes, when Francisco Gento's daisy-cutter rolled past the desperate flailing fingers of Milan goalkeeper Buffon.

Immediately following the final President Bernabéu dedicated the victory to those killed in the air disaster and offered the trophy to United who, despite being overwhelmed by Bernabéu's magnificent gesture, politely declined. Too much blood had been spilled for the trophy to be handed on a plate – they would earn their holy grail the hard way.

As for Puskás, during his early training sessions as he sweated to lose the extra pounds gained during his enforced lay-off, there were signs of a worrying stand off with Di Stefano. Both masters of their profession, they seemed intent on quietly eyeing each other up, unsure as to the other's thinking. Many seriously wondered if Madrid would prove big enough for two egos such as these?

But the Hungarian was no fool, he knew it unwise to antagonise the powerful Argentine who he believed ruled Madrid and not Franco and so he plotted a way into Di Stefano's heart. Puskás began by reversing his traditional method of running out first. Instead he would make an equally dramatic entrance by appearing last out of the tunnel. A jovial character with a kind word for all but not a man to cross, Puskás soon became a popular figure amongst his new *compadres*. Francisco Gento remembers him, *"Juggling with a bar of soap in the showers"* while the other players watched on in astonishment, including a bemused Alfredo Di Stefano.

Slowly even the Argentine fell under the *Major's* spell and as Puskás sweated blood to achieve match fitness and a fighting weight, Di Stefano came to the opinion that here was a worthy *Madrileño*. There was one who remained unconvinced about the cocky, if brilliant Hungarian. Argentine Madrid coach Luis Carniglia took an instant dislike to Puskás and the feeling was mutual. On first sight of the hugely overweight Hungarian he declared to his President: *"What am I supposed to do with him?"* *"Make him pretty,"* came Bernabéu's legendary reply.

Come the start of the new season, Puskás had lost almost a stone and half in weight and was ready to be unleashed. After so long out it came as no surprise that his start was relatively unspectacular but ever so slowly the magic was coming back. Once Christmas had passed Puskás hit top form and started to run riot. No more so than in a 10-1 dismantling of Los Palmas when he and Di Stefano scored hat tricks.

For the Real supporters, whilst not love at first sight, it was an affair that in time would become all consuming. They christened him *Canononcito Pum, the Little Cannonball*. Puskás' finishing style was unusual; a short backlift to give himself an inch, then hit it like a rocket. He had a magical left peg capable of wreaking carnage and opening the tightest defence. At times he was unplayable, deadly, blessed with wonderful technique – he was also tough and streetwise, laced with guile and a touch of the devil when needed. The Hungarians worshipped their

Galloping Major, another life a different time. Ferenc Puskás was reborn; *Canononcito Pum*. Like Alfredo Di Stefano many years before him he had arrived at his spiritual home.

As the season reached its conclusion both men were going head to head for the title of *La Pichichi* - the league's top scorer. In Spain this prize came with huge prestige and for one like Di Stefano, whose ego needed constant massaging, such prizes were essential. Here would be where the wily Puskás would engineer a way to seal his illustrious partnership with Madrid's finest. It was during Real's last home game against Elche that the Hungarian made his move.

With time almost up and the *Madrileños* romping away Ferenc Puskás beat the offside trap to race away with just the goalkeeper to beat. With both him and Di Stefano still level pegging in the goal scoring charts it looked set to be a pivotal moment. As all Madrid stood ready to hail their adopted Magyar as *La Pichichi, the* Hungarian had other ideas. Seeing Di Stefano unmarked into the penalty area he simply drew the goalkeeper before tapping the ball sideways for his *compadre* to tap into an empty net. In that moment any doubts that this truly formidable duo would not succeed disappeared. It was a partnership that would send shivers across Europe as those clubs already struggling to hold onto Real Madrid's coat tails found themselves once more cast off.

The generosity of spirit shown by Puskás boded well for the future and the sporting phenomenon that had dominated the fifties looked set to conquer a new decade. The *Blond Arrow* ran across to warmly embrace the Hungarian before taking his hand and holding it high. Together they took the acclaim of an adoring crowd. Ferenc Puskás had been granted the royal decree.

The 1958-59 season saw Real Madrid once more reach the European Cup final. A prize now regarded at the *Bernabéu* as personal property. During the campaign Puskás played an integral role and it was his winning goal during a mighty struggle against Atlético Madrid in the semi-final that finally saw Real through after a play-off. However come the final against Rheims he found himself out of the team and banished from sight. An argument had blown up with coach Carniglia who, tired of being belittled, dropped the charismatic Magyar. The player was informed an hour before kick off and the shock of both his team-mates and club President was obvious. The excuse from Carniglia given to a fit Puskás was that *"You are injured"*.

Fortunately this spiteful decision by the coach made scant difference for on *3rd June 1959,* in the Neckar Stadion, Stuttgart, Mateos and Alfredo Di Stefano scored the goals that sent the capital soaring into a fiesta mood. Amid the official post-match banquet there was one who cut an unusually sad figure. Finding it hard to join in the celebrations, a distant and quiet Ferenc Puskás was cornered by his President and asked why he had not played. The Hungarian replied that Don Santiago should ask the coach. After consulting with Di Stefano, Bernabéu acted and soon after Luis Carniglia was gone. It proved that in Madrid success carried little security for a coach, for this team managed itself.

Madrid's Hollywood approach was shown again that summer when Bernabéu dipped once more into his treasure chest to deliver from South America the great Brazilian Didi. He was famed for his free kicks, in particular the legendary *Fol ha sec, (dry leaf)* banana shot. It was said that the venom and dip caused crowds back in his home town club of Botofago to dive for cover, only for the ball to then swerve back into the goal.

Here was a legendary figure who arrived at Madrid airport with huge pomp and ceremony amid great excitement. Thousands had gathered to welcome the World Cup winning Brazilian superstar to their castle on the hill. His performances during Brazil's 1958 success were spellbinding and meant Didi's fame and bewitching talent went before him. Named player of the tournament, he was offered a name your price move to Spain by Raimondo Saporta. Here was a special footballer who fitted Bernabéu's profile for a *Madrileño.*

However there was one though who begged to differ… wild rumours swept the city that Didi had been brought in to replace Alfredo Di Stefano. Such tales caused ructions in the Real corridors of power. There was trouble and a smell of sulphur in the air when the two first met. The Argentine was not happy and their opening meeting has become immortalised in Madrid folklore. In front of the entire team at pre-season training Di Stefano confronted the thirty-one year old Didi and informed him that he was *"Neither good enough or young enough to take my place."* Didi would last just over a season in Madrid, his card marked from day one. Knowing he was fighting a losing battle so long as Di Stefano ruled the roost, the Brazilian simply gave up and went partying! In fact Puskás would later claim that *"Didi put on the weight that I had fought so hard to lose."*

The truth as ever probably lies a little in between for basically Didi had jumped to the foregone conclusion that he had finally made it on arriving at Real. Not realising, as Puskás had, that the hard work only truly begins when the plane door opens in Madrid and the Spanish heat gushes wildly into your face.

The Hungarian's last words on the Brazilian: *"He simply became too fat and slow to play for the great Real Madrid."* As for Didi, once safely ensconced back home following a generous pay-off secure in a Rio bank vault, he claimed that he was the victim of a *"Dressing room boycott orchestrated by Alfredo Di Stefano."* Didi also went on to moan that he suffered because of not paying lip service to the Argentine. In Madrid this was sacrosanct. Refusing to bow before the *Blond Arrow* meant it was hardly worth unpacking his suitcase. A short loan spell at Valencia helped ease the tension at the *Bernabéu* before Didi was finally got rid of the following summer with a return to Bofotago.

With Luis Carniglia deemed surplus to requirements, former captain and *Madrileño* legend Manuel Muñoz, with of course Di Stefano's blessing, became Real's next coach. It was a popular decision amongst all at the *Bernabéu*, Muñoz understood the problems and pressures associated with wearing the white shirt of Madrid. He had no issues in consulting senior players on matters of tactics and selection. For he also understood more than most that to survive in the bear pit of intrigue and bitter in-house politics that was Real Madrid, he needed allies like Di Stefano and Puskás fighting his corner, otherwise he would become just another managerial casualty at Real.

In early 1960 Don Santiago Bernabéu cast his eyes across the world once more in an attempt to strengthen even further his already illustrious armoury. There was one who caught his eye. One signing that if successful, would have seen the rest of Europe throwing in the towel; armed as ever with endless charm and even more Spanish gold, Raimondo Saporta travelled to Brazil in an audacious attempted to sign Edson Arantes De Nascimentes, known worldwide simply as Pelé.

However this time it was not to be as Santos, backed by the Brazilian government, refused point blank to do business. The magnificent Pelé, Brazil's most precious jewel, was not for sale at any price and Don Raimondo was gently warned advised to leave on the next available flight back to Madrid. For Saporta it was a rare failure and the Spaniards reluctantly admitted defeat. Don Santiago was disappointed but hardly forlorn. How could he be? With the holy Real trinity of Di Stefano, Puskás and Gento already mounting the *Bernabéu* walls, Pele very swiftly became an after thought. As for the rest of football, when word slipped out of Real's intentions and subsequent failure to sign Pelé, a collective sigh of relief swept across the continent. No more so than in Barcelona. For something was stirring in Catalonia.

The Magic Man: As Real Madrid vanquished all before them on the European scene, events on Spanish soil were proving much more interesting. The arch enemy Barcelona had acquired, at a fearful price, the Argentine mercenary and master tactician Helenio Herrera nicknamed *Il Mago (The Magic Man)* Herrera deserved his reputation as a footballing miracle worker who possessed few equals when it came to motivating players and getting teams to perform at their peak. Nevertheless he was a controversial figure who sought any advantage whether fair or unfair to obtain victory. His methods often bordered on the bizarre and left Catalan journalists bemused. Herrera's first action on arriving at the *Nou Comp* was to try to rid the players of an inbuilt inferiority complex regarding Real Madrid. He inherited a team that, on its day, was the equal of the *Madrileños*. Barca bristled with power, skill and attacking flair but seemed crippled by a deep rooted self doubt that verged on paranoia regarding their detested rivals. The Catalans had convinced themselves all referees were totally biased in Real's favour and with Madrid being General Franco's first footballing love, their hatred knew no bounds towards Di Stefano and his all-singing and all-dancing superstars.

Helenio Herrera would use this in his psychology but only to the Catalan born players. For they would react best to the chest thumping speeches at which Herrera excelled. They would listen in awe as their coach demanded they sweated blood to defend the banner of Barcelona. *Il Mago* had them enraptured by demonizing Real Madrid and all they stood for. He would remind them of the times when the bombs rained down on Barcelona. As for the foreigners, he spoke about money. The unbridled pots of cash available should they succeed in overcoming the great enemy. He understood more than any the psyche of the mercenary, for Herrera was the ultimate soldier of fortune. It was said Herrera would coach the Devil's eleven in hell if the money was right. Huge bonus schemes were set in place and almost immediately he began to work wonders.

World class talent such as Ferenc Puskás's old team-mates and close friends Zoltan Czibor and Sandor Kocsis began to show form reminiscent of when they had been in their 'Marvellous Magyar' pomp. The pair had badly underachieved before Herrera's era but not anymore as they battled with Real Madrid to win the championship. Among their number was the heavenly gifted Ladislao Kubala; he of the thunderous right foot and devastating skill. It has been said that he remains the finest player ever to wear Barca colours and when one considers the claims of the likes of Cruyff, Maradona, Rivaldo and Messi, that may illustrate the heights to which this player could soar. Loved by the supporters, the Hungarian born Kubala drank with the fans and played for his adopted Barca with heart felt conviction. He was a man whose love for beer was bettered only by an adoration to perform on the field. An immense attacking midfielder of sublime touch he was, on his day, unplayable.

Then there was the explosive Luis Suarez, another wonderfully sublime talent that bore easy comparison to anything on show at the *Bernabéu*. Armed with such a heady concoction Herrera set about bullying, cajoling and bribing Barca out of a self-induced slumber to take on Madrid. And then Europe. His first season brought instant success as a league and cup double was gained at Madrid's expense and the Catalans celebrated like they'd won a war, which in a sense they had. At the very least it was one in the eye for Franco and his fascist bully boys that forbade their language and freedom of speech. A government that caused so much senseless carnage that Catalonia became stained blood red with the thousands slaughtered. A civil war for which they paid a torrid price for defying the despised *Generalissimo* until its bitter end.

For bringing joy to the people Herrera found himself all but canonised by the euphoric Catalans. Finally they could raise a one fingered gesture in Madrid's direction. This strange, charismatic figure who had arrived amongst them after surviving a plane crash had restored some pride. More importantly for Herrera, his rewards were astronomical as a grateful Barca filled his pockets and more.

Now, as champions, they would enter the European cup with an opportunity to end the golden era of Real Madrid domination. The opportunity to take from Real their most coveted prize – what would the Catalans pay for that? Fate decreed a semi-final showdown and all Spain held its breath, as the two clubs prepared to do battle.

Yet on the eve of the first leg in Madrid, Barca set about slitting their own throats. Helenio Herrera found himself entangled in a slanging match with his star player Kubala. The two had never seen eye to eye with each merely tolerating the other for Barca's sake. However only hours before arguably the most important match in the club's history they all but came to blows over bonus money.

A Real player, rumoured to have been a mischievous Ferenc Puskás, had let slip to fellow Hungarian and Barca rival Zoltan Czibor their astronomical cash rewards for winning the match. Czibor repeated the sum to Kubala who confronted the coach demanding parity with the *Madrileños*. Backed by Czibor, an insistent Kubala complained to such an extent that Herrera finally snapped and told the rebels they were dropped. Both were said to have thought their coach would never dare go through with such a threat, but he did, and Barca entered the *Bernabéu* without their two best players. It was to prove a ghastly error on *Il Mago's* behalf, and on hearing the news Puskás and the *Madrileños* danced with glee.

The following evening, a Barca side still in shock from such vicious in-fighting were ruthlessly put to the sword by Di Stefano and his electrifying white knights. With a fearful glee Real ripped apart the Catalans. They delivered a sumptuous showing. The *Blond Arrow* twice hitting the back of Barca's net whilst Puskás smashed home a third. A 3-1 defeat saw the visitors escape lightly and much to the delight of an enthralled 100,000 Madrid crowd, the Real players teased their opponents by keeping the ball in the final moments while the crowd mockingly shouted "*Olé*" across the cavernous *Bernabéu*.

On returning home to Catalonia, Herrera had some serious explaining to do. His controversial decision to leave out Kubala and Czibor had rebounded on him to such an effect that his neck was now on the line. If events went awry in the second leg, he was gone. Mercilessly pilloried by an outraged Catalan press, they demanded Herrera's head. *Il Mago* bowed to pressure and recalled both players for the all or nothing *Nou Comp* showdown. It proved to be a final curtain call for Herrera as Real Madrid blew Barcelona away. In an intimidating atmosphere brimming with hatred and hostility, the dark memories of recent history filling every sinew of the stadium, the *Madrileños* played as only they appeared able.

With Di Stefano conducting the orchestra, an irrepressible Puskás slammed a brace, whilst Francisco Gento added another in a 3-1 rout to confirm their place at Hampden Park for a fifth consecutive appearance in the European Cup final against German champions Eintracht Frankfurt. Helenio Herrera was sacked shortly after the final whistle and later that evening his night got considerably worse when a seething Catalan mob besieged his hotel baying for blood. *Il Mago* performed one last magic trick and disappeared into the night, considerably richer but more importantly still alive.

For Real Madrid their incessant, triumphant march into the annals of footballing legend showed no signs of abating. With the *Blond Arrow* in tandem alongside the *Little Cannonball* the fairytale looked set to run into a new decade and beyond. Glasgow's Hampden Park was calling. The *Madrileños* were set to soar ever higher.

CHAMPIONS OF HONOUR I

It had been a heartbroken Real Madrid treasurer Don Raimondo Saporta who broke the news of the Munich air crash to Alfredo Di Stefano. Saporta telephoned the player at his home, a call which the player would later rememeber as amongst the "saddest moments of his life". As news filtered through to Madrid, the extent of the disaster shocked Santiago Bernabéu. He spoke solemnly of this great tragedy and of his prayers for the dead and the survivors. None more than so than his great friend Matt Busby, who by God's grace had survived the crash but now hung on for dear life in a Munich hospital. Twice to be given the last rites...

O f the eleven Manchester United players who had lined up against the *Madrileños* in the two legged semi-final, five died instantly; Roger Byrne, David Pegg, Eddie Colman, Tommy Taylor and Liam Whelan while Duncan Edwards fought on valiantly but lost his battle a few weeks later. Edwards' death touched Alfredo Di Stefano immensely and he told of the "magnificent impression" Duncan Edwards had made on him during the second leg in Manchester.

"Such will to win and power in one so young. None deserved more the fullness of a great career."

What truly moved Di Stefano was being told how, in his last ailing days, Edwards had called out for the gold watch that had been presented to him the previous season by Santiago Bernabéu following the semi-final in Madrid. It was a gift cherished by Edwards and after a swift investigation, a taxi was sent to the crash site where, astonishingly, it still lay amongst the debris, and was returned to its rightful owner. Placed into his hand the watch for a short period appeared to have a revitalising effect on the player – sadly such was the extent of Edwards' internal injuries that he passed away in the early hours of Friday 21st February 1958. His solid gold watch nearby calling time on a footballing colossus respected and feared by the *Madrileños*.

Now six lay dead. *Los chicos*, the *Busby Babes,* were all but gone.

In an act of wonderful generosity the three times European champions offered to hand the grieving Mancunians the European Cup they won that season but United politely refused, thanking in turn the Spaniards for their deep friendship. For this trophy had suddenly come to mean so much more to all connected with Manchester United and had to be one fought for and won. Too much blood had already been spilt, too many hearts had been broken to accept such an offer.

There was also much talk of Bernabéu loaning United the services of Di Stefano for a season with the Madrid club offering to pay half the Argentine's exorbitant wages. Whilst it was claimed the player was willing, again the Old Trafford club baulked. Whether through pride or rumours that the petty pen pushers and insular attitudes of the Football League would refuse point blank the notion of a foreigner taking the place of a British player, it was hard to tell.

Perhaps more disturbing was the League's shabby at best decision to bar United from competing in the 1958–59 European Cup competition, after being invited by UEFA as a grateful thank you for their *"Service to Football."* United initially accepted and found themselves drawn against Swiss champions Young Boys of Berne, only to later be informed that their participation had been denied following an objection by Wolverhampton Wanderers backed by Football League secretary Alan Hardaker.

But despite such ill feelings directed towards them on home soil, in Madrid at least hearts went out to the Mancunians in their darkest hour. In an act of extraordinary support they came up with a special memorial pennant. It was conferred by Real Madrid to commemorate the destroyed English team and was entitled "*Champions of Honour*". On it were the names of the dead players of which all considerable proceeds were sent to Old Trafford. A further show of Real's nobility of spirit came that same summer when they contacted Manchester United offering free holidays in Spain to Munich survivors with all expenses paid. Finally, and most importantly, a series of matches between the two clubs were swiftly arranged. Santiago Bernabéu not only agreed to Matt Busby's plea for help but waived the normal £12,000 appearance fee charged by the Spaniards. A meeting took place in Madrid between Busby and Bernabéu where the United manager asked if they would consider accepting reduced fees, due to the cataclysmic effect the crash had placed upon his club. A generous Bernabéu insisted that the cash strapped United should, "*Pay us what you can afford.*" With the Mancunians out of Europe and severely weakened, Busby realised how vital it was they retained the experience of playing against the world's best. Therefore both teams agreed to treat the games as serious affairs. All would prove to be occasions with goals galore, the vast majority being scored by the team in white.

After a remarkable 1958-59 season during which United defied all odds to finish in runners-up position, the Mancunians had begun the 1959-60 campaign in more prosaic fashion, lying in sixth position at the time of Real's visit. The previous Saturday they had been taken apart 4-0 at Preston North End who, inspired by veteran Tom Finney, were unlucky not to reach double figures. United were terrible as the wheels came off a half decent start to the campaign in gruesome style. Whilst dazzling going forward, defensively they were atrocious.

Busby was desperate for reinforcements before a bad run morphed into a relegation battle. Fine defenders such as Blackpool's Jimmy Armfield, and Rangers' Eric Caldow were targeted without success. He also bid for Burnley creative

Northern Irish midfielder Jimmy McIlroy but a move was turned down by chairman Bob Lord with a warning to the Mancunians not to return. Lord had little sympathy for United after Munich and hardly appreciated them attempting to take his best player from Turf Moor. It was the second time Busby had gone for McIlroy, the first time just before the crash. He would not go back again.

These were worrying times, at this stage of their recovery, a season where United veered from the sublime to the ridiculous on a weekly basis was driving supporters to despair. Following United has never been for the faint hearted, and that particular period they were capable of anything. A thrilling goal-laden 6-3 win at Stamford Bridge over Chelsea watched by 66,000 evoked the best of memories pre-Munich, as had a 6-0 home crushing of Leeds. Then the dark side, a new phenomenon; a humiliating 5-1 drubbing at Old Trafford by Spurs and a feeble 3-0 surrender in the Manchester derby in which City outfought their neighbours was hard to stomach. As the inconsistency stretched into October there were many furrowed brows on the Old Trafford terraces.

The expectation that the Munich survivors; Bobby Charlton, Harry Gregg, Bill Foulkes, Albert Scanlon and Dennis Viollet would carry the team were huge and perhaps unfair but all had shown incredible bravery. None more than Charlton, on whose slim shoulders United fans placed most faith and the pressure was therefore the greatest. Charlton was regarded as one who spanned the pre- and post-Munich era; he was a living and breathing epitaph for the fallen who evoked the spirit of the *Babes*. With him around the future remained palatable.

It was hoped that Real Madrid's arrival in Manchester would provide a welcome break from the weekly pitfalls of First Division football. It was a friendly match with nothing at stake; just take a deep breath, relax and enjoy the football of a Madrid team whom would simply go through the motions...

However under orders to perform at full throttle and on £50 a man win bonus, Real Madrid came to Manchester and cut loose in terrifying manner. United received a dose of cruel reality as they were handed a footballing lesson, the 6-1 scoreline saw United get off lightly and did little justice to the imperious *Madrileños* that night as Busby's patched up team were thoroughly outclassed. Even more formidable than the pre-Munich team, the Spaniards lit up Old Trafford with an irresistible concoction of European and South American artistry and guile. None was more dazzling than the irascible Magyar genius Ferenc Puskás. Rescued from footballing exile by Bernabéu, Puskás' god-sent ability and personable character added immensely to Madrid's already perfect storm. As wise as he was talented, the Magyar played the role of loyal Lieutenant to Di Stefano to perfection, he preferred to waltz gloriously in the shade of the all consuming shadow of the *Blond Arrow*.

Also arriving in Madrid to perform alongside the holy trio of Di Stefano, Gento and Puskás was that other huge summer signing, the deceptively languid but utterly brilliant Brazilian playmaker Didi. He was joined by fellow countryman Canario and the wickedly gifted Uruguayan defender Jose Santamaria who was a marvellous footballer blessed not just in his ability to play and begin Madrid attacks, but also in the finest tradition of Uruguayan stoppers, willing when necessary to commit atrocities in defence.

With an emotional but deafening 63,000 crowd roaring them on, United started brightly and Bobby Charlton twice went close with thunderous strikes that Real goalkeeper Dominquez did well to save. Then on seven minutes, as if annoyed that Charlton possessed the cheek to attempt such acts, the visitors opened the scoring. A delightful through pass by the dazzling Didi to Puskás caused gasps of awe from the terraces. The Hungarian maestro waited for Harry Gregg to commit himself then, with great audacity, slipped the ball beyond the big Irishmen into the net. It was all done with the ease of genius.

It was soon 2-0 when on twenty-five minutes Francisco Gento set up Puskás who once more looked up and flashed a ridiculous, swerving drive past a flailing Gregg into the net.

It was bewitching football. On the half hour it was 3-0: Real were relentless; with what appeared effortless skill Didi supplied a dagger of a pass into the path of an electric-heeled Alfredo Di Stefano who, without slowing, took the ball in stride before beating a besieged Harry Gregg with ease. Yet the best was still to come when moments before the interval Di Stefano delivered a moment of wizardry that bamboozled the United defence and made many in Old Trafford believe they were witnessing something quite unworldly. Standing by a goalpost, he produced an outrageous back heel after trapping the ball with his heel before turning and flicking it past a befuddled Gregg.

At 4-0 Madrid left the pitch to huge applause from a home crowd that watched through disbelieving eyes their beauty and majesty. The breathtaking images of those gleaming white figures under the Old Trafford floodlights re-ignited memories of heroes lost. None more so than Di Stefano whose magical piece of artistry for Real's fourth goal earned him a moving reception as he vacated the stage from an adoring, if still silently grieving, audience.

United came out for the second half determined to save face; Albert Scanlon went close before Bobby Charlton sliced apart the Real Madrid defence allowing winger Warren Bradley to run through from the halfway line and score from a tight angle. Maybe consolation only but for Bradley, loaned to Manchester United by famed amateurs Bishop Auckland as they strove to regain their feet after Munich, it was a special moment.

Warren Bradley's bravura effort served only to irritate the Spaniards and Real swiftly moved back into top gear. The ball was passed with a tenderness and technique but kept from United's grasp like a child clutching his favourite toy. On sixty-three minutes a grateful Puskás accepted Didi's delightful pass before crossing for the unmarked Pepillo to make it 5-1 from close range. Pepillo had signed that same summer from Sevilla and was yet another Madrileño superstar in the making. As for Didi this night, under the hazy glare of the Old Trafford floodlights, was arguably his finest hour during a short and turbulent career in Madrid. Twelve minutes from time and with United being dangled, toyed and prodded Francisco Gento suddenly got bored and exploded past a bedraggled United defence before almost breaking the back of the net with a ferocious finish past a desolate Harry Gregg. Beaten six times and at fault for none, Gregg was thoroughly fed up and cut a disconsolate figure.

Come full time and Real Madrid gathered in the centre-circle to take the acclaim of an adoring Mancunian public. Even the United players stayed behind to applaud the *Madrileños* off the pitch. It had quite simply proved a mis-match. Dennis Viollet, speaking to the *Manchester Evening News* afterwards, summed it up best, "*It seems an odd thing to say after losing 6-1 but I have to say I enjoyed that! They were special.*"

Munich had decimated Manchester United and a long time would pass before they could resemble a team good enough to give the European champions a real challenge. After the match Matt Busby was brutally honest in his summing up: "*They have walloped us 6-1 and in doing so confirmed what I already know, that we have a long, long way to go to close the gap.*"

The newspaper headlines next day extolled Real Madrid's bravura showing:

THE DAILY HERALD:
REAL GIVE GREATEST SHOW ON EARTH!
NEWS CHRONICLE:
SHOOTING SEÑORS SMACK IN SIX!
DAILY MIRROR: **REAL PERFECTION!**

Two days later a touch of Di Stefano and Puskás must have rubbed off on Manchester United as 41,000 returned to Old Trafford to witness the *Red Devils* thrash Leicester City 4-1. Charlton's opener on five minutes was followed by Viollet (2) and another from Quixall. The grim realities of this post-Munich, though ever present, were for once temporarily put aside for ninety minutes as United on an Old Trafford pitch still sprinkled with *Madrileño* gold dust sent supporters home smiling. That itself a small miracle in such trying times.

WEDNESDAY 11TH NOVEMBER 1959

Six weeks on from the 6-1 massacre at Old Trafford, a return match was staged in Madrid with Manchester United and Matt Busby given the red carpet treatment by Santiago Bernabéu from the moment they landed till the moment of their departure. A pleasant stay was tinged with real sadness at memories of events only two and a half years before when the *Babes* had arrived so full of life and captured the hearts of the Madrid public.

United went to Spain on the back of a 3-3 draw away to Fulham in which a late Bobby Charlton goal salvaged a draw. Lying in sixth place, their league form remained patchy and infuriating – a bookies' dream and a pundit's nightmare. However on their better days, they remained a match for any team in England. A fact soon to be confirmed with events in the *Bernabéu*.

The affection and admiration for Manchester United was obvious amongst the *Madrileño* faithful as they handed the visitors a stirring welcome on entering the Bernabéu. As for the game, it turned out to be a remarkable match with United scaring the living daylights out of Real before finally going down in a 6-5 shootout! It was Boy's Own football.

An 80,000 crowd watched on in astonishment at the *Estadio Bernabéu* as the visitors raced into a shock two goal lead after only fifteen minutes. The first a penalty on twelve minutes after Bobby Charlton was cynically chopped down by Jose Santamaria, a man who clearly did not believe in friendlies. The goalkeeper Dominquez saved the initial shot from Albert Quixall, only to lie helpless as the United man got lucky and lashed home the rebound. Signed by Matt Busby to help rebuild his fallen empire in September 1958 from Sheffield Wednesday for a record fee of £45,000, Albert Quixall was nicknamed *"The Golden Boy"* and cost £10,000 more than the previous highest transfer. His time up to that point had been disappointing at Old Trafford.

Although rated highly, Quixall struggled to live up to the huge sum spent on him. The fee for both sides was important though but for vastly different reasoning. Busby would later admit: *"I was determined to keep the name of Manchester United on people's lips. We always had to look as if we were doing something. Having been the greatest we could not settle for anything less. Quixall was part of that."* As for Sheffield, their General manager Ernie Taylor was alleged to have said of the Quixall fee, *"The real price was £25,000. The other £20,000 was for Mark Jones and David Pegg."* Both Yorkshire schoolboys who Wednesday had expected to have a career at Hillsborough and not Old Trafford, where fate's cruel hand clipped their wings far too early.

Sixty seconds later Albert Scanlon skipped clear of Marquitos and his long searching pass was picked up by Warren Bradley. Racing past the defender Pachin, Bradley let fly and his shot deflected off Santamaria and beat Dominguez to silence the stadium. The Madrid crowd were shocked and they soon let their heroes know about it.

However at the opposite end they had no quarrel warmly applauding Harry Gregg, who after his nightmare experience at Real's hands in Manchester was busy banishing ghosts. Two sensational saves by the big Irishman as the Spaniards turned up the heat from Enrique Mateos and Alfredo Di Stefano brought the *Bernabéu* to its feet, as Gregg staged a one man show of defiance. He was finally beaten on twenty-one minutes but only by a debatable penalty after a very soft handball was alleged against Bill Foulkes. Up stepped Di Stefano to thrash the ball past Gregg and halve the deficit. Immediately the crowd's spirits were raised and they shook life into a so far listless home side.

Yet just as it was thought Madrid would switch into overdrive, United struck again. On the half hour the reds broke out en masse and a four man move between Freddie Goodwin, Albert Scanlon, Bobby Charlton and Dennis Viollet saw the latter sweep the ball past Dominquez from five yards. It was football *Madrileños* style by the boys from Manchester! A feeling of bemusement filled the *Bernabéu* for, though classed only as a friendly, it was thought unthinkable for Real Madrid to be 3-1 down on home soil. The natives were restless.

Gregg's heroics in the United goal hardly helped their mood as he threw himself around in order to keep out a barrage of shots. However good fortune favoured the Spaniards once more when moments before the interval a clearly offside Mateos was allowed to run through and score. At 3-2 they had been handed a lifeline. It was cruel on the Mancunians who knew they now faced a second half onslaught from the European champions.

Five minutes after the break normal service appeared to have been resumed as Real drew level. A brilliant through ball was latched onto by their latest wonder kid, nineteen-year old Seville born Manuel Bueno, who fired the equaliser past a diving Harry Gregg. A frustrated Gregg pounded the turf in frustration at being beaten. Bueno was a truly outstanding talent but due to such riches of talent at the *Bernabéu* his appearances were limited. Now the *Madrileños* turned up the gas. They pinned Manchester United back and hardly needed the helping hand of a clearly out of his depth French referee Monsieur Barberan who, on fifty-four minutes, produced another shocking decision by awarding a penalty for an innocuous challenge by Goodwin on Mateos. This proved the last straw for the visitors whom blazed in anger at the inept official. After having a quiet word with the United players, Alfredo Di Stefano appeared to gesture an apology to the crowd before purposely hammering his penalty over the bar.

There was class and then there was Di Stefano.

Two minutes later United had edged back in front when winger Albert Scanlon released Bobby Charlton to crash a powerful shot in off the post past Dominguez. Charlton had been wonderful throughout and appeared comfortable playing on such a stage. He was turning heads in Madrid and was the subject of overt flattery from Madrid officials which included an unexpected encounter at Madrid airport with Don Raimondo Saporta. The charismatic fixer embraced the startled United player before asking *"So what do you think Bobby, would you like to come play in Madrid?"* Happily for Manchester United supporters, Bobby Charlton politely turned down the offer. He had no ambition to ply his trade elsewhere and no amount of Spanish gold would tempt Charlton abroad. Madrid had its attractions; the money, the sun, playing alongside Di Stefano and Puskás every week but it wasn't Old Trafford.

In the immediate aftermath of Munich it was Charlton, still only twenty years old and now without doubt the most talented of those still plying their trade at United, who dragged them through the dark days. Though scarred from the loss of dear friends and forever to be haunted by his experiences in the crash, Charlton played like a man possessed in the red shirt.

The last half hour saw Real up their game significantly with Alfredo Di Stefano seemingly on a mission to make up for his deliberate penalty miss. The *Blond Arrow* proved unplayable, like a ghostly white wind he flitted across the pitch, impossible to mark, thrusting passes like swords through the United defence. Three times he shredded the thin red line and each was put away with aplomb past Gregg by the sensational Bueno. It was a superb twenty minute hat trick that left the visitors reeling, Harry Gregg speechless and the match surely safe for the home side.

Out came the white handkerchiefs in tribute; a rare moment in the sun for Bueno who acknowledged the crowds chanting his name. But still United came back, refusing to lie down they scored again in the dying embers of the contest when substitute Alec Dawson, cut in from the touchline and hit a scorching drive past Dominguez making it 6-5.

A classic encounter finally ended and despite being light years away from the *Madrileños* in terms of class, Busby's men had shown a spirit that boded well for the future. Come full time both teams were cheered to the rafters as the *Bernabéu* showed their appreciation for a memorable spectacle. That evening Santiago Bernabéu spoke at a money raising banquet organised by the Spaniards for the families of those killed at Munich. In a speech the Madrid President revealed once more

Santiago Bernabeu: *For sixty eight years until his death in 1978 his enduring love affair with Real Madrid, first as player then President, burned bright. He turned the club from also-rans into Europe's leading club. His formula for success was simple - buy the best and success will follow...*

The Blond Arrow: Alfredo di Stefano - *the greatest player in not just Real Madrid's rich history but arguably the finest of all time. A fact made all the more galling for bitter rivals Barcelona who were victims of the footballing coup of the century.*

Tracksuit managers: *In contrast to Bernabeu's 'Galactico' approach, Jimmy Murphy and Matt Busby corralled the finest British talent for Manchester United. Their innovative approach to scouting, coaching and training produced the only serious challengers to Madrid in the 50s.*

Boys to Men: *The Busby Babes had conquered England, winning the league title in 1956 with an average of just 22. Here Roger Byrne, Tommy Taylor and David Pegg relax ahead of the 1st leg o the 1957 semi-final in Madrid.*

Tommy's War: *Tommy Taylor scores to pull a goal back in the Bernabeu but United's fightback was stymied by a late Madrid goal. A 3-1 defeat meant the English champions would have a mountain to climb back at Old Trafford.*

Rivalries renewed: (left) *A pair of senoritas are presented to the teams ahead of the second at Old Trafford.*

Manchester United Captain Roger Byrne and Madrileño captain Miguel Muñoz (later to become club coach) shake hands before battle recommences. An astounding first half performance saw Real surge into a 2-0 lead. Goals by Bobby Charlton and Tommy Taylor spared United's blushes but a 2-2 draw ended United's hopes.

Evening Chronicle

Berry and Edwards still in danger: Busby improving

UNITED VICTIMS WILL LIE AT OLD TRAFFORD TONIGHT

LATEST BULLETIN

Funerals to be private

'HAS HE ANY MONEY?' REMARK ALLEGED

3 a.m. NEWS

THEY QUEUE TO SEE RE-BORN UNITED

The worst of times: *The tragic tale that brought two cities together. Newspapers of the day showing the grim tidings of that far off southern German runway. A football club decimated and a city with it's heart ripped out.*
(top left) Surivivor Bill Foulkes picks through the rubble in Munich.
(below) Wednesday 19th February 1958: On an emotionally traumatic evening at Old Trafford against Sheffield Wednesday Munich survivors Bill Foulkes and Harry Gregg lead out the 'new United'.

Champions of Honour: Santiago Bernabeu's generous offer to play United in a series of fixtures set in train three seasons of memorable games.

(top left) the match programme from the first friendly - 1st October 1959.

(top right) Bobby Charlton heads for goal in the 1960 game at Old Trafford.

(above) Alfredo di Stefano illuminates Old Trafford with a sublime back flick in the same game.

(right) Denis Law is foiled by Vicente as United triumphed at last in the Bernabeu.

Hungarian maestro Ferenc Puskas gives a master class as Real Madrid scale new heights of perfection in the 1960 European Cup final at Hampden Park. The final score of 7-3 now etched in footballing folklore.

Glasgow's heart belongs to Real Madrid. In the midst of his beloved Madrileños, Don Santiago Bernabeu appears the proudest man in the world. The Spaniards had touched the stars as they secured their fifth successive European Cup.

(left) A star is born: *The Belfast boy George Best makes his first team debut for Manchester United against West Bromwich Albion and a new era dawns for the Old Trafford club.*
(below) *Fans celebrate United's 1965 title success, the club's first since Munich.*

The disappointment of failure in the 1966 campaign almost forced Matt Busby into retirement Given one last chance following United's 1967 title success, the club made it to the semi-fina where they faced their old friends from Madrid.
Wednesday 25th April 1968 - European Cup semi final, 1st leg. *Real Madrid return to Old Trafford. The fans greet them warmly and chide them with chants of 'Franco out Busby in'! Georgie Boy smashes home the winner at Old Trafford against Real Madrid as United grab narrow 1-0 to take to Spain.*

ck from the Brink: *United saw their slender lead wiped out before* alf-time as Real stormed into a 2-0 lead. However Zoso (Madrid's . 6) gave the reds a glimmer of hope, slicing wildly into the net hen under no pressure.

evertheless Amancio restored Real's advantage seconds later and ited seemed as good as out...

elow) *David Sadler celebrates as United pull level on aggregate* fore Munich survivor Bill Foulkes scored late on to win the tie.

REAL MADRID

EUROPEAN CUP
19 68
SEMI-FINAL

MANCHESTER UNITED

Miércoles
15 de mayo de 1968
Precio: 10 Ptas.

The Final Whistle: *the emotion of the occasion clearly gets to Bobby Charlton as he is helped to his feet by United supporters and 18 year-old Brian Kidd after United's 4-3 aggregate victory.*

Redemption: *Bobby l the cup after United's Wembley win as fell Munich survivor Foulkes celebrat* his huge respect for the United manager. He told the assembled guests that "*Matt Busby is not only the bravest, but the greatest man I have ever met in football.*"

They were words spoken from the heart. They would meet again.

A GLASGOW TALE

For one man, a Major without the stripes but a football God to countless thousands, the 1960 European Cup Final could not come round fast enough. For ten years his had been a football tale of epic scale. One rich in drama, laced with unbridled passion, tears and joy but, so far, without a single major trophy. On 18th May 1960 the opportunity would finally arise to end such an undeserved famine. For Real Madrid, victory over Eintracht Frankfurt would signal a fifth consecutive triumph, another notch on a gloriously unfolding dynasty. The Madrileños prepared to unveil the curtain and present for eternity an abiding epitaph. They were the angels without wings weaving a masterpiece...

Now fast approaching his thirty-fourth year, the sands of time were shifting quickly for Ferenc Puskás. Like lightning striking through the night sky the *Major* had illuminated the European game for a decade. Surely in Glasgow he would finally receive due reward? However there was drama in the lead up to the final when it appeared Real's opponents were set to pull out of the competition.

An incident in the bitter aftermath of the 1954 World Cup final had returned to haunt him when a raging Ferenc Puskás had claimed, after Hungary's incredulous defeat to Germany, that their opponents were, *"Doped up to the eyeballs."* He also told all who would listen that he had witnessed *"Needles on the German dressing room floor."*

These serious allegations had never been forgotten by the German football authorities and they banned all their teams from playing clubs in which he featured. For years Ferenc Puskás had refused to back down. However once the team had come through the semi-finals and it became known that Real would be up against German opposition, Don Santiago Bernabéu acted. He persuaded the Hungarian to agree for his signature to be added to a letter of apology drafted by Raimondo Saporta. Whether Puskás actually signed it remains highly dubious but it was delivered personally to the Germans by Saporta who, with typical charm, solved the problem and thoughts quickly returned to football.

There were journalists and footballing realists who proclaimed loudly beforehand that events at Hampden Park could well be Puskás' and perhaps more so Alfredo Di Stefano's swansong. The *Blond Arrow* was approaching his mid-thirties and many thought his force was waning - although none dared ever suggest such to Di Stefano's face.

The city of Glasgow found itself torn in two on who to support. The Protestant supporters of Rangers were firmly behind the Germans, whilst Celtic's Catholics formed in procession behind the pride of the Spanish church. Sadly when it came to the putrid question of Sectarianism, Glasgow society remained stricken more than most. It was shameful that a sporting occasion as the European Cup final should have been dragged down to such ridiculous divides. Luckily, Real were set to show the city that football, *Madrileño* style, crosses all borders and faiths, no matter how dark or bigoted. For on a gentle, warm Scottish evening 127,000 would gather to witness football from heaven. Glasgow was set for a religious enlightenment.

Real's opponents were arguably their toughest opponents in a final to date. A crack German outfit bristling with pace and skill, they were doggedly resistant and technically astute. Eintracht had all but obliterated Glasgow Rangers over both legs of the semi-final. The Scottish champions were totally unaware of their little known opponents' qualities when they had arrived in Germany, to such an extent that Rangers manager Scott Symon declared he had never heard of them. It was a comment he would soon regret when the Scots found themselves totally outclassed and thrashed 6-1 in Frankfurt. Then there was the double embarrassment at Ibrox where the Germans tore them apart 6-3. Symon knew them well enough by then. Eintracht travelled to Glasgow for a second time feared, respected and threatening to hand Real Madrid a most severe examination of their legendary status.

The Germans began in the same form that demolished Rangers. Playing fast, incisive and utterly gripping football they broke quickly down both flanks and rocked Madrid early on. When left-winger Eric Meier smashed a shot violently against the Real crossbar from close range in the opening minutes, the shock reverberated across Hampden as the reality dawned on all present that the *Madrileños* had a real game on their hands.

Real hit back. Their latest superstar, twenty-five year old Luis Del Sol, had signed the previous January from Betis for six million Pesetas and was a darting left-sided winger with gazelle like pace and swift balletic feet to match, He brought the Eintracht goalkeeper Egon Loy to his knees with a low shot that signal that Real had woken up. Yet still the Germans swarmed forward and twenty minutes in Hampden was in rapture when they took a deserved lead. A superb cross from Eintracht's centre-forward Erwin Stein was missed by Jose Santamaria and landed at the feet of experienced right-winger Richard Kreis, who slammed a fierce shot at the near post past a dumbfounded Dominguez. Madrid appeared stunned and an irate Di Stefano handed Santamaria an aristocratic mouthful for allowing Stein to escape his shackles.

As if *Madrileño* pride had been pricked by the temerity of going behind, the white shirts suddenly switched gears; their football became typically whiplash, deadly and cajoling. Six minutes later the Brazilian Canario careered downfield and crossed for the *Blond Arrow* to steer an equaliser past Loy. Di Stefano had now scored in every European final played so far, it was a stunning record from a player who, along with his *compadres,* was set to inflict wanton devastation on the unsuspecting Germans.

Eintracht were pushed back, overpowered and unable to get near the ball. On thirty minutes the incessant pressure on the Frankfurt rearguard told when a nervous Loy fumbled, allowing a quick thinking Di Stefano to swoop making it 2-1. The Germans found themselves in a strange world; treated like stooges on a conjurer's stage.

With a nonchalance born of the fact they were good enough to do what they wanted, the Real players began to strut and stroll in possession. They had that whiff of blood, German red. Eintracht were a proud side, reduced to chasing after teasing *Madrileños* like a dog chasing a newspaper caught in a fierce wind. It was the beginning of the greatest footballing show on earth.

Time and again Gento, Del Sol and Canario ripped like dervishes past alarmed defenders to feed the lurking Ferenc Puskás. The Hungarian joined the carnival right on the interval when he let fly a thunderous strike from an impossible angle that somehow roared past Loy to secure a fifth trophy for Real.

At witnessing such an audacious strike the Glasgow audience applauded this tubby little figure laced with awesome talent and possessing sticks of dynamite in his left foot. The second half saw little respite for Frankfurt as nine minutes in they were 4-1 down. The electric pace of Gento took him past the flustered Eintracht stopper Lutz before finally being brought to earth by the shattered German in the penalty area. A little shimmy and Ferenc Puskás placed his shoot past Loy with tormenting ease. Embarrassed, humiliated and crestfallen they may have been but the Germans refused to throw in the towel. Meanwhile Madrid showed off, they teased their opponents. Cruel but beautiful; the ball was stroked amongst the *Madrileños* with a rare forte of bewildering flicks, all performed with an intent to hurt and grind Eintracht into the turf.

On sixty minutes Gento flew clear of Lutz, who trailed in a weary if dogged pursuit of *El Motorcycle*. Waiting for Gento's cross was an impatient Puskás who struck to complete his hat trick and Madrid's fifth. Instigated by he of the balding pate and strutting manner, the carnage continued. Ten minutes later Puskás had a fourth, his best of the evening when he killed the ball dead in the penalty area and lashed home a ferocious shot past a shell-shocked Egon Loy. It was the *Major's* defining moment on a Glasgow night full of footballing sorcery and brought a moving reaction from an astonished crowd, who were struggling to believe it with their own eyes. Maybe the gallop had turned more into a trot but the Hungarian's star still shone bright.

On seventy-two minutes and showing huge defiance, Frankfurt regained a modicum of self respect when they pulled back a goal and earned a standing ovation in doing so. Stein lowering the deficit if not the feeling of humiliation which had engulfed all in Eintracht's colours. The time was almost upon Glasgow for a last cameo to crown a performance that would echo in eternity as the greatest ever by any team. Enter stage right the *Blond Arrow* to deliver a *coup de grace* and seal this bloody if magnificent slaughter. Playing any number of intricate passes in his own half, though only on the understanding he got the ball back, Di Stefano glided around and past Eintracht shirts, before letting fly on the edge of the German penalty area – it was a snapshot of all that summed up arguably the finest footballer of all time. A lone klaxon roared out in Teutonic defiance across Hampden as fifteen minutes from time Eintract pulled back another consolation. Stein earning himself a brace and some small satisfaction on a night when his team had been torn apart .

The final whistle was sounded by English referee Jack Mowatt with Alfredo Di Stefano and Ferenc Puskás competing to have the last touch so they could claim the match ball. The *Majors* four and *Blond Arrow's* three ending any semblance of argument that Real's finest remained untouchable.

It was a show of strength unrivalled in the tournament's short history and a message to any who dared to take their crown. As for the ball? Puskás won out, only to then hand it to a

Frankfurt defender who pleaded with him for a memento. After the pain inflicted by he and his team, how could the Hungarian refuse? The Scottish spectators stood en masse to acclaim the Spanish masters as the BBC commentator that evening Kenneth Wolstenholme aptly described their football as "*Swan Lake on turf*". High regard was paid to the distraught Germans who remained on the field and performed a guard of honour for the victors. Eintracht would return home well beaten and humbled but proud of the fact they had played a part, albeit unwillingly, in perhaps the greatest match of all time. A testament to a glorious era – Real Madrid 7 Eintracht Frankfurt 3.

On the terraces many simply refused to leave, desperate to soak up the atmosphere and hold on to the sweet memories. Long after the *Madrileños* had bade a fond farewell from the centre-circle and disappeared into the dressing room, thousands of Glaswegians remained gazing out onto the pitch. The unforgettable scene of magic and wonder where Di Stefano and Puskás had run riot. The Spaniards were going nowhere as that night Glasgow's huge heart belonged to them. The Scots celebrated as if the victory were their own. The next day saw the players paraded around the city on an open-top bus, nursing giant sized hangovers – the result of all night partying with more than receptive hosts.

Finally, after a civic reception at Glasgow town hall where the European Cup trophy took pride of place, they retired to the relative sanctity of the airport. Though even there the party continued, as thousand of Scots awaited to wish them well and a safe journey back to Madrid. As the plane soared off the runway taking the European champions home, the cheers of Glasgow still rang loud. In a city hardly rich in gold but the possessor of poets in abundance, and a love of the beautiful game to rival anywhere, 18th May 1960 entered local folklore; in a way Real Madrid never went home.

Finally the *Major* Ferenc Puskás had a much deserved medal to show for a glorious career and as the sixties dawned the *Madrileños* were quite literally on top of the world. A goodwill orgy towards Real ensued by all, except one, Barcelona: the Catalans not appreciative of the admiration and affection shown towards a football club they despised with a vengeance. It was time to curtail this love fest for it had become clear the only team capable of ending the nightmare was FC Barcelona. A time of reckoning drew near between the warring clubs, one set to shake the foundations of European football.

CHAMPIONS OF HONOUR II

Wednesday 13th October 1960

Manchester United were entrenched in a desperate struggle for survival; 1-0 down at Bolton Wanderers with just fifteen minutes remaining these were traumatic times for the Old Trafford club. The first three months of the season had proved horrific with only two games won and First Division survival looking dubious. It was the worst start to a campaign for United since World War Two and relegation from the top flight now seemed a real possibility. As the Burnden Park hordes rejoiced in the misery of their famous big city neighbours, an eighteen year-old Manchester United débutant called Norbert Stiles stepped forward to save the day...

The former altar boy from the United hotbed of North Manchester set up his close friend and team-mate, Irish midfielder Johnny Giles, to run on and finish superbly past Bolton goalkeeper Hopkinson. The Daily Express next day summing up United's relief. **STILES TO GILES: ALL SMILES!** A valuable point was earned by two boys brought through United's youth scheme to prove some things at Old Trafford never change.

Five months on from their historic 7-3 victory over Eintracht Frankfurt at Hampden Park, Real Madrid again took on Manchester United in the latest in a series of friendlies that were starting to take on a life of their own. The relationship between the two clubs had grown to something quite extraordinary in Munich's shadow. A typical example came when it was thought

Alfredo Di Stefano and Ferenc Puskás might not be fit to travel, Santiago Bernabéu phoned Matt Busby and asked if he wished to postpone the game until Real's leading lights were fit? Not wishing to appear ungrateful to the *Madrileños* Matt Busby insisted they come anyway. Busby informed the Real President that *"Real Madrid had become like family and whether bearing their most fabulous gifts or not Manchester was eagerly anticipating their visit."* On hearing this Bernabéu relayed Busby's message to Di Stefano and Puskás, who then decided to travel and if possible at least play some part of the game.

"You are playing with my money!" - Alfredo Di Stefano

With the *Little Cannonball* and the *Blond Arrow* in the visitors' line-up, 50,000 supporters welcomed back Real Madrid to Old Trafford. The dazzling sight of those gleaming white shirts under floodlights was the stuff of dreams. Memories were still fresh of the *Madrileños* in their absolute pomp ripping apart the unfortunate Germans at Hampden Park. Many on the terrace feared total carnage if Madrid were in similar mood and after just nineteen minutes a delightful pass from Puskás found Di Stefano who slammed a wonderful shot past Harry Gregg. Old Trafford held its collective breath then warmly applauded. Lancashire's ground sat only within short walking ground of the football stadium and with a cricket score looking set for the evening a wag in the crowd joked maybe they should have played the game there!

Amid the spellbound masses that night was one boy who stood enraptured as the *Madrileños* performed their pre-match warm up routine - fifteen year-old George Best. The Belfast boy had just arrived in Manchester and felt unable to take his eyes off Francisco Gento as he performed for an awe struck audience. The Real goalkeeper Vicente drop kicked the ball to a waiting Gento twenty yards away. *El Motorcycle* dragged down the ball in mid air with a magician's ease. Then, as if passing back to Vicente, Gento's intended hit suddenly stopped on contact with the ground and spun back towards him. Gasps fell down from the terraces as Francisco took a bow. Applause broke out. The greatest footballing show on earth was once again set to descend on Old Trafford.

Like rain falling in the northern city, a goal for Alfredo Di Stefano against United was equally expected. Real appeared in troublesome mood as the ball was moved waspishly across the field. There did however not appear the intent to twist the dagger any deeper into the hospitable Mancunians – the visitors had come to put on a show, display a few tricks and go home. Di Stefano could sense this and began to lose his imperial temper with strutting team-mates. He feared complacency.

United began to make their own opportunities; Bobby Charlton, who always impressed against the Spaniards, let fly only for Vicente to leap magnificently and tip over the bar. Roused by Charlton's effort the noise level soared and on thirty minutes to the utter disgust of Di Stefano, the home side equalised. Charlton's in-swinging corner was headed clear by Jose Santamaria, only for Albert Quixall to launch it back into the penalty area. As Vicente came to meet the ball a quick thinking Mark Pearson reacted first to flick it home from six yards. Pearson was a big favourite of Jimmy Murphy's; an inside forward, small but tough and brimming with talent. He had been plucked from the reserves to carry the flag after Munich and made his début like so many on that tear-stained night against Sheffield Wednesday. Now, Mark Pearson had rocked the European champions.

Suddenly it was all United as Real Madrid, seemingly stuck in showboat mode, were forced back. Again Bobby Charlton cut a swathe past chasing white shirts before flashing a shot inches wide and into the side netting. By this time the *Blond Arrow* was apoplectic with rage! Reacting and probably a little fearful for what awaited them at the half-time interval, the *Madrileños* moved through the gears. Puskás, who had walked around disinterestedly for the previous thirty-eight minutes, revived to leave three players on their backsides, before laying off a pass for Jose Maria Vidal to hammer from twenty-five yards past Harry Gregg into the goal. As the half-time whistle was set to blow a now focused Puskás lashed in a ferocious left footed shot that Gregg did well to see never mind save – it was a timely reminder that inside the squat number ten lurked one of the all time greats.

Alfredo Di Stefano wasted no time venting his spleen as he began tearing a strip off a shocked Ferenc Puskás even before they had reached the privacy of the Old Trafford tunnel. A public dressing down was not appreciated by the Hungarian who appeared to just shrug his shoulders at the Argentine, as if to suggest, *"It is just a friendly Alfredo. Why are you getting so wound up?"* But an irate Di Stefano was not for softening and the wagged an accusing finger at Puskás because he knew that Real Madrid could never afford to let down their guard. The same effort must apply in every game, be it a meaningless friendly or European Cup final. The path to ruin lay in complacency and Di Stefano was not about to let such happen on his watch.

Watching on fascinated was United youngster Nobby Stiles who could not believe what he was witnessing, as two of the greatest players in the world almost came to blows with so little at stake. But for Stiles it was an important lesson, one he would learn well. For fate had decreed a magnificent career for this unlikely looking hero, a short sighted youngster from the Saint Patrick's congregation on Livesey Street. On the day of the crash he had raced into the church where he prayed desperately for the lives of his idols, only then to be left desolate as Manchester faced the grim realisation that most, including Colman, had been killed.

Now as he watched the great Alfredo Di Stefano, the integrity of such a man to give his best at all times and insist others did the same made an impression. Nobby Stiles realised just what separated the mortals from the great Argentine. The heated debate continued on in the Real dressing room as Di Stefano turned his considerable wrath on others who he deemed as falling below the expected standards. Through the walls shouting could be heard, with one voice above all. Any cynics in the vicinity who ever doubted Real Madrid's professionalism and ambition to treat these matches as ultra serious affairs would have changed their opinion as Di Stefano was heard yelling and demanding more from his under-performing *compadres*. None dared disagree, others preferred to say nothing and just hope Alfredo's temper would blow itself out if the game was won and that the £60 win bonus offer would help soothe matters. Even as the *Madrileños* re-entered the field, arguments were still raging with a visibly fed up Puskás still on the receiving end of Di Stefano's tongue lashing.

The second half saw a Real Madrid team with their ears still ringing intent on proving a point to a certain Argentine. Francisco Gento, a particular target, left home defender Shay Brennan in a heap before being stopped at the last by the long legs of Bill Foulkes. Brennan's brave attempt to halt Gento as he sprinted clear left him unable to carry on and, making his début, eighteen-year old Irish full back Tony Dunne replaced him, another like Stiles destined for glory in a red shirt.

As Madrid looked for a third to kill off United, a defence which had been pilloried all season somehow held firm. It was no longer a friendly as tackles flew and the game's competitive edge was evident by Real's Santamaria, whose challenges if committed off pitch would have seen him spending the night in a Manchester jail cell. On seventy minutes a fierce, hard fought encounter was decided in the visitor's favour when the gazelle-like Brazilian Canario sprung free to fire past Harry Gregg and seal the result. It could have been 4-1 moments later when Puskás, now busy trying to ram Di Stefano's words back down his throat, played in Gento, whose first time cross found the *Blond Arrow,* only for his goal bound shot to be blocked by substitute Tony Dunne on the goal-line much to the Argentine's chagrin.

To Manchester United's credit they kept going and despite a series of further Real opportunities, all wastefully scorned, two minutes from time they grabbed a deserved second; Bobby Charlton, forever involved as he ripped dangerously down the left wing, crossed dangerously, only for a Madrid defender to head clear. The ball fell thirty yards out at the feet of twenty-one year old Belfast born midfielder Jimmy Nicholson. Looking up the Irishman picked his spot and thundered a stunning effort into Vicente's top left hand corner. It was a goal that electrified Old Trafford and proved a fitting finale to what had been yet another fascinating clash between two football clubs still seemingly heading in opposite directions.

Nevertheless this had been by far United's best performance of the season. The final whistle saw the home players form a guard of honour and applaud the *Madrileño's* off stage. Though not before Di Stefano and his *compadres*, all friends again, bade *"Adiós"* from the centre-circle to a crowd they never tired of delighting.

Once more, under the Mancunian stars, it had been a special night. It was unfair maybe to measure United's progress since the crash against such vaunted opponents, but ever so slowly, despite their league showing, Matt Busby felt they were coming back to life. He appreciated more signings would be needed, fresh blood to go alongside the likes of Bobby Charlton, Nobby Stiles and Tony Dunne and though not blessed in being able to see into the future, Busby for the first time since Munich sensed hope as the battle to restore his ravaged club continued unabated.

The following Saturday United returned to league action at champions Burnley and despite a Dennis Viollet hat trick went down 6-3. It was a dreadful result which left them second from bottom and facing an uphill task to survive in a hellish season. United had not been out of the last four all season and with the referee that day a certain Mr Hemingway, it appeared the bell was tolling for an ailing football club.

AUTUMN

6th August 1936: A blazing red sun set low over the Guadamarra mountain peaks in Northern Spain as FC Barcelona president Josep Sunyol was led out into a Nationalist army courtyard. Condemned to death by firing squad, a blindfold was placed over Sunyol's eyes as a priest administered the last rites. The President awaited his fate with courage and seconds later militia loyal to Franco took aim and shot him dead. Sunyol's crime had been to drive accidentally into Fascist territory, and when his identity was made known the sentence was a hail of bullets through his Catalan heart...

Twenty-four years, 3 months and 19 days later came the momentous events of *25th November 1960* when the memory of President Sunyol could be suitably honoured with revenge for his execution as all Catalonia rejoiced in knocking Real Madrid off their European perch. Press wires across the continent blazed and few could believe it was really all over. Only six months on from the *Masterpiece* in Glasgow, the *Madrileño's* reign was brought to an abrupt end. The *Bernabéu* walls had been breached by their most ferocious enemy and in Barcelona the fireworks erupted and the celebrations began.

Following Helenio Herrera's traumatic departure the previous season and after being beaten and humiliated by Real at the semi-final stage, Barca had recovered sufficiently to hang on to their league title by the slightest of margins, thus gaining entry back into the European Cup and another opportunity for revenge. Herrera's replacement was the veteran Yugoslav coach Ljubisa Brocic. A former Juventus and PSV Eindhoven coach, he had arrived in Catalonia with a fine reputation, which was further enhanced amongst the Barca supporters when he managed to prise away the great central defender Jesus Garay from Athletic Bilbao. A serious and thoughtful man, Brocic had one agenda – to rid the Catalans of the eternal stone in their shoe called Real Madrid. Immortality beckoned early on in his *Nou Comp* career when fate intervened to ensure Barca were sensationally drawn to play the European champions in just the second round. As all Spain held its breath the opportunity arose for Ljubisa Brocic to finish off a legend and earn for himself a place in Catalan folklore.

The animosity between the two clubs did not always extend to the players, especially the foreign contingent and the Hungarians in particular. Having shared so much before, fellow Magyars Ferenc Puskás together with Zoltan Czibor and Sandor Kocsis maintained a close friendship. Whenever the teams played in Barcelona the three would quietly arrange a meeting where they would talk of times gone by, toast old comrades – these were men who had witnessed their own nation erupt into fire and flames, who had lost close friends and family in a doomed uprising and were not about to fall out over somebody else's war.

The rampant hostility which existed between Catalonia and Castille showed itself in many forms and on this occasion the Magyars felt unable to meet up when the two clashed in the Spanish capital. They daren't risk it. For in an atmosphere teeming with the rancid odour of the civil war, the visitors never hung around long in Madrid to swap handshakes, never mind pleasantries. Here General Franco, the devil on earth for all Catalans, still resided and the horrific memories of Stukas dive bombing, screaming low over Barcelona and slaughtering innocent civilians remained fresh in their minds. Their officials were never prepared, unless left with no option, to drink champagne in President Santiago Bernabéu's hospitality suite.

And yet amid such hatred the Hungarian trio's relationship remained strong. Until the fateful European Cup draw in which they were paired together for the second time, then the laughing stopped, as even they realised the consequences of defeat. The controversial events of the two forthcoming matches would test their bond of unity to its extreme. For this was truly war without the shooting.

Madrid hosted the first leg and, as was their wont, FC Barcelona arrived at the latest possible hour – they were hardly keen on sight-seeing. Come kick off on *November 9th 1960*, the *Estadio Bernabéu* was awash with tension and excitement. A spectacular sea of white flags covered the stadium. Fireworks crashed, flares whizzed and flew. Rockets shot high into the Madrid sky. The noise from a nervous but expectant crowd utterly deafening 100,000 demanding Catalan blood. They did not have long to wait for in the opening minutes Enrique Mateos swooped to hand Real a dream start. Stirred by Mateos' opener Real went for an early kill, but despite close shaves Barca survived. Then, against all odds, they struck an unlikely equaliser on a rare foray over the halfway line. On thirty minutes a Luis Suarez free kick deceived Vicente and soared into the net. A deathly silence descended on the *Bernabéu*, the celebrating Barca players saluted their bench as a hail of abuse fell upon their heads. Words were not deemed necessary to appreciate just what the goal meant to the Catalans.

The massacre expected by the home crowd after such a promising beginning failed to materialise and as the interval drew near Barca looked to have survived the worst excesses of Di Stefano, Puskás *et al*. As groans and whistles accompanied every misplaced Real pass the tension rose, only then for Francisco Gento on thirty-three minutes to latch onto a loose pass and fire his side back in front. It was so unexpected but delighted this footballing cathedral. Gento's lightning finish looked to have restored confidence amongst home players and fans, handing new found belief to all of a *Madrileño* persuasion that Barca would be finished off in the second half. But Real had not played well, their brightest stars struggled and appeared at all too human.

As the contest wore on Real seemed content with a 2-1 lead and sought not to lose rather their gain further advantage. The *Bernabéu* terraces whistled with disdain, a support spoilt beyond all measure by success now turned on a team that had only ever brought glory. Two minutes from time came the sting in the proverbial tail when Barca midfielder Evaristo split the home defence and put Sandor Kocsis clear on goal. The Madrid defenders appealed desperately for offside and for a second were relieved when the linesman put up his flag. Only to watch aghast as the English referee Arthur Ellis ignored his assistant's claim and waved play on. On went Kocsis into the penalty area, only to be sent sprawling by Vicente. To the disgust of almost all in the *Bernabéu*, Ellis pointed to the spot. As the *Madrileños* surrounded both the referee and linesman Luis Suarez prepared for a defining moment in the history of both clubs. Ellis had no intention of backing down and when the arguments calmed Suarez swept the penalty past Vicente to ignite wild scenes of joy in Catalonia and send Madrid into mourning. It finished 2-2 and for the first time Real Madrid had failed to win a home tie. The mood was dark as the champions vacated the arena to muted boos.

An irate Ferenc Puskás seethed over the last minute drama and manhandled Kocsis accusing him of diving; the strains of *El Classico* finally breaking the bonds of friendship. Puskás later recalled that his old friend, *"could not look him in the eye"* and swiftly retreated into the safety of a joyful Barcelona dressing room. Those Madrid supporters present on that momentous evening all suspected that one day the sword of defeat would fall upon their incredible run of success, but for it to be plunged into them by the demonic Catalan hordes! In just a fortnight's time the European champions would be going into the lion's den of the *Nou Comp* battling for their imperial lives. It had been a bad night in Madrid.

25th November 1960

The Barca players delayed their entry into the *Camp* Nou to allow their crowd full and unmitigated licence to unleash hell upon the heads of the visiting *Madrileños*. The abuse that rained down from the spiritual home of the Catalans came laced with the rancid memories of that proud region's recent history. The appearance of FC Barcelona and the volume of noise that followed could be heard as far away as the mountains of Guadamarra. Where ghosts of the past listened in and prayed for revenge. It was to be another English referee, Reg Leafe, who was given the dubious honour of handling this game. Leafe was to have the type of evening on which nightmares and conspiracy theories thrive. Yet he was more likely hapless and inept than corrupt.

After an opening half hour that seethed with passion but little flowing football, the deadlock was finally broken and again it was Sandor Kocsis who caused mayhem for the Madrid defence when his cross deflected off Pachin into the net to leave Vicente stranded and on his knees in despair. Barca led for the first time on aggregate in four meetings. Twice, as Real rallied, they had the ball in Barca's net, only to see both efforts disallowed by the English referee. Surrounded by infuriated white shirts, Leafe, like his countryman Arthur Ellis in the first leg, cared little for popularity contests and was not for turning.

Half-time came and went with the Catalans holding on grimly to their narrow lead. Knowing disaster loomed Real surged forward, Di Stefano smashed a ferocious low drive past Ramallets in the Barca goal, only for the ball to rebound off the post. It was all Madrid but the Barca defence was unyielding, a wall of red and blue. Puskás became frustrated, lashing out at the lack of service whilst the *Blond Arrow* dropped ever deeper in sheer desperation to begin attacks. Never in their golden era had the *Madrileños* sailed so close to the wind. The *Nou*

Comp prayed as the white shirts surged forward in search of redemption. Nerves were shattered and all Catalonia was closer to hell than heaven at the thought that any moment a *Madrileño* would break their hearts.

Nine minutes from time Real Madrid were dead and buried. A lightning counter attack by Barcelona caught the visitors with men short in defence. Away they sped on the break with the roar of the living and dead behind them. Finally a cross into the Real box saw a leaping Evaristo direct a looping head past a frantic Vicente to surely end Madrid resistance? In a wild frenzy of madness, tears and undiluted joy the *Camp Nou* self combusted! Across the pitch *Madrileños* fell to their knees, exhausted and spent. Needing two goals just to stay alive all looked lost.

Step forward Alfredo Di Stefano who stubbornly refused to accept the inevitable. The shaken knight roused himself for one last rally – a cavalry charge ensued as Real fought against the dying of the light. Two further goals were ruled out by Mr Leafe who appeared totally out of his depth in such an intimidating atmosphere. The *Madrileños* fumed, none more than Puskás who glared towards Leafe with what could only have been murderous intent. Told by Di Stefano to forget about the Englishman until after the game, the Hungarian appeared dumbfounded at Leafe's decisions.

Three minutes from time a chink of light appeared when, to the Catalans' horror, Real grabbed a goal back. The Brazilian Canario stabbing the ball past Ramallets to set up a storming finale; Barca panicked, the weight of history choking them and their confidence falling away. Old self doubts returned and Real Madrid went for their throats. Hanging on by the darn of a thread, the unlikely Manuel Marquitos was handed the god given opportunity to level the tie when, with just Ramallets to beat from twelve yards, he inexplicably shot over the crossbar. The Real defender dropped down in tears, for he knew. Even for a warrior like Marquitos it was hard to take.

With Di Stefano trying in vain to orchestrate one more attack Mr Leafe blew to send all of Catalonia dancing in the streets and Madrid into a veil of tears. Trouble erupted post-match with Real players, notably Puskás and Di Stefano, confronting the referee before being hustled away. It would not end there as Reg Leafe and his linesmen had later to be smuggled out of the stadium, amid rumours of severe *Madrileño* retribution. Leafe and his terrified colleagues were put into a waiting getaway car and driven by an English journalist into the safety of the Catalan night. They left behind a Madrid lynch mob searching the *Camp* Nou high and low to wring their necks in utter frustration. It was only the intervention of Don Santiago Bernabéu who calmed tempers and told his players to show some dignity in defeat that matters settled down.

When asked later for his thoughts on Leafe's "strange performance" Bernabéu declared with a straight poker face, "He was Barcelona's best player." Hardly a lover of Barca, being a former Nationalist officer in the civil war, the Real President had infamously once claimed, "The only thing wrong with Catalonia is the Catalans." It was a comment not forgotten in Barcelona. Along with his fallen team, Bernabéu returned to Madrid.

Meanwhile the Catalans were in dreamland. The spell had been broken and they felt it was almost their given right to sail onto the final in Basle, Switzerland and beat an emerging Benfica. An unhealthy over-confidence bordering on arrogance consumed Barca before the match. All that is except their two marvellous Hungarians, Zoltan Czibor and Sandor Kocsis. The venue of the Wankdorf stadium was where the Magyars had lost in an unforgettable manner in the 1954 World Cup final against the Germans. Both claimed to have dark premonitions beforehand. Their psyche permanently scarred by the torrid events of that day, as were all Hungarians when they fell at the last. The Magyars' strange experience beforehand proved to be uncannily correct for despite Barcelona swamping the Portuguese for long periods, they went down rather unfairly 3–2.

Barca's presumptive claim to be heir apparents to the crown

worn with such majesty by their bitter rivals proved unwise. The realisation was they had to win, victory was more than essential, it was expected. *"We must win or die!"* exclaimed General Manager Juan Gish. Ferocious competition with Madrid had left them mortgaged to the hilt on a new stadium on which it was said £1 million was still owed. To fulfil their finance payments Barca had been forced into an agreement to transfer one of their great stars, Luis Suarez, to Inter Milan for £160,000 after the final. Also, with the title going to Real Madrid, beating the Portuguese was their only guarantee of a place in the following year's competition as holders. And yet on a beautiful Swiss evening in the glorious shadow of the Alps, it all went horribly wrong.

Two unforgivable errors by goalkeeper Anton Ramallets ultimately cost them. As the nightmare unfolded they struck the Benfica woodwork an astonishing six times as, on the greatest night in their history, fate conspired against them. Barca's Hungarian duo finished the final in floods of tears. Zoltan Czibor was inconsolable, lightning had struck them twice in the same place. The scant consolation for Czibor was that he scored one of the finest goals ever witnessed in a European final; a thundering thirty yard rocket that hit the net with such a ferocity that the Benfica goalkeeper could only stand and stare. On hearing of his countrymen's lament Ferenc Puskás could not help but raise a wry smile. *"I heard they were on a huge bonus,"* he claimed, *"Maybe that is what brought tears to their eyes?"*

After the distress following their loss in the *Camp Nou,* Real had stormed back to life with a point to prove. Just weeks after their European exit at Barca's hands they returned to the scene of the crime and destroyed Barcelona 5-3 with a stunning performance.

Alfredo Di Stefano defied the many critics who claimed he and his team were a busted flush after losing their European crown. Never more dangerous than with a point to prove, the *Blond Arrow* wreaked mayhem on enemy territory. The loss of the European Cup acted as motivation for the *Madrileños* and they stormed back to take the Spanish title off Barcelona and end the season as champions. Though no longer holders, Real would take on Europe's elite once more. They wanted to show a doubting public that the magic remained, that the candle still burned bright. Sadly Di Stefano and Puskás would be up against an opponent who even they would find impossible to overcome.

Father Time.

The autumn leaves were falling.

CHAMPIONS OF HONOUR III

Wednesday 13th December 1961:
For the first time since these two great clubs came together, Real Madrid were no longer European champions. Defeat to Barcelona in the previous season's competition led some cynics to suggest their annual visit to Manchester, though still special, had lost just a smattering of glamour. Yet such thoughts disappeared as cameras clicked furiously to create a minor supernova of flashes around the tunnel area, momentarily blinding Spanish eyes, before the crowd's roar welcomed them onto the Old Trafford turf. Honouring a promise made in the wake of United's darkest days the Madrileños had returned to a city in which they remained footballing gods...

Coming into this match, Matt Busby's struggling team sat two places from the bottom of the First Division. A disastrous run from early October had seen them incur terrible losses; 5-1 at Arsenal, consecutive 4-1 reverses against Ipswich and Burnley and a gruesome 5-1 slaughter by Everton. United fell like a stone and early hopes for a decent campaign when they appeared settled in the top six became the bitter memories of a false dawn.

The normal full house which had accompanied every Real Madrid visit to Old Trafford was for once not forthcoming as only 43,000 turned up on a freezing December evening. Home crowds had dipped alarmingly as patience finally snapped. Many stayed away because they had little wish to see United treated like cannon fodder by the still reigning champions of Spain, if not the continent.

Real Madrid themselves were not in the finest of health. Age more than ailment troubled the *Madrileños*, Father Time was an enemy that even a side of their calibre could not overcome. And yet even with Puskás injured, the likes of Di Stefano, Gento, Del Sol and Santamaria made the trip to Manchester, all four a class above any plying their trade in red, so the possibility of a rout remained.

Once again free from the stress of their First Division survival battle, the United players relaxed and began against Real in menacing attacking form. With only fourteen minutes on the clock two United youngsters combined intelligently to beat the Real rearguard. The beguiling little schemer Johnny Giles setting up his team-mate, Manchester born inside-forward, nineteen-year old Phil Chisnall to race on and hammer past goalkeeper Araquistain. Chisnall was an astute passer of the ball with considerable natural talent who was viewed by Busby and Murphy as one with a chance. It was a rare chink of light for United supporters in a season that up until Chisnall's fine strike had driven them mad with frustration.

Undeterred by this minor setback Real swiftly regrouped and laid siege to the home goal but with a back four of Brennan, Dunne, Setters and Foulkes, United held their own. It couldn't last and three minutes before the interval Di Stefano picked his spot from fully twenty-five yards and crashed an unstoppable shot into the top corner to level. Di Stefano's customary goal on the Old Trafford turf proved a worthy addition to his glittering collection of strikes against the Mancunians. As he made his way back to the halfway line he was congratulated by his jubilant *compadres,* yet hardly a smile passed the Argentine's lips. For this was not so much a personal vendetta but something splendid for United supporters to remember him by.

Normally a moment such as this would signify a home collapse but instead it was United who came storming back. Three minutes into the second half a Jimmy Nicholson pass found the recent signing, £35,000 Scottish International David

Herd. Herd's United career began well before the goals dried up. Tormented by injury and lack of form the pent-up twenty-seven year old drove a clinical low shot past Araquistain to delight the home crowd and bring a little solace and light relief to his under pressure manager Matt Busby.

Immediately on the ball hitting the net Real coach Miguel Muñoz appeared to lose interest and substituted Di Stefano, Gento and Santamaria to save their ageing legs for more meaningful contests. Sensing a pivotal moment in the match the Old Trafford masses respected the trio's departure with a grand ovation but then switched their attention to roaring their own side on to a morale-boosting victory.

The clock ticked on with both teams creating chances. David Herd had what looked like a good effort ruled out for a foul, while Johnny Giles fired in a shot that beat Araquistain, but was cleared off the line by Pachin. Real struck back and inside forward Antonio Ruiz sneaked behind Shay Brennan before finishing with ease past Gaskell, only to raise his hands in disbelief when he was deemed offside. Then, with just ten minutes remaining, Herd scored a deserved second and United's third. Substitute Albert Quixall, who had replaced the injured Giles, split the Madrid defence and the forward gleefully lashed the ball past Araquistain's grasp - Old Trafford went wild!

United rejoiced in the 3-1 scoreline – finally, at the seventh attempt, the spell had been broken. Though the Spaniards were clearly not the team of yesteryear, for Matt Busby and Jimmy Murphy, indeed all associated with Manchester United, it was a moment to cherish. The final whistle bore witness to the fact that Real Madrid handled defeat with the same dignity and class they treated victory. The *Madrileños* applauded both the crowd and their opponents before leaving the pitch to return home and leave the stage clear for the victors to receive some much deserved acclaim.

Busby hoped the result would act as a spur for them to take into their league performances. Yet typically the following Saturday disaster struck once more; a paltry 29,000 turned up at home expecting United to see off a West Ham side whom had not won there since 1935. An early goal from Herd looked to have set the *Red Devils* on the way to a convincing win, only for two late strikes from the Hammers to deny them the points. As a result United remained only two places off the bottom of Division One and any good will earned in beating Real evaporated amid a chorus of boos across a half empty stadium. For Matt Busby, still in considerable pain from the crash, redemption had never felt so far away. Any thoughts of conquering Europe now seemed to have disappeared..

GOLD

Like an aged movie queen who steadfastly refutes the onset of old age, so Real Madrid refused to go gently into the night, and in 1962 once more reached the European Cup final. The Blond Arrow and the Major, both thirty-six years old, basked in the dying embers of an empire that was once thought invincible. Retirement was a notion that scared both into continued levels of performance defying both age and nature. Theirs had been a wonderful partnership; Alfredo and Ferenc. Names etched forever in footballing folklore to be spoken of with awe. Theirs was a lasting legacy that would stretch beyond the dimming pages of history books and one that both intended to crown with a last shot at glory...

However these were changing times, it was in Lisbon and specifically Benfica's *Estadio da Luz*, where the banner of European champions now flew high and proud. Their nickname, the *Eagles*, was relevant to the height to which they had soared following their dramatic victory over Barcelona the previous season. As if the footballing gods were not handing out enough gifts to the Portuguese, they had in hiding a young colt who in time would come to be remembered and spoken of in the same hushed tones as Di Stefano and Puskás.

From the dirt strewn back alleys of a rat infested shanty in Mozambique, the *Black Panther* sprung onto an unsuspecting world. Eusebio da Silva Ferreira was one of eight children raised by his widowed mother. As a child he had played from dawn till dusk with a ball tied together by rags. As night fell he would stare upon the Mozambique sky with longing eyes and dream of escaping such a miserable existence, never realising that already he had been selected to live his life a world away amongst the glittering stars. For the *Eagles* had come calling, Benfica awaited for this extraordinary young footballer.

His rise began as mere gossip in a Lisbon barber shop. The Benfica coach Bela Guttman was being attended to in his favourite chair, happily relaxing when Carlos Bauer, an ex-player of Guttman's, now acting as a scout, came hurtling through the front door, with the air of one who had just witnessed the second coming. A breathless Bauer stood staring at his boss before stating, "*You are not going to believe what I have found for you.*" Bauer told Guttman how he had just returned from a scouting trip to Mozambique and had unearthed a prodigy. "*He is not of this world*" the German exclaimed, "*I swear he is not of this world.*" After hearing similar reports regarding the boy from others whose faith he trusted implicitly, plans were made to bring the young African to Lisbon.

But there was a problem. Eusebio had already played junior football in Mozambique for one of Sporting Lisbon's junior teams. Sporting were Benfica's deadly city rivals and there was mutual hatred on both sides. Sporting were sure to resist Benfica's attempts to lure away their most precious asset. Word had already reached them of Bela Guttman's intent and plans were made to keep him at bay.

Unluckily for Sporting they found themselves up against a wily old gypsy whose plans to snare his prize would concentrate on the lair. Guttman met secretly with Eusebio's mother and offered her the princely amount of $20,000 for her offspring's signature. Like any good son he did as she insisted, for such a sum went a long way to putting food into the mouths of his brothers and sisters.

Benfica had their man, but this was only the first stage of Guttman's plan. Eusebio had now to be smuggled out of Mozambique and out of Sporting's sight. Already they had people at airports both in Portugal and Africa looking out for the player, and with orders to hold on tight to the Panther's reins. The dictat came down: do whatever it takes to prevent him wearing a Benfica shirt.

Always a step ahead, Bela Guttman had Eusebio disguised and discreetly got him on a plane to Lisbon. On landing he was whisked straight off the runway to a Benfica hideaway. All the while the Sporting welcome committee waited in the airport lobby wondering where on earth he had got to - they would soon realise and pay a heavy price for many years to follow.

Once Eusebio's kidnapping had been made legal, Benfica felt sufficiently confident to allow their new star to join his fellow *Eagles* in a training session. The sixty-two year old Bela Guttman could not believe his own eyes. He was said to have whispered on his first sighting up close of the teenage African. "*This boy is gold!*"

This was a man who had witnessed the best and worst of this world. Who had suffered and survived the horrors of a Nazi concentration camp. He was reduced to believing that after living through such terror, nothing could ever make his heart soar again. Guttman was wrong, for Eusebio had relit a spark in his soul. He was a footballer of limitless power and skill, blessed with a Panther's spring and speed and lethal in front of goal. A true predator: Benfica could not believe their luck.

Like a punch drunk boxer who cannot live without the sound of the bell and the smell of battle, so it was the *Madrileños* gathered in Amsterdam for what was being deemed a last stand. The path to their sixth European final had been as dramatic as any before. A quarter-final clash against Juventus saw Real clinch a 1-0 win in Turin courtesy of Di Stefano. However the game will be forever remembered by both sets of supporters for a clash between Juve's giant centre-forward John Charles and the visitor's Uruguayan henchman Jose Santamaria. It was a ferocious struggle that continued after the game in the tunnel. Only the timely intervention of Ferenc Puskás, who wrestled Santamaria away and quite literally threw him into the Madrid dressing room, ended the duel.

If the Spaniards thought the job complete, events in Madrid left them staggered as a lone strike from the diminutive Argentine maestro Omar Sivori silenced the *Bernabéu* and led to a Parisian play-off. Suddenly at the final whistle, after being beaten for the first time on home soil, men such as Di Stefano and Puskás looked their age. Finally succumbing to the harsh realities of the rapidly advancing years, they looked ripe for the taking.

Still the swansong was put on hold as Real Madrid found they had enough left in their armoury to put Juventus away 3-1 in Paris. Sadly it was a famous win tarnished by the on-going vendetta between Santamaria and Charles, who found himself victim of a Real defence that at times appeared intent on sending him to an early grave. The fine line between professionalism and butchery was crossed in sickening fashion as the financial incentives offered to Juve and Real players in that particular match meant they resorted to methods that shamed both clubs.

Goals from Luis Del Sol and Puskás saw Madrid through in the semi as they eased past Standard Liege. Benfica awaited in the final for a team who simply refused to go quietly away. The old movie queen may have overdone the make-up to cover the wrinkles but the *Madrileños* still had a puncher's chance of knocking out the reigning European champions. Yet with Eusebio ready to be unleashed upon their waning legs few held hopes for a last miracle.

The seventh European Cup final turned out to be an enthralling match with a first-half performance from Real Madrid worthy of a glorious epitaph. For thirty-five minutes Di Stefano and Puskás rolled back the years. The Hungarian scored a remarkable hat-trick, all three laid on by the *Blond Arrow*. It was astonishing football; Puskás scored the first with great poise after Di Stefano's deft, defence-splitting pass was hit with perfection. The second came from a drilled left footed shot that screamed past Benfica goalkeeper Costa Pereira. Finally the *Major's* crowning glory saw him side-step two Portuguese defenders before finishing with typical aplomb. But this was no one way romp, for in an outstanding opening period Benfica scored twice themselves to keep Madrid in sight. Though out-played Bela Guttmann's men had power, pace, flair and more importantly youth on their side.

Come the half-time whistle, Puskás found himself mobbed as he left the pitch by the Real coaching staff. He looked weary, as did his *compadres*. Such an effort had robbed them of much energy. Guttman watched like a hawk eyeing its prey as the Madrid players trooped slowly down the tunnel.

In the dressing room he instructed his versatile all action midfielder Domciano Cavém to man-mark Di Stefano, he could no longer allow him to prowl at will but would have to content himself with sitting deep and launching attacks. The Argentine may have had a battle plan in the head, but his legs would be unwilling and unable to carry it out. Cavém was told to stick tight and harass and deny the great man decent possession. Guttman's logic was sound – if you cut off the head, the body will fall. Real were finished.

Eusebio had experienced a relatively quiet first period. Overawed at being so close to his boyhood idol Di Stefano, he struggled to find form. All that would change after a tongue-lashing from Guttmann. With their young talisman fired up, the second half began with Benfica turning the screw and going hell for leather at the wilting *Madrileños*. The dazzling pace, movement and tenacity of Eusebio, Augusto and Simões tortured the Real rearguard. Miserable through lack of service, Puskás dropped back to help out his beleaguered *compadres*, only to immediately lose possession as red shirts jumped upon him. Away went the towering Angolan midfielder Mario Coluna towards the Madrid goal. Coluna took aim from fully twenty-five yards and swept a skimming drive past Jose Araquistain - 3-3.

The Portuguese now swarmed all over the Spaniards. A

distraught Di Stefano was close to despair as Cavém all but cut off his air supply, rendering him helpless as Real folded around him. The Madrid of yesteryear would have simply found another gear but not anymore. This was the endgame.

Eusebio was on fire, hurdling tackles, getting off shots, collecting the ball and running through a writhing masse of Spanish defenders. On sixty-five minutes Pachin erred and chopped down an unplayable Eusebio in the penalty area as he streaked past him like a runaway train. The *Panther* got up and dusted himself down before lashing his spot kick into the net.

Madrid heads dropped and they bore the look of a team resigned to defeat. There was to be no let off from Benfica as, urged on by Guttman, they went for a fifth killer goal. Three minutes after his penalty strike Eusebio robbed a flagging Santamaria and from just outside the box let fly to see his deflected effort inch past Araquistain, to clinch a second successive European cup. At 5-3 it was all over and come the final whistle Benfica supporters raced in celebration onto the pitch to raise their heroes high. Amid the mayhem and wild scenes of jubilation, Di Stefano sought out Eusebio and embraced the young tormentor before handing him his shirt. It was a moment to cherish as the baton was passed, the old guard giving way to the new.

Real returned to Spain still refusing to believe it was the end of the road. The fact that Benfica had ripped them to pieces at will in the second half appeared lost on the *Madrileños*. The doors of the *Bernabéu doors* had truly been blown open by the winds of change and the power base of European football now resided in Lisbon. The aged movie queen had been unmasked, the golden era of Real Madrid was over.

CHAMPIONS OF HONOUR IV

Wednesday 19th September 1962:
In the aftermath of Real Madrid having their hearts ripped open by
Benfica in the 1962 European Cup final at the Olympic stadium
in Amsterdam, Matt Busby secretly met Torino's Mr Fix-it, the
dapper Luigi "Gigi" Peronace. Their conversation centred around
a young Scottish international centre-forward who was currently
plying his electrifying talent in the Agnelli motor kingdom of
Turin. The debonair, thirty-three year old Peronace specialised in
the transfer of British players to and from Italy, Jimmy Greaves
and John Charles being the two most notable. However, neither
compared with what "Gigi" was set to secure for United. If they
were willing to a pay a record transfer fee of £115,000 then Denis
Law was theirs. Over a handshake the deal was done and The
Lawman was Old Trafford bound...

These were sad times in Madrid, the dying days of a football empire. The barbarians were not so much at the gates, they had come roaring through and taken away what the *Madrileños* valued most, their cherished European crown. To rub salt into an already festering wound, Real had just been held 3-3 on home soil by Belgium champions Anderlecht in the first round stage. The Belgians refused to lie down in the *Bernabéu* as three times they hit back to cancel out Gento, Zoco and Di Stefano strikes. Among the visitors was exciting twenty year old prospect Paul Van Himst, who terrorised the Madrid defence throughout. It was the beginning of a wonderful career for Van Himst, who in time became established as his nation's greatest ever player.

They were left facing a hazardous second leg in Brussels with the real possibility of being eliminated. Gone were the guarantees of sailing amongst the stars, on a pedestal of one, for suddenly they had been outed as mere mortals. With Di Stefano and Puskás now both the wrong side of thirty-six, it felt mad to even suggest another shot at the crown could be had without a massive transfusion of new blood. But who in Madrid possessed sufficient heart or courage to tell these two living legends their time was over?

There were those ready to step up, a new breed of *Madrileños.* Amancio Amaro, Ramon Grosso, Pirri and Manuel Velásquez. All were being groomed to lead Real into the next golden age. However in terms of sprinkling gold dust, technical excellence and sheer glamour, none could hold a candle to Di Stefano and Puskás, but their spirit, togetherness and never-say-die attitude meant that behind the scenes in the *Bernabéu,* hopes were high for better days to return.

To honour the thirteen year career of Real Madrid stalwart Jose Maria Zarraga, Matt Busby took his Manchester United team to Spain, continuing a tradition borne out of tragedy, and one highly valued by both clubs. Despite the arrival of Denis Law, United were enduring another poor start to their league campaign. The previous season they had recovered sufficiently to finish a lowly fifteenth, when at one stage around Christmas they appeared certainties for the drop. Busby's acquisition of Law had seen hope abound in Manchester and the Scot began in sensational manner by scoring on his home début. Yet that goal became a high watermark in a disastrous run that, by September's end and their arrival in Madrid, saw them languishing in sixteenth place.

Four days earlier they had suffered the embarrassment of a home derby defeat to Manchester City, when even two goals from former Maine Road favourite Law proved insufficient to save an appalling day for the red half of Manchester. A crowd of 49,455 had watched in horror as the Blues new signing Alex Harley crashed home a winner with the game's last kick.

The match against Real Madrid would, as on previous occasions, provide brief respite from domestic turmoil. A Madrid audience of 80,000 welcomed back Manchester United onto the sacred *Bernabéu* turf. Both line ups were shadows of their successful pasts but the sheer imagery of *Madrileño* white and Mancunian red still captivated the Spanish public. It was a footballing romance that showed no signs of waning.

The game began in typical manner with Di Stefano now more selective in his choice of forward runs, but still dictating all aspects of the Real performance. Forever demanding the ball, pushing others into position, telling them where they should run, and finding team-mates with exquisite range of long and short passing. He was still an artist who retained a wondrous ability to paint beauty on the *Bernabéu* canvas, even if nowadays he was unable to complete it. Alfredo The Great was getting old and it was killing him inside.

Following the *Blond Arrow* wherever he strode was United's Nobby Stiles. A constant irritant to the Argentine, the great man struggled to shake off Stiles' limpet like attentions. Niggling and harassing; the Mancunian was no respecter of reputation on the pitch but away from the action Nobby Stiles adored Alfredo Di Stefano. He had no bigger admirer. On it, Stiles, like his idol Eddie Colman seven years before, was driving Di Stefano to despair. On a torrid, sweltering evening in the *Bernabéu,* the Collyhurst boy was winning hands down. To such an extent that Madrid's famed number nine gave up the ghost and lost interest.

With Di Stefano under lock and key, elsewhere Denis Law was causing gasps of wonder from a *Bernabéu* crowd that were normally reserved for their own. Law was at his simmering best, playing on the edge and willing to start a fight or finish a move. Prowling; his slim figure moved into scoring mode as if electrified. Law was a flashing red streak that tormented Real defenders. A predator the likes of which they rarely faced.

The interval came with no score but the visitors much in the ascendancy. As the second half began the crowd became increasingly impatient at their team's lack of coherence. Looking to spark some life and urgency Miguel Muñoz brought on four substitutes, only then to find himself a goal down moments later. Mark Pearson picked up a loose pass on the edge of the Real penalty area and hit a first time left-footed snapshot that Vicente failed to hold. As the groans from the terraces poured down, the ball bobbled under the goalkeeper's body and into the net. Real supporters screamed abuse at the forlorn Vicente. These were changing times in Madrid.

The incredibly hostile home crowd resembled a baying, howling mob. Incredibly spoilt and incapable of handling what these present *Madrileños* were serving up, they were reduced to silence with a masterly second United goal. Again it was the explosive Law who proved impossible for the opposition to handle – the Scot split two home defenders with a deft pass to the feet of Johnny Giles, the little Dubliner had lit up this grand arena all night with his touch and guile. With space and time Giles' perfect cross found David Herd whose powerful header slammed into the top right hand corner of Vicente's goal. From that moment people began leaving the stadium in their droves. Those left behind stayed only to shout abuse at the unfortunates they felt were white shirted impostors. The final whistle brought a polite ripple of applause across the stadium for United's fine showing.

The managers shook hands, not knowing that the next time the clubs clashed would be for a place in the European Cup final. Since Munich the clubs had grown increasingly close off the pitch and now, significantly, on it there was little to separate them. It was a true friendship; when most of their domestic rivals had seemed content to let United suffer, Real Madrid had shown themselves true Champions of Honour.

★

For Matt Busby and Jimmy Murphy any faint hopes that Manchester United's breathtaking *Bernabéu* display would help ignite their league performances was shot down four days later when they faced Burnley at Old Trafford. The same line-up that excelled in Madrid were mercilessly ravaged 5-2 by their Lancastrian neighbours. Those two results were typical of one of United's most dramatic seasons. A battle against relegation ensued and supporters faced a rollercoaster of emotions that left them exhausted by season's end.

Yet just as the dogfight depressed the faithful, so an unexpected FA Cup run provided joy unconfined. By the end of it United fans sensed that the dark clouds enveloping Old Trafford for the past five years would shortly lift, and a welcoming ray of sunshine was set to warm the hearts of all associated with Manchester United football club.

THE SUMMER OF '63

Since Munich, Old Trafford had become a turbulent and at times poisonous place to ply your trade. With Matt Busby suffering physically and mentally following the crash, he was incapable of exerting the same authority that once held power over everything that moved at the club. To make matters worse, Busby's decision making in the transfer market had became erratic. Between 1953 and 1957 he hadn't needed to buy one player but needs must. United desperately required new blood and players arrived who, in normal circumstances, would not have been allowed a space in the Old Trafford car park, never mind the chance to pull on the sacred red shirt, were signed. With little time to double-check character and nurture technique, they existed as a human life support machine for a club that many still expected to wane...

Somehow they got through. Cliques formed, money a burning issue, there was never enough, the players remained on pauper's wages even after the maximum wage was lifted in 1961. The constant whiff of rebellion was a fragrance smelt by all. Sadly for new recruits, they also were joining a troubled club. A wretched world where red ghosts haunted every corner of The Cliff training ground and the Old Trafford dressing room. The frequent Mancunian downpours hinted at a city still in grief.

A flood of tears: lost voices echoed down every corridor, the players forever compared with the illustrious departed.

The survivors fared little better. There were strained

relationships in the wake of Munich. No longer brothers-in-arms, a loathing developed amid the fortunate few with claims that Bill Foulkes for one *"ran away"* instead of trying to help their trapped, injured and dying team-mates. Harry Gregg and Bill Foulkes hated each other's guts, *"You should have seen that big bastard run"* the Irishman joked.

Where there were once shiny apples, now there were rotten eggs and it only took one to cause a stench. Old established training methods were mocked; in November 1960 Busby splashed out £29,500 for West Ham's cultured, left sided defender, twenty-eight year old Noel Cantwell. Behind his manager's face Cantwell was incandescent with rage at what he felt was a shambolic set-up. Cantwell had come from the self-styled West Ham Academy, a band of players who had began to think deeply about the game. Malcolm Allison, John Bond and Bobby Moore would gather after training in an Italian café around the corner from Upton Park and dissect the merits of English football. How things had to change and adapt or be left behind. None were more vocal than Cantwell. Moving salt and pepper pots across the table to make a point, the group exposed the myth of the long ball and dissected the attributes that made Real Madrid, Benfica and Inter Milan so superior in European competition.

Then Cantwell came to United, supposedly a far bigger club than his previous employers, only to find petty arguments over a practice kit deemed not fit for tramps. He would complain about everything: the preparation was beyond contempt, there were no tactics or talk of defensive formations. Set-piece moves seemed anathema and in the manic training sessions players appeared content to kick lumps out of each other. It all came to a head when criticism of trainer and former United goalkeeper Jack Crompton went too far.

Crompton implored Busby to intervene. It was explained to Cantwell there was the *"United way"* or the highway. Soon the sophisticated Irishman and his sky high West Ham ideals settled down to become an integral part of the new Manchester

United. So much so that in time Busby made him captain. While Cantwell was a thorn in the management's side, he clearly had a point. There were others, though, who needed to be weeded out of the Old Trafford dressing room.

Infrequent tales of match-fixing surfaced during the period between 1960 and 1962. It was the ultimate, unforgivable sin and signalled that defeat no longer hurt United players, quite the opposite. Unexpected hammerings, such as a notorious 7-2 mauling at Newcastle, caused eyebrows to be raised.

Events came to a head one sad Saturday at Highbury when certain United players appeared disgusted at a team-mate when he scored and it all nearly became public knowledge when *Daily Mail* journalists confronted goalkeeper Harry Gregg. It was quickly explained to the volatile Irishman that he was not involved but that it was clear others were guilty. The players involved were household names who would have been lynched in Manchester had they been outed. The shocked United goalkeeper had had his long running suspicions confirmed. He was sick to the stomach and knew there was only one man who could put things right.

"I knew it! I just bloody knew it!" raged Busby, when Gregg confronted him. The United goalkeeper suspected that his manager had an inkling but needed genuine proof. A meeting was called of all the playing staff, the reason unclear. There were worried faces as rumours persisted that something big was going down. Surely the boss had not found out? In came Busby flanked by Jimmy Murphy and Jack Crompton. The atmosphere was intense. Pulling a letter from his pocket, Busby read out a letter of apology he had received from the editor of the *Daily Mail* for the behaviour of his two reporters in Blackpool regarding their "*incorrect*" allegation against United players throwing matches. Matt Busby had called in every favour to extract this apology from the Mail. The guilty had got the message. The boss knew and it would happen no more.

On Saturday 5th May 1963, Manchester United made the short journey across town to take on local rivals City, in undoubtedly their most important match since Sheffield Wednesday had to be overcome in Munich's grim aftermath. Both clubs had three games left to play and were enmeshed in a spider's web, seemingly incapable of escaping the bottom of the table unless one used the other for leverage to jump clear.

52,000 had claimed their place on the terraces hours before kick off, as outside chaos reigned on Maine Road's forecourt. Thousands attempted to gatecrash by wrenching open the stadium's main doors in a mad rush to watch what threatened to be a relegation death knell for whoever lost.

To the joy of Manchester's blue side the player who had grabbed a last gasp Old Trafford winner in a 3-2 victory earlier in the season, struck again after just eight minutes to ignite Maine Road. Twenty-three year old Scotsman Alex Harley looked to have handed his team a lifeline and at the same time doom United. Harley should have scored again shortly after, only for United's reserve goalkeeper David Gaskell, standing in for the injured Harry Gregg, to deny him from point blank range. It was an occasion full of tension and petty fouls. A war of attrition broke out. The visitor's attack led by Bobby Charlton, Denis Law and David Herd were being denied by blue shirted defenders, throwing body and heart in to deny United.

Passions ran high and fists flew; none more so than in the tunnel at half-time when United's latest signing, former Celtic midfield schemer Paddy Crerand, punched City defender David Wagstaff to the floor for an adverse comment made during play. On being challenged by a member of City's backroom staff the fiery Scot warned him that he could expect similar treatment, only for the person in question to quickly disappear through a Maine Road side door. A furious Matt Busby confronted Crerand in the visitor's dressing room. When asked outright if he had floored Wagstaff, Crerand vehemently denied it!

Signed on 6th February 1963, exactly five years after Munich, Crerand was the type of character both on and off the pitch that the United manager had sought since the crash. A no-nonsense, loyal lieutenant who would never back down when the boots were flying. He possessed a passionate will to win that sometimes overstepped the mark as many opponents would discover in time. However what charmed Busby most was his vivid imagination and wonderful passing, both short and long. Though hardly blessed with pace it mattered little, for Paddy Crerand was quicker in mind than most and became an integral part of any United team sent out by Busby as the sixties unfolded. As for the unfortunate Wagstaff, his day would only get worse.

The second half wore on with United becoming increasingly desperate for an equaliser. Six minutes remained when Maine Road erupted in controversy. Wagstaff underhit a backpass towards goalkeeper Harry Dowd and the ball was chased down by Denis Law, whose ankles appeared to be grabbed as he tumbled over. As the blue majority of the crowd howled and screamed venom at Law, the referee Mr McCabe awarded a penalty. Showing great bravery, when other team-mates turned their backs, Albert Quixall, a player many Old Trafford supporters remained unsure of, fired nervelessly past Dowd, to secure the point that ultimately saved United and relegated City.

And yet just three days later Matt Busby's master under-achievers almost blew it at home to Leyton Orient. At half-time they trailed 1-0 to former legendary United captain Johnny Carey's team. Again the 33,000 people present were being made to sweat and boos swept around Old Trafford. Early in the second half a Bobby Charlton cross was turned into his own net by Bobby's namesake, Orient defender Stan Charlton's diving header. It was an equaliser that did little to change the mood on the terraces as they waited in trepidation for their team to slip up again. Once more the air was fraught with uncertainty until the last ten minutes, when Denis Law pounced to soothe red brows. Then, as news filtered through from Upton Park of Manchester City being savaged 6-1 at West Ham to confirm their plight, Bobby Charlton smashed a third United goal to end all doubts. United were staying up and all thoughts could now turn to their forthcoming appearance in the 1963 FA Cup final.

The winter of 1962-63 had been the worst any could remember and the backlog of fixtures meant there was little football played between Christmas and February. United were forced into playing eight games in a manic March including three FA Cup ties and, as their league form continued to drive both Busby and Murphy to distraction, suddenly, without really thinking about it, they were in the cup semi-finals.

On Saturday 27th April 1963, United took on second division giant killers Southampton at Villa Park, and in a grim semi-final clash that few remember with any fondness, Denis Law struck after twenty-two minutes to clinch a Wembley appearance. For Matt Busby the opportunity had arisen to show the world that his efforts to rebuild Manchester United were starting to take shape. A team that tried to play football in a manner befitting the memory of those lost at Munich. In Charlton, Law and Crerand, the manager felt he had the bedrock of greatness. Only time would tell.

The 1963 FA Cup final
Manchester United v Leicester City
Saturday 25th May 1963

After finishing fourth to complete their best ever league season, Leicester started as favourites to win the cup. They were a hard working if unspectacular team who had proved themselves difficult to beat; they were precisely the type of First Division team that Manchester United so often struggled against and yet even though fourteen positions separated the two sides, the mantle of underdogs did not sit well with United players and supporters.

Matt Busby had selection problems, notably with Nobby Stiles who had suffered a hamstring pull in the recent Manchester derby. United's plight that day was such that Stiles played on in considerable agony, thus aggravating the injury and all but ruling him out of Wembley. Into the side came Stiles' best friend and future brother-in-law Johnny Giles. In terms of natural talent, Giles was arguably the best player at Old Trafford, but a tetchy relationship with Busby meant this dark haired, tough and technically gifted little Irishman would soon seek footballing solace away from Manchester. He was later to haunt the United manager for a decade at Don Revie's up and coming Leeds.

In attempting to rebuild after Munich, Busby had never been afraid to spend big and the side that took to the field at Wembley back in 1963 cost in the region of £300,000. They were easily the most expensive team to reach an FA Cup final. The quality of footballer available to Busby was the highest since the crash and if they clicked on the day capable of giving anyone a game.

Twenty minutes before kick off drama occurred in the United dressing room when it was discovered Paddy Crerand had disappeared. In his eagerness to witness the crowd singing "*Abide with me*" the traditional cup final hymn, a curious Crerand had gone walkabout to stand in the tunnel. There he watched the pomp and ceremony unfold. On returning, a frantic Busby quizzed his fellow Scotsman, before the bell rang and it was officially time to enter the pitch.

Led by captain Noel Cantwell, Manchester United stepped back onto the Wembley turf for the first time since 1958. Football writers predicted widely that Leicester's strong defence would win the day and send it to Filbert Street. With the highly rated twenty-six year old Gordon Banks in goal, and a defence marshalled superbly by their commanding Scottish centre-half and captain Frank Mclintock, many claimed Leicester were more than capable of handling the high-explosive concoction of Law, Herd and Charlton. Whilst at the other end of the pitch,

United's much discussed Achilles heel, their own rearguard, was deemed likely to concede against a nun's eleven.

At first, all talk of a spectacle looked to have been muted as Leicester's tactics appeared to be to sit back and play on the break. Indeed early on eight white shirts stood in their own penalty area as United's Maurice Setters took possession still inside his own half. When the *Foxes* did move forward, the uncertainty in the Mancunian defence showed itself and at any time could prove their undoing. Goalkeeper David Gaskell was a case in point. Three times in a mistake-littered opening fifteen minutes the error-prone Gaskell flapped to present Leicester players with clear cut opportunities, only for centre-forward Ken Keyworth and his fellow strikers to miss them all. Having survived United breathed more easily. Wembley was hard on both legs and minds. Bill Foulkes for one experienced cup final nerves. He, along with Bobby Charlton, were the only crash survivors left in the starting eleven. The sheer emotion of an already draining occasion and the pressure to finally win silverware taking a heavy toll.

United hit back, Denis Law's menace and guile played in Albert Quixall with a superb pass. Quixall's inability to control allowed Banks to dive courageously at his feet and clear the danger. Nevertheless, orchestrated by a probing Crerand, United built an incessant passing rhythm; they dominated possession, their football neat and incisive. Bobby Charlton went soaring through and unleashed a typical rasping effort that Gordon Banks did well to save. Banks' ensuing kick out to Scottish inside-right Dave Gibson was intercepted by countryman Paddy Crerand. A typical act of swift thinking saw Crerand intercept and spot Denis Law arriving in the penalty area. Law got the ball ten yards out and with his back to goal let the pass run behind him, turned and then in an eye blink lashed a low shot past Banks into the net. Manchester United led and their mass travelling support went mad. On the bench Busby was up celebrating but a season long torment meant any thought of victory remained folly, for he knew his team was capable of anything – good or bad.

Shortly before half-time it should have been 2-0 when the scintillating Law sped like a red blur past Banks, shot goalwards and missed by an inch. It was all United, their play calm and progressive. Leicester were rocked but as the interval came they remained only a goal down and the game was anything but over. The second half saw a brief flurry from the Midlands club and a still shaky Gaskell dropped the ball at the feet of onrushing City midfielder Graham Cross, who inexplicably shot wide. Sadly for their supporters, who tried in vain to rouse Leicester, they fell back into a first half mode of careless passing and on fifty-seven minutes paid a heavy price. A long goal kick by Gaskell found the cunning Johnny Giles lurking wide on the right. A touch of class followed as he beat his man before flighting a precise cross-field pass to an unmarked Bobby Charlton. Racing with deadly intent into the box Charlton let fly a shot straight at Gordon Banks. As Wembley held its breath the Leicester goalkeeper failed to hold and United striker David Herd swept the ball home.

Across the Wembley terraces a sea of red simply exploded in delight. A victorious, deafening chorus of "*When the reds go marching in*" erupted amongst them. With United so on top many felt that the cup was already won. As Paddy Crerand controlled the centre of the pitch with a calm but tough authority with Albert Quixall alongside having undoubtedly his finest match since arriving at Old Trafford, even Matt Busby appeared relatively content. He should have known better for from seemingly being down and out Leicester struck back.

Ten minutes from time Keyworth's diving header beat Gaskell's flailing fingers to halve the deficit and reignite City hopes. Suddenly the Leicester faithful raised the volume and the 1963 FA Cup final was back on. Stunned but determined not to throw the cup away, United roared back. Denis Law switched play to David Herd then sprinted forty yards forward into the penalty area for the expected return. When it came the *Lawman* smashed a brilliant arcing header past a desperate Banks, only for the ball to agonisingly hit the post and roll rather shamefully back into Bank's grateful hands. Ever the showman Law, in mock histrionics, collapsed to the floor.

On eighty-five minutes all doubts vanished when from another precise Johnny Giles cross, Denis Law jumped with Gordon Banks, who for the second time erred and dropped the ball at the feet of David Herd. Taking aim, a prowling Herd took advantage and flashed a skimming drive past two desperate Leicester defenders trying to block on the goal-line.

At 3-1 there was unbridled ecstasy among the red hordes. The cup was going to Manchester and five long painful years after Munich, the Mancunians could once more glimpse silverware. Even when Captain Noel Cantwell threw the cup high, few worried he would not catch it on the way down. For on that sunlit Wembley afternoon it had been United's day. When interviewed after the match by the BBC's David Coleman, Busby claimed, "*Having so many big time players won us the cup.*" As for Leicester City, their manager Matt Gilles spoke for thousands of United supporters when he said, "*I can't understand how they can play like that today and finish where they did in the league!*"

Free from the lament of a trophyless period, there now existed the fervent hope of better days ahead. Mancunians revelled in glory. On returning home a city ignited in joy at being back amongst the land of the living. Hundreds of thousands lined the streets. Every sightseeing vantage was taken. People hung off lamp posts, on top of bus shelters. Others climbed rather warily onto high narrow window ledges. The bus carrying the victorious United team edged its way at snail's pace, showing off a trophy that was so much more than a simple prize. Munich still cut deep, those lost never to be forgotten but now life could go on.

On entering its final destination for a civic reception at the town hall, the bus went under a huge man-made red and white arch. A moment in time perhaps that signified when Manchester United had moved on from the end of that German runway.

No longer did their supporters feel guilty at looking forward. As Matt Busby raised the cup high to the ecstatic crowds in Albert Square, it was clear United were back.

RENACIMIENTO

Whilst foreign fields continued to be laced with pitfalls that wrecked their ageing legs, on home soil Real Madrid continued to reign supreme. As the 1963-64 season dawned the Madrileños had collected four consecutive Spanish championships. With arch-rivals Barcelona suffering a hangover dating back to their mugging by Benfica in the 1961 European Cup final and loss of Il Mago, Helenio Herrera, to Inter Milan, they were a club in disarray.

So it was that a Madrid team obviously in decline and in a period of transition were able to continue their domestic dominantion. With Alfredo Di Stefano and Ferenc Puskás both now thirty-seven, but still making themselves available for selection, a modicum of gold dust remained. They remained deadly in Spain, as the arrow flew and the cannonball fired but come entry into the European cup, surely it would not be enough to expect a renaissance?

Sustained by sheer will and with a capacity to inspire team-mates and retaining enough firepower to destroy any defence, Alfredo and Ferenc re-entered Europe's premier competition with the clear intention to win it. After romping home by twelve points the previous season, Miguel Muñoz led his team once more into the romance, drama and intrigue of the European cup.

They began in Glasgow on 25th September 1963, scene of their greatest triumph, this time against Scottish champions Rangers at Ibrox. Rangers had recently completed a league and cup double and in their attacking left-sided midfielder Jim Baxter possessed a talent on a par with any in Madrid. *Slim*

Jim was the idol of the Ibrox terraces. However a tendency to party and drink heavily was said to have cost him a transfer to Manchester United, with Busby preferring Denis Law.

Against Real Madrid, Baxter was given short shrift by a Real defence led with vicious intent by Jose Santamaria. He was ably abetted by a new generation of hatchet men when the situation required; Isidro, Vincente, Miera, and Pachin. In a fiercely fought contest Rangers dominated but were undone by one flash of *Madrileño* genius three minutes from time. Caught pushing forward in an attempt to grab a late winner, Rangers lost possession to the electric-heeled Francisco Gento, who raced half the length of the pitch before crossing for Puskás to fire high into the net and silence 81,000 Glaswegians.

On a night when Real had only really performed in short spurts and were at times almost overrun by a rampaging home side, it remained unclear whether this had been a wonderful hit and run showing by the Spaniards, or just sheer good luck. Many thought the latter, nevertheless it had been a distinguished showing by Marquitos and his defenders whose tenacity had kept Rangers at bay, but overall, judged by their own esteemed standards, they were poor at times – it was a performance that was unlikely to set alarm bells ringing in Milan or Lisbon.

For like a mugger in the dark, age had crept up on Alfredo Di Stefano and he was afflicted with sciatica. The clock was ticking loudly for the Argentine to win a priceless sixth European cup. It was now or never. However events in the second leg against the Scots may well have had the Italians and Portuguese scurrying for cover! Real cut loose in the *Bernabéu* to savage Rangers 6-0 with a portly Ferenc Puskás grabbing a hat-trick with further goals from Gento, Ruiz and Evaristo. The latter had signed from Barcelona despite scoring with the diving header that had ended their golden era. The versatile, energetic Brazilian was a great acquisition for a Madrid side with weary legs.

Madrid's progress all of a sudden seemed stately, unruffled: a contemptuous dismissal of Dinamo Bucharest followed. The 8-4 aggregate score was a fair reflection of the gulf in class between the two sides but come the quarter-finals there was dismay when the Spaniards were drawn against holders AC Milan; a side containing the prodigious attacking prowess of Sandro Mazzola and Gianni Rivera. Surely they would finish off this proud, though vulnerable, ageing giant.

Few dared to tip Real, a team deemed by most experts to be ripe for a dose of football reality. But on 29th January 1964, on a glorious Madrid evening, the *Madrileños* defied father time once more to hand the champions a 4-1 thrashing. Goals from Amancio, Puskás, Gento and Di Stefano delighted a home crowd who watched in disbelief as the champion *Rossoneri were* torn apart. The magic burned still, the white handkerchiefs waved, the *"Olés" s*oared into the Madrid sky. The years, if not the weight, fell from Puskás and the pain that wracked Di Stefano's ailing physique, disappeared. Next stop *San Siro*.

Milan waited with baited breath for the Real Madrid old school who, like an old flame appearing at your wedding, had come so close to wrecking all that the *Milanistas* held dear. Not prepared to risk disaster, Miguel Muñoz chose to adopt a safety first attitude and select a blanket defence. This seemed anathema for a club brought up on an attacking mentality – it was akin to having a bath fully dressed.

During a nightmare first half showing AC pulled two goals back and with Real trembling on the precipice the *San Siro* boiled over with expectations for a sensational comeback. Yet, by the interval, an exasperated Muñoz retained sufficient demeanour to reorganise and somehow inspire a Real defence to hold firm. An assortment of courageous defending, luck and rank bad finishing meant the Spaniards survived an incessant *Rossoneri* second half whirlwind. But Di Stefano and Puskás had been passengers throughout, and never again could Muñoz risk employing the same tactics with these two in the side.

There were few worries in the semi-finals as Grasshoppers of Zurich were effortlessly put away 8-1 over the two legs, as all eyes then focused on the final in Vienna and the opportunity to renew acquaintances with an old foe. *Il Mago* had re-appeared at Inter Milan and prepared to end forever the era of the *Madrileño*.

After employing thirteen coaches in five years, it was time to go for the best. He was back. Helenio Herrera had pitched a tent and thrown in his lot with the Milanese aristocrats, Internazionale. Bankrolled by the oil billionaire Angelo Moratti, Herrera had arrived in May 1960 with the taunts of the Barca supporters still ringing in his ears. He swiftly set about rebuilding their fortunes and presented the Inter faithful with a first title for eight years. Whilst the long suffering supporters took him to their hearts, *Il Mago* promised them more, much more and for this he was adored by the *Nerazzurri*. Of course, what Herrera desired most was a last shot at a team whom had caused him so much pain, the club whom had had the temerity to make the magician appear a fraud. Now, back in the rarefied atmosphere of the European Cup final, he wanted to finish off Real Madrid.

In the beautiful Austrian capital of Vienna on 27th May 1964, Herrera was handed the opportunity to make the *Madrileños* vanish from the face of the earth. On arriving at Inter, Herrera swiftly decided the vibrant open game practised at Barcelona would never work in the cutthroat, ultra cautious, counter-attacking world of Italian football. Herrera changed tack and imposed upon his team an iron discipline and win at all cost mentality. A dark spell was cast, the *Catenaccio*, or *lock out* was born - a defensive system that if played correctly strangled the life out of opposition forwards, rendering them ensnared in a spider's web.

Herrera employed four man-marking defenders and a *libero or* sweeper whose task was to pick off loose balls. Once nullified, the system emphasised the use of devastating quick counter strikes to steal goals and win matches but few friends. At Inter, Herrera was blessed with a set of players perfect for such a system. In goal the experienced Sarti; holding everything together at Libero, dictating events around him, was inspirational club captain Picchi. Out wide a full-back pairing that had no equals, the formidable Burgnich and Facchetti. They were helped at all times by defensive midfielders in Tagnin, Guarneri and Corso, who were relentless at hunting down their targets.

Above all Inter were ruthless, they would wear down opponents, then strike like a cobra against a chastened and broken opposition with a front three capable of winning matches in the blink of an eye. Brazilian Jair was an elusive, fast and deadly winger. The irrepressible, magnificent Spaniard Luis Suarez, European Footballer of the Year in 1960 and brought to Milan by Herrera for a world record fee from Barcelona, was supplemented by Italian wonder kid nineteen-year old Sandro Mazzola who would go on to play his entire, esteemed career in the blue and black stripes. This frightening trio wreaked mayhem on the break as their team-mates behind locked up the bolt and threw away the key. For Madrid special preparations were made; Burgnich would hang tight to Gento, Facchetti to the darting Amancio, Guarneri to Puskás and the seemingly boundless, energetic Tagnin was handed the golden ticket to destroy Di Stefano.

On the eve of the final the master of mind games Herrera claimed he feared the still serious double threat of Di Stefano and Puskás, whilst secretly knowing that if the game was still alive after an hour, then Inter's extra youth and stamina would surely prevail. Inside the Madrid camp the atmosphere was far from relaxed as players complained about facilities and the press roamed the hotel looking for stories. All hell broke loose when a photographer sneaked out pictures of both a topless Puskás and Di Stefano, which were plastered on front pages under the squalid headline: *WHO IS THE FATTEST ?*

An infuriated Argentine complained bitterly but to no avail – as his powers on the field waned, so went his influence off it. This was a man who had demanded the best from both himself and team-mates, who had earned the respect from all, yet was now humiliated. There was worse, much worse to follow for Di Stefano, as team coach Miguel Muñoz, in compliance with his President, was already mulling over the unthinkable whatever happened against Inter.

In an atmosphere of cataclysmic change, and with the assassination of John F Kennedy still on people's minds, this was regarded by most as Alfredo's last stand.

And so at the *Prater* stadium, in front of 72,000 people, the last rites of a glorious era in the history of the European Cup were pronounced. Inter and Real appeared to a marvellous reception, with Ferenc Puskás, as ever, bringing up the rear. Real still dazzled in their all white strip, so vivid and delightful as, capturing the moment for the history books, hundreds of flashbulbs exploded. It was a snapshot of a rainbow's end; the romantics versus the cynics. Inter, business-like in their *Nerazzurri* stripes, played the pragmatist, football's accountants; calculating, cold.

Nevertheless in a tightly contested first half Madrid were only beaten by a cleverly struck, clipped drive from Sandro Mazzola's right foot shortly before the interval. Vicente could only look on in horror as Mazzola's fine effort flew past him to ignite the Inter support and dismay Madrid's. Moments after the break Real went so close to equalising when Puskás for once found an inch of space to thrash a rasping cross shot against the Inter post. The *Madrileños* continued to press but struggled against a blue/black wall of defiance. With Di Stefano unable to exert an ounce of influence, the Spaniards floundered. Age and Herrera's tactical chains proved unbreakable.

Inter held firm, measured and always ready to strike out. On sixty-one minutes two horrific errors in the Madrid defence gifted the cup to Milan; a rare lapse of concentration from Santamaria let in the prowling Mazzola, who laid off a pass for fellow striker Aurelio Milani. Taking aim Milani's weak shot was misjudged terribly by Vicente, whose flailing attempts to stop the ball only helped it bobble over the line. The stricken goalkeeper held his head in hands that appeared unable to catch a beach ball, as a truly forgettable evening under Viennese stars unfolded for Real Madrid. As the ball hit the net, Helenio Herrera raced off his bench in jubilation and stood hands aloft facing the crowd.

He knew the game was over. A new era dawned. *Catenaccio* had drawn an unholy veil over the golden ball players of Madrid. The demons that had wracked Herrera since his time at Barca had disappeared. *Il Mago* had his revenge.

Then, a twist, as with twenty minutes remaining and Inter already coasting and celebrating victory, a Francisco Gento corner was spectacularly hooked home from six yards by midfielder Felo. Suddenly new life and legs breezed into the Spaniards. Muñoz urged his players for one last great effort. Bernabéu, who had hardly shifted in his VIP seat, now bore the look of a man praying for one last miracle. Momentarily rocked, the Italians made mistakes. Amancio flew down the right wing and his cross, met by Puskás, was blocked by two Inter defenders on the line. White shirts stormed forward, the weight of history demanding they go for broke. Then on seventy-six minutes with Real throwing everything into attack they were handed a last gut-churning moment; a desperate mistake again from Santamaria saw the badly tiring Uruguayan robbed by the speeding legs of an effervescent Sandro Mazzola. Racing clear on goal Mazzola fired past Vicente to clinch the match 3-1. There could be no more arguments. There would be no *renaissance*. The dreams of a sixth European cup had gone and the fall out in Madrid would prove just as cataclysmic.

When it was casually suggested to Di Stefano by Muñoz that perhaps the time had come to hang up his boots and take a position on the club's technical staff, the Argentine erupted and demanded to see his President. Alfredo may have been thirty-eight but surely he could count on the old General for support in this his darkest hour? Forty-nine goals in a hundred and forty appearances in Europe's most prestigious competition demanded loyalty, surely?

However on meeting Santiago Bernabéu the Argentine was shocked to discover that he too was ready to twist the knife. Bernabéu advised him to sign a much reduced non-playing contract or risk departure. Still seething, Di Stefano went away licking his wounds, only to later return puffing out his chest and demanding a new playing contract? He was the *Blond Arrow,* without him the *Madrileños* would never have flown so high for so long. Would this once great star be consigned to walk on parts in B movies? Bernabéu lost patience with his adopted son telling him *"Sign or go!"*

Refusing point blank, Di Stefano issued a public statement: *"Real Madrid have maliciously terminated my contract."* Such contentious words meant there could be no way back. He had also in his actions sacrificed a golden handshake and this for Di Stefano must have felt like a dagger through the heart. With neither party willing to back down, a tragic finale occurred and Di Stefano left to manage Espanol. An emotional Madrid President, angered by what he considered the Argentine's betrayal and sheer insolence declared: *"Di Stefano will never again tread the hallowed Bernabéu turf, whilst I am alive."* These sad words ended eleven wonderful years – the love affair was over. It was a crying shame and the *Blond Arrow* would soar no more.

Postscript: Tempers cooled in time prevailed and on 7th June 1967, Alfredo went home. The Estadio Bernabéu bade a magnificent farewell to the man who had been so instrumental to their golden era, Alfredo Di Stefano. 130,000 gathered to watch the Madrileños take on newly crowned European champions, Jock Stein's Glasgow Celtic and pay respect to The legendary Blond Arrow.

Fifteen minutes in the lights were switched off in the Bernabéu and a single spotlight picked out Di Stefano illuminating him in the centre-circle. As the crowd went mad the great man left the stage for the final time. The noise as he trotted off rocking the very foundations of the stadium, what a fitting exit for the finest player in the history of Real Madrid. It had been a wonderful journey for the boy from Barracas on the outskirts of Buenos Aires.

BEST INTENTIONS

On Saturday 14th September 1963, 50,453 people packed Old Trafford. They came to watch and be enthralled by Denis Law, Bobby Charlton and Paddy Crerand. They left speechless and in a state of wonder - it wasn't an electrifying Law scissor-kick or thundering Charlton shot into the top corner that dazed the senses of the home support. Instead it was a skinny slip of a seventeen year old from Belfast, who dazzled. His dancing feet moving to the staccato rhythms of the city's burgeoning music scene - the red half of Manchester watched as if the second coming was unfolding before their eyes. Matt Busby had been biding his time, but could hold the leash no more, and now the moment had arrived for the world to witness for themselves, the phenomenon that was George Best...

Graham Williams was a no nonsense left full-back for West Bromwich Albion, a twenty-six year old Welsh international with a fierce reputation for dealing with wingers who dared to ever spread their wings and go by him. Then he met George Best. As Old Trafford swayed and rocked with each turn and twist of their bewitching Irish teenager, Williams bore the impression of a man caught in a house fire trying desperately to find a way out. Best tortured Williams in their first encounter, he actually nutmugged the defender to huge cheers from the terraces! Whether it was simply putting the ball past him to race clear or waiting for the fraught Welshman to lunge in before leaving him for dead with a sleight of foot, Williams' attempts to kick Best out of the game were fruitless as he simply could not get near him - except once.

Shortly before half-time, he earned the home crowd's wrath by sending Best hurtling through the air. To the crowd's great relief their new hero simply picked himself up, dusted himself down and once again went looking for the ball before tormenting Williams some more. Busby had seen enough and in the second half he switched Best to the opposite wing to ensure Williams didn't dish out more serious retribution to his Belfast boy.

Shortly after the game finished Williams went looking for Best in the tunnel and, on finding him, simply glared at the young Irishman. A worried Best quizzed what was the problem, to which Williams replied, *"I just wanted to see what your face looked like because I got sick of seeing your backside!"* George Best had arrived in Manchester and the city itself would never be the same again – the sixties were about to swing.

Easter Monday: Champions Again!

On *26th April 1965,* in front of an emotional Old Trafford crowd, Manchester United clinched their first title in eight years and prepared to paint the city red. A 3-1 defeat of Arsenal with two goals from Law and another from Best ensured that Matt Busby's quest for the European Cup could begin again. It finally extinguished some of the demons of Munich; the clanking metal, bitter snow and the coats and rags that had covered the bodies of those who had perished amid the fire and flames. A football club torn apart by tragedy had risen from the grave in an attempt to claim a trophy they had sworn a blood oath to win. It meant everything.

Their first attempt back in eight years saw United coast to the quarter-final stage where the draw handed them a foreboding task against two-times champions and the previous season's finalists Benfica. Once again under the astute guidance of Bella Guttman, whose original departure over money left a sour taste in the mouths of Benfica supporters, they were a force to be reckoned with. Once the manager and the directors kissed and made up, thousands greeted his return at Lisbon airport.

On Wednesday 2nd February 1965, 64,035 paid club record receipts to witness a five-goal thriller. The home side triumphed 3-2 but it was hardly a healthy advantage for the return match in Lisbon, where at the magnificent *Stadium of Light* Benfica remained unbeaten in European competition. Nevertheless Old Trafford hosted a classic first leg, full of passion and quality football with the Portuguese quite happy to take on the home team, content in the knowledge any damage could be put to right in Lisbon.

United began on fire when after just five minutes David Herd lashed a header from a George Best free kick that rattled a Portuguese post: but it was Benfica who silenced the deafening crowd to strike first on the half hour. An unguarded Jose Augusto side-footing home from a Eusebio corner to leave Harry Gregg incandescent with rage. Seven minutes later United roared back when Stiles, Law and Best combined to rip apart Benfica's defence, setting up Herd to slot home an equaliser.

The Portuguese seemed taken aback by the sheer volume of noise coming from the terraces. A raw passion, Mancunian emotions were overflowing for they were not just cheering this present team on to victory, they were raising the roof for red ghosts. Flagging Benfica players were left chasing shadows as the midfield fell under the spell of Crerand's precision passing and the biting, snarling Stiles. Twice United hit the woodwork as the pressure became all consuming. The visitors could not escape their own penalty area and looked ripe for the kill.

Another goal had to come for the home side and three minutes before half-time a Charlton cross was finished in mesmerising style by Law, whose reactions and quicksilver finish left goalkeeper Costa Pereira helpless. Again the stadium erupted and the interval whistle was greeted with raucous applause from a crowd whom could ask for no more from their team. On sixty minutes they took a deserved 3-1 lead when Bill Foulkes made a rare sortie forward to hammer a diving header past a mishandling Pereira. Now Benfica awoke, Eusebio came to life, unplayable at best he ripped past red shirts with alarming ease, his pace frightening and causing gasps from the worried terraces. An all action Nobby Stiles tried everything to rein in the *Panther*, but it was proving to be a nigh on impossible task - akin to trying to catch the wind, as the boy from Mozambique sprang free. Three times he let fly thirty-yard rockets that skimmed the bar, causing supporters to duck for their lives behind the goal, and Harry Gregg to believe Irish luck was going his way - only for Gregg to curse it when Eusebio's stunning cross left him stranded, as it landed at the feet of deadly centre-forward Jose Augusto Torres. This heaven sent gift for Torres was not wasted and at 3-2 what appeared a relatively impressive showing by Manchester United, suddenly resembled a dangerous result. They needed another, and in the dying moments Denis Law went within inches of grabbing a priceless fourth; Costa Pereira leaping to his team's aid with a magnificent save from close range to tip Law's goal bound header onto the crossbar - as the ball bounced back the Scot miraculously leaped skywards to hook in another shot, only to see his acrobatic effort blocked on the line.

The final whistle sounded and amid the applause at Old Trafford there were worrying grumbles that come the second leg on Portuguese soil, Benfica would tear United apart. Their home record was immaculate – in an astonishing eighteen games, thirty-seven goals had been scored, a record so formidable as to suggest the Mancunians did not have a prayer when battle resumed in front of a fanatical 100,000 crowd at the *Stadium of Light*.

Matt Busby insisted that they would go to Portugal and attack but few believed him. It sounded like false baravdo in the face of inevitable defeat. Attempting to take on the *Eagles,* most notably Eusebio, in their own backyard was regarded as footballing suicide. Better teams than United had gone there in the past claiming they would attack Benfica, only to receive beatings of murderous proportions. The previous season Real

Madrid had been given a 5-1 thrashing at the same stage of the competition, part of run of home legs that yielded 19 goals in just 4 games.

Bobby Charlton hinted after the first leg that maybe a one goal lead would just not be enough to survive what was certain to be an inferno. Many were mindful of United's recent record in Portugal - just two seasons before they had hammered Sporting Lisbon 4-1 at Old Trafford in the Fairs Cup, only then to succumb to a 5-0 humiliation in Lisbon.

The coming of Georgie Boy:

On the morning of Wednesday 9th March 1965 the city of Lisbon awoke to count down the hours before their beloved Benfica took on and destroyed the famous Manchester United. Portuguese confidence was sky high. As the United coach made its wary way to the stadium, Benfica supporters held up five fingers to remind the visitors just how badly they were beaten when they were last in the city.

Always wise to any outcome, Bela Guttman intended to use all possible advantages. A ten o'clock kick-off wholly alien to the English champions would be delayed even further by the presentation to Eusebio of the European Footballer of the Year trophy in the centre-circle. It all added to an atmosphere of fanatical showmanship. Wary of the attacking threat posed by United, Guttman, though confident, had reason to feel edgy. Benfica had not enjoyed a great season. Trailing heavily to Sporting Lisbon in the league meant success in Europe had become all consuming. There was intense pressure on him and his players to succeed and privately he forecast a troublesome evening.

In the Manchester United dressing room before kick-off tensions ran high. Nerves were fraught, players sat with their own thoughts as they listened to the crazy decibels rising through the walls. Already the bell had rung to see them line up in the tunnel, only then to have to return whilst Eusebio received his award. Nobody spoke and few moved, all except one - Paddy Crerand. The Scottish midfielder busied himself by playing

around with a ball, only to cause ructions when he smashed a full length wall mirror, shattering glass all over. Crerand felt the wrath of team-mates who already feared the worst and now had to contend with the seven years bad luck thrust upon them by their midfield lynchpin's clumsiness.

Busby glared angrily towards Crerand but was too pre-occupied to comment. He called everyone together for a last team talk, imploring them to "keep it tight in the early stages and not to give anything away." A red faced Crerand for once kept his own counsel, not daring to risk opening his mouth for fear of being jumped on. As for George Best, well his thoughts must have been elsewhere...

Finally both teams entered; firecrackers deafened and rockets ignited high above the stadium. A full moon disappeared behind a huge plume of red smoke. From the floodlight pylons the proud eagles of Benfica lit up in neon against a velvet black skyline. The *Estadio da Luz* paid homage to their heroes.

Named after the parish where the ground stands, *Nossa Senhora da Luz (Our Lady of the Night),* many a silent prayer was said by the Portuguese to their holy mother, who it was claimed had paid them a visit to *Fatima* only forty-eight years previously in the *O Milagre Do Sol (The Miracle of the Sun).* Very shortly they were soon to witness another one of God's miracles, this one hailing from Belfast.

It took just six minutes for the Belfast Boy to work his magic – a foul on Bobby Charlton resulted in a free kick which Tony Dunne flighted into the Benfica box. Waiting to pounce was George Best who soared over two defenders to head past Costa Pereira and horrify the locals. Now two goals down on aggregate the home side roared forward, only to be caught again on twelve minutes by a quick kick out from Harry Gregg that found David Herd midway inside Benfica's half. Swift thinking by Herd saw him guide a header into the path of an onrushing George Best. As the *Stadium of Light* watched transfixed, Best accelerated, took on and left for dead three Benfica players, before firing low past Pereira from a narrow angle. It was an outrageous goal from the Irishman; blistering pace, wonderful control and a devastating finish and it all but finished off Benfica.

Across the huge terraces they watched grim-faced but fascinated by this slight red demon, who slipped tackles with ease, then teased and tormented their world class players. George Best appeared unplayable as at one stage five white shirts were left trailing in his slipstream, dazed and confused as if hit by a smoke bomb. Later on, recalling this memorable Lisbon evening, Paddy Crerand summed everything up by claiming *"Besty just went daft!"* With the game continuing almost in silence, Best looked to have completed a thrilling hat-trick, only to be judged offside by famed Italian referee Concerto Lo Bello.

On fifteen minutes the visitors scored again! Charlton, Law and Herd all combined superbly to dissect the Benfica rearguard and set up winger John Connelly to lash a sensational third past a disbelieving Pereira. At 3-0 and 6-2 up overall, United were home and dry. For Benfica it was a collapse unparalleled in their history. A monumental thrashing, they were totally taken aback by the English champion's attacking play and like a boxer they hung from the ropes reeling.

They had anticipated a tactical contest, only to be caught by surprise when their opponents had come out swinging. Bela Guttman bore a resigned look on the bench. No longer concentrating on how to pull back the tie, he instead wished only to avoid further humiliation. The myth of Benfica's invincibility at the *Estadio Da Luz*, like the mirror in United's dressing room, had been well and truly shattered. The old man knew well when a fight was up. This night belonged to the men from Manchester.

Half-time came, and with the Portuguese players and fans in utter despair, Paddy Crerand, who had been magnificent throughout, declared to his jubilant team-mates in the dressing room. *"Anyone got another mirror?"* Seven minutes after the interval Shay Brennan misjudged a lob and sent it soaring horribly over

Harry Gregg into his own net. The sight of Eusebio rushing to retrieve the ball and restart proceedings momentarily galvanised the Portuguese crowd but as United continued to carve open their defence at will, there remained little hope of a miracle. Guttman's men were a ghost of the team whom had terrorised Europe for the previous five years. With Eusebio under Nobby Stiles' lock and key, Benfica played without any conviction or belief.

It came as no surprise when ten minutes from time United increased their lead further, Paddy Crerand scoring a much deserved fourth as he slid home after being put through by Law's deft side-footed touch. If George Best had been the catalyst and the fury, then Crerand had been the instigator of this unforgettable Manchester United performance. It was already a well stated fact that when Crerand played well United performed and this was never truer than on that unforgettable evening in the parish of *Nossa Senhora da luz*.

In the dying moments Bobby Charlton capped a marvellous showing with a stunning run through the heart of a bedraggled Benfica rearguard before rounding Pereira and slotting home. The home supporters who had waved five fingers at the United players beforehand had proved to be correct but they could never have dreamt it would have been in this manner. The final whistle signalled total mayhem on the pitch as hundreds converged from the stands to remonstrate with the Benfica players. Cushions rained down and fires started on the terraces. Some United players were jostled as they made for a quick exit down the tunnel. As for George Best, he found himself stranded in the centre-circle amid scenes of bedlam. Surrounded by Portuguese riot-police the Irishman was the focus of a hysterical mob who were desperate just to be near him.

One crazed fan surged towards Best with a knife demanding a lock of his hair but was swiftly wrestled away. These were strange scenes unfolding in Lisbon. An adulation normally reserved for rock and roll stars was being heaped upon this United youngster's head. Matt Busby declared the performance,

"My finest hour." As for Benfica, their season simply fell away. Guttman left that same summer for pastures new - the footballing gypsy off wandering once more.

The plaudits and acclaim for Best's individual performance had wordsmiths struggling to find phrases suitably apt. Geoffrey Green of the *Times,* in describing the Belfast boy's second goal penned a memorable line: *"There was Best, gliding like a dark ghost past three men to break clear and slide the ball home. A beautiful goal."*

But the most famous would be by local sports paper *Bola* that summed up the evening with its sensational headline: ***A BEATLE CALLED BEST SMASHES BENFICA!***

A legend was born.

The following morning at Lisbon airport Best bought himself a huge sombrero and egged on by team-mates put it on as they landed back in Manchester. Walking down the gangway a hundred cameras flashed and clicked and a smiling, Sombrero wearing Best entered the realms of Beatlemania. Cue the next day's headlines with the photograph entitled ***EL BEATLE!*** The boy from Belfast in time would become the world's first instantly recognisable footballer. It was a monster that for a while would see him ride with angels, before he ultimately fell from a great height. But events in the *Stadium of Light* had been a rite of passage - George Best had arrived.

Matt Busby was ecstatic. Manchester United were back in the European cup semi-finals. Even better, United had avoided Real Madrid and holders Inter Milan and were paired against Partizan Belgrade. A fine side, tough and resilient but limited and surely beatable. Already there was much talk in Manchester of a trip to Brussels' *Heysel* stadium and a possible showdown against the *Madrileños.* What finer way to honour the memory of those killed at Munich. Supporters began making plans for the final, there were even rumours of United pre-booking their Brussels hotel. And yet... nothing cuts worse than complacency.

BAD TIDINGS FROM BELGRADE

For Matt Busby it had been eight years since Munich, yet still the physical and mental pain remained to give him more sleepless nights than not. To be given the last rites once and survive must be a humbling experience, to have them delivered twice must make you doubt your own mortality and treat every new day as a gift. For Busby there was also the guilt, an obsession with conquering Europe and remaining dominant on the home front had, in his mind, resulted in carnage. Before the crash he was keen to push his boys on, afterwards it became a holy grail. Those lost had to have died for something, otherwise what was the point in going on? A deeply religious man, Busby had come close to losing faith in a God who at times appeared intent on breaking hearts. A path to salvation that came laden deep with traps and pitfalls had yet another in store for the Manchester United manager. A return to Belgrade…

Belgrade: *Wednesday 13th April 1966:* Hiding any fear or angst at returning to a city where his *Babes* played their final match, a buoyant Matt Busby declared publicly on the eve of the first leg against Partizan, *"Manchester United have never played for a draw before and we will not start now!"* True to his word Busby's team attacked from the off in Belgrade. With Partizan experiencing stage fright at being cast amongst such acclaimed company, United attempted to take swift advantage, and as eight years before, hit early and hard. With both George Best and Denis Law far from full fitness, they each missed more than presentable chances in the opening ten minutes.

First Best shot wastefully wide when all of Yugoslav descent in the *People's Stadium* had resigned themselves to going one down. None seemed more surprised than the wistful Irishman who, it appeared, was already limping. Then, as if determined to make amends, Best left two Yugoslav defenders for dead, went round the goalkeeper before setting up Denis Law, who inexplicably lashed his shot against the crossbar from two yards out. The Partizan goalkeeper Milutin Soskic stood relieved and a little bemused that his goal had remained intact after the normally deadly Scotsman's uncharacteristic miss. Both misses combined to leave a feeling of dread among United supporters listening back home.

Seemingly in awe of their big name opponents, the Yugoslavs had begun nervously and the passionate 55,000 capacity crowd had been reduced to a grumbling slumber. The visitors pinned back their hosts for long stages of the first half, but apart from a lone instance when a clearly unfit Law again struck the Yugoslav woodwork, they failed to take advantage of almost overwhelming possession. At times United appeared complacent, such was their complete dominance. A European cup semi-final was not meant to be this easy.

Though not playing well, a Partizan team on an unusually attractive win bonus of a third of the gate were taking no prisoners. Hacking and slashing, they picked out their worst tormentor, the pulsating George Best, for particularly special attention. Already feeling the effects of a painful leg injury suffered in a recent FA Cup tie at Preston, and far too brave for his own good, the United forward at one stage actually stood on the ball to avoid the blood curdling swipes aimed towards him!

In truth, Best should not even have been out on the field but, not wanting to let his manager and team-mates down, when asked by Busby beforehand if he felt fit the young Irishman claimed he was fine. In reality his knee was close to collapse and Best had made a serious mistake - one that was soon to cost him and United dear.

Content with his team's performance up until this point Busby knew the pitfalls of a wonderful but unforgiving competition and remained wary. Opportunities at this heady level had to be taken when offered. On leaving the pitch at the interval United's reserve Noel Cantwell, who had watched proceedings from the visitor's bench, implied to Paddy Crerand that it was just a matter of time before they scored. This irked Crerand for he knew Partizan could not be as bad again in the second half. He was right. Two minutes after the break a revitalised home team took the lead. Looking sharper and quicker on the ball they caught United cold with a quick throw in, Partizan's raiding full-back Jusufi raced clear to place a high cross into the penalty area. Totally misjudging the ball, a despairing Harry Gregg allowed prolific Serbian born striker Mustafa Hasanagic, the idol of the Belgrade terraces, to smash home a glorious header. Suddenly United were rocking.

Stunned by Hasanagic's goal, and taken aback by the technical brilliance and sheer fury of Partizan's football, a siege ensued. On the hour, with Best and Law reduced to walking wounded, United cracked again. Partizan's finest players had risen to the occasion, the scheming box of tricks and lightning fast left-winger Milan Galic was a constant thorn, whilst their classy sweeper Velibor Vasovic, now freed from defensive duties, moved up field and busied himself ripping apart the United defence with a series of sublime passes. After intense pressure with the home white shirts swarming all over their English opponents, it came as no surprise when a typically incisive ball from Vasovic wreaked havoc. Raiding midfielder Radoslav Becejac controlled instantly before firing past Gregg to send Belgrade delirious and the Mancunians into turmoil.

It was a devastating knock-out blow for Manchester United and clearly rattled them. Still, Partizan roared forward in search of a third killer goal. In fear of being overrun, Nobby Stiles and Paddy Crerand attempted to stem the tide by crashing into tackles that erred towards street brawling. One instance involving the quick tempered Stiles saw beer bottles hurling down upon the Mancunian's head from the terraces. Belgrade was not a place to pick a fight.

Crerand and Stiles swiftly decided it wiser to live and fight another day. The game descended into a series of nasty and niggling incidents that did not bode well for the return at Old Trafford. At the final whistle, the Yugoslavs antagonised their opponents by celebrating like they had already won the European cup.

Outwardly Matt Busby accepted defeat with good grace. *"I think we can still win in Manchester despite the two goal loss. My players are sick with the chances we missed and at half-time I would have given any odds on our victory. But congratulations to Partizan."*

Secretly Busby was reeling. The European Cup seemed further away than ever. Memories of Belgrade first time around must have swept through Busby's head. Bobby Charlton's scintillating grass-cutting effort making it 2-0. The huge tension of the final moments as Harry Gregg refused to be beaten. The after match party, the laughter and the songs. Enduring friendships, some doomed to last no longer than a day. *"We'll meet again,"* Roger Byrne sang, *"Don't know where, don't know when. But I know well meet again…"*

There was more bad news for United as Best had badly aggravated the knee injury fifteen minutes from time and would require a cartilage operation, curtailing his season. Best's courage and youthful exuberance had backfired spectacularly. For in seven days time when Manchester United attempted to pull back the 2-0 deficit, their most precious diamond would be sat amongst the crowd praying like the rest that the *Red Devils* could pull off a most unlikely comeback.

Manchester: Wednesday 20th April 1966: On a night tinged with high emotion and sheer unadulterated passion, Manchester United threw everything they had at a resolute Partizan

Belgrade defence. Roared on from the whistle by a deafening 62,000 crowd, they went for broke. However George Best's replacement, John Anderson, proved inadequate at this exalted level and a Yugoslav team desperate to make it to Brussels by any means necessary simply swatted him aside.

Partizan coach Abdulah Gegic had shown great tactical acumen in plotting Partizan's route to the semis. So much so that Europe's elite clubs, including Real Madrid, had inquired about his services. But as the Mancunian skies turned black and the noise from the home crowd threatened to rip the roof off Old Trafford, Gegic's final team talk came solely down to one simple instruction, *"Defend for your lives!"*

This was an experienced, battle-hardened Partizan and the vast majority had played vital parts in Yugoslavia's impressive showings in recent European championships and World Cups – reaching the final in one and the semi in the other. Old Trafford held no fears and they stood ready to go to war with Manchester United.

The first half saw United bombard the Partizan goal without creating anything resembling a decent opportunity. Every long ball and mishit pass came etched with hints of desperation. As the clock ticked down tempers on both sides frayed – a simmering undercurrent from the match in Belgrade that threatened at any time to erupt. Finally it exploded when Nobby Stiles snapped after one to many attempts by Partizan defender Ljubomir Mihajlovic to dissect him at the midriff.

With the Swiss referee Dienst's back turned, Stiles took retribution and punched Mihajlovic to the floor. Suddenly chaos reigned as players from both sides became involved in a free for all. In an unfortunate case of mistaken identity by his linesman, Dienst took the wrong advice and sent off Paddy Crerand for allegedly flattening Mihajlovic. An irate Crerand tried desperately to argue a case without actually naming Stiles but it was to no avail. As if to confirm Dienst's highly dubious decision, Crerand became involved with Partizan winger Pirmajer, who was taunting the Glaswegian and telling him to get off the pitch. This was before Crerand clocked him with a left hook that would not have shamed Cassius Clay! And so with just twenty minutes remaining a tearful Crerand was finally led away, knowing that if United did pull off a late miracle, he would be barred from the final.

As for Nobby Stiles, his night took an even more frenetic twist when with just seventeen minutes remaining he finally grabbed a goal back. Running into the penalty Stiles shot past a fumbling Soskic from twelve yards out. Old Trafford went mad and Matt Busby came onto the touchline urging his team for a last great effort. The dream was still alive and just one more goal was needed to level the tie.

A fraught Partizan steadied themselves for a final onslaught. United came again, this time Bobby Charlton let fly a tremendous volley that hissed inches over Soskic's crossbar into the Stretford End. With time almost up few could hardly bear to watch. Busby stood and stared, as if in a trance, his dream in tatters once more. There was to be no ten man miracle and at the final whistle Partizan celebrated a ferocious backs-to-the-wall showing. They would go on to play Real Madrid in the European Cup final. For Manchester United there was only utter despair as for the third time running they had been eliminated at the semi-final stage.

In the dressing room no one spoke. A spluttered cough and the clack of boots being the only sound. One by one the players drifted off before finally only Paddy Crerand and his manager remained. The two men had grown close over the years, a distraught Busby opened up to his fellow countryman to tell him it was over. Crerand recalls the moment, "*I was sitting in the dressing room and Matt was the only other person there. He was in a bad state and looked crushed. He kept mumbling about never winning the European Cup. But I said 'you hold on here, because in two years we will win this thing'. I really believed it.*"

That same evening there was a banquet for both teams at the Midland hotel in the city. A still fuming Paddy Crerand angrily confronted Partizan's Mihajlovic, who he accused of getting him sent off. The Yugoslav ended up locking himself in a toilet cubicle to escape the Scotsman's wrath! Finally the night ended and a miserable episode in the history of Manchester United came to a close. For Matt Busby a decision had to be made on whether he could summon the strength to go on, and his mood hardly improved when the following Saturday saw United suffer further heartache by losing to Everton in the FA Cup semi-final.

However an incident occurred two days later when he was travelling to Old Trafford for training that made up Busby's mind. "*I was fed up and everything else, but driving along I stopped at the crossing near the blind school. There I witnessed seven little children with sticks being led across the road. I just sat in the car and thought, 'Matt what problems have you got? You've got no problems compared to these poor kids.' At that moment I thought one more go. Just one more go!*"

LA SEXTA

The chosen few were handed a baton that glistened with gold dust - a group of players talented and dedicated to the Bernabéu cause. They were called the 'Ye ye generation', named after the Beatles number one hit "She Loves You". Respecters of the past, but eager to cement their own brand of Madrileño magic into the annals of football history their number included the likes of Amancio, Grosso, Velásquez, Sanchis and Pirri. They were new names destined to walk in the shadow of giants. Of the all-conquering side of seasons past, only thirty-three year old Francis Gento remained consistently on the team sheet. Puskás and Santamaria had been reduced to walk on parts in testimonials and lucrative friendly matches. As for the Blond Arrow, he had flown to pastures new. Following a tragic exit tinged with sadness. Their time, though glorious, had gone, now a new era dawned...

On the same evening Manchester United were being frustrated against Partizan Belgrade, a thousand miles away in Italy, Real Madrid were ridding themselves of demons that had haunted them for years. Internazionale, still under the spell of Il Mago, Helenio Herrera, were looking for a hat trick of European Cup victories; a period of domination that had all but strangulated a tournament once noted for the beauty and majesty of the white storm.

The first leg was typically tense, a lone Pirri goal from a typical slice of Gento magic won the day in a fierce contest at the *Bernabéu*. Herrera found it hard to disguise his hatred of Real in his post-match comments, declaring that come the second leg, *"Madrid will burn in the San Siro."* Stirred by Herrera's bloodcurdling call to arms, a record crowd gathered in Milan to see their team wipe away a miserly 1-0 deficit.

Yet it was Inter who dissolved into flames on an historic night as the new Madrid produced a stunning display, full of class and guts to grab a 1-1 draw and shove Herrera's spiteful words back down his throat. With the Real sweeper Pirri producing a masterful display of man-marking on Inter's main danger Luis Suarez and the lightning Amancio latching onto yet another priceless Gento pass to sweep Real in front on the night, the Spaniards advanced through to an astonishing eighth European Cup final appearance. The magician's hoodoo had been laid to rest, it was time to claim *la sexta*. Waiting to stop them in Brussels at Heysel was the pride of Belgrade, a team who Manchester United discovered were notoriously tough to beat, and one guaranteed to rock the *Madrileño's* world if underestimated.

Running like the wind

Of the glorious white shirted trio who had illuminated the European game for over a decade, only one remained. And yet despite advancing years, *El Motorcycle* Francisco Gento, still ran like the wind. As a child Gento dreamed only of playing for his home town club Racing Santander, never knowing he was destined for a higher plane. Such rampaging speed on the run and ability to produce precision crossing at breakneck pace was god sent to provide the likes of Hector Rial, Ferenc Puskás and Alfredo Di Stefano with an abundance of bullets. Widely regarded during that era as the finest left-winger in the world, Francisco Gento enchanted and enthralled. Now captain of a group of players who understood the values associated with being a *Madrileño,* and although not darned of quite the same imperial silk as heroes past, they bridled with a fervent passion and an abundance of talent. The *Ye ye,* with the blistering Gento at the helm, prepared to make their own history.

On *11th May 1966*, in the *Heysel* stadium Brussels, in

front of 55,000, Real Madrid and Partizan Belgrade clashed in the European Cup final. For the Spaniards it was their eighth appearance at the continent's top table, for Partizan the greatest night in their history, a monumental first. And it was the Yugoslavs in an impressive opening who looked by far the better team. Constantly pushing forward, opportunities arose for both centre-forward Hasanagic whose deflected effort flew narrowly wide and winger Josip Pirmajer who cut a swathe down the right before his low cross went agonisingly across the goal face.

Real struggled; high expectations, epic tradition and pre-match favouritism overwhelming them. More worrying for the Madrid supporters they were dangerously hesitant at the back. Only once did the Madrileños threaten to spark, their only genuine goal scoring effort missed by forward Ramon Grosso who sliced through the Partizan rearguard, only to shoot horribly wide with just Soskic to beat.

Then on fifty-five minutes, the shock. Partizan's sweeper Velibor Vasovic powered home a Pirmajer corner to stun Madrid and send their own fans into dreamland. Immediately on scoring Vasovic gathered his team-mates around him and implored them to hold onto their priceless lead. Yet there was no instant reaction from Real, their attacks instead came in spurts laced with panic stricken errors. Stung at going behind they were almost seen off when Partizan striker Milan Galic broke out, only to fluff a golden opportunity to seal the cup with just Araquistain to beat. Sadly for the normally reliable Galic, it was to prove a costly miss as the Madrileños finally awoke from their slumbers to come roaring back.

Real motored, their football becoming swift and typically incisive. It was if the spirit of Di Stefano had suddenly sprung upon them, demanding more, mauling egos and screaming white murder. Now Partizan dropped off, just twenty minutes away from a triumph that would echo forever in Belgrade folklore. Marshalled by the brilliant Vasovic, the Yugoslavs defended for their lives, but were outfoxed by a sensational through ball from Grosso that landed perfectly in Amancio's path. For the player nicknamed *El Brujo (the witch)* it was time to truly earn his *Madrileño* spurs. Amancio had first made his début back on a Madrid tour of Africa in 1962. Playing in Ghana he noticed whilst pulling on the famed white shirt that it had no club shield on the breast. Amancio made the fearful mistake of mentioning this to a dismissive Alfredo Di Stefano who curtly informed him *"You've got to sweat for it first, sonny."* The fleet-footed Amancio swept clear to slide his shot past a floored Soskic to equalise and make Madrid hearts beat a little easier. Now Amancio had sweated!

The Spaniards sensed blood and went for a dramatic late winner. As Partizan backed off, unsure whether to stick or twist, the *Madrileños* claimed *La Sexta* with a goal befitting such a grand achievement. Twenty-four year old right-winger Fernando Serena, born within a stone's throw of the *Bernabéu*, had promised the Madrid press beforehand he would score the winning goal. On seventy-six minutes and with Real now in full flow, Serena remained true to his word by lashing in a vicious left footed volley from fully thirty yards past a diving Soskic to seal the match. The Yugoslavs visibly slumped as the ball hit the net. It was all over and Real Madrid's *Ye ye* generation had stamped their own particular brand of *Madrileño* magic on a tournament they regarded as their own.

Intriguingly, for a club whose rich tapestry of success had been built on the cream of foreign imports, they had won with a team of eleven Spaniards. It was a point not lost on President Santiago Bernabéu, who had taken a conscious decision to overhaul club policy and attempt to conquer Europe with home grown talent. Once more Don Santiago had triumphed and his presence in the dressing room was a scene of undiluted joy for a club that had again placed itself at the forefront of European football.

For one man, Francisco Gento, a lasting link to the past and a still potent force to go forward into the future, huge satisfaction was claimed from the victory over Partizan Belgrade. "For *me winning the final was a proud moment. This team is young and has different qualities from those of the past. But we struggled well and it was a great achievement to win once more the European Cup."*

On returning to Madrid, the team received a magnificent reception from thousands of supporters who stood impatiently to greet their heroes. It had been too long and the city was not used to such a famine. First down the steps into view, smiling widely and grasping on tightly to the hard won trophy, was Francisco Gento. The roar from the gathered masses on seeing this living legend back on home soil was the cue for the fiesta to truly begin. It was party time in Madrid – champions once more!

However many seasons would pass before the *Madrileños* again revelled in such joy.

WELCOME TO SARAJEVO

Sarajevo was known as the Jerusalem of Europe, where for centuries different faiths lived and prospered together in peace. Yet here amid religious tolerance occurred an incident that sparked a fire to ignite a murderous conflict - one that cost the lives of countless millions. On Sunday 28th June 1914, twenty-three year old Gavrillo Princip, the son of a postman and member of the Black Hand, assassinated Austrian Archduke Franz Ferdinand. It was an act that ultimately let to a slaughter of humanity on an unprecedented scale - World War One. Later of course the city was to become infamous as the cockpit of another conflict.

To such a city of contradictions travelled Manchester United Football Club, as once more back in the exalted echelons of the European Cup, their quest for the Holy Grail continued. A place of haunting beauty, of ghost and devils both past and future... Welcome to Sarajevo...

On Saturday 6th May 1967, at West Ham's Upton Park, Manchester United secured another pathway back into the European Champions' Cup. With only the match against the Hammers and a final home game versus Stoke City to play, United required two points to secure the title. On a sun-drenched afternoon in London's East End, Busby's team wrapped up the league with a scintillating 6-1 rout.

The visitors were three up within the first ten minutes. A typical rasping drive from Bobby Charlton, a rare Paddy Crerand header and an even rarer goal from Bill Foulkes stunned the home supporters and sent the travelling Mancunian hordes into ecstasy. An hour before kick off the gates had been locked as a capacity Boleyn Ground crowd of *38,424*, their largest since the war, were treated to a footballing master class. Playing in an all white strip United were sensational and on twenty-five minutes went four up; Nobby Stiles playing in George Best who left West Ham full-back John Charles dizzy before firing past goalkeeper Colin Mackleworth.

At half-time, in an ecstatic United dressing room, Busby was shocked to learn the actual score after taking his seat late and missing Charlton's opening goal. Two minutes after the break West Ham defender Charles smashed a shot past Alex Stepney from fully thirty yards, though this served only to irk the champions in waiting who went on to score twice more; Denis Law inevitably grabbing a brace, first from the penalty spot before, six minutes from time, he hit a devilish shot into the top corner to cap a magnificent afternoon in the London sunshine for Manchester United. Amid the celebrations an ecstatic Matt Busby was already planning ahead, *"We would obviously like to win the championship again. But we all feel that we must have a real go to win the European Cup."* Busby knew time was no longer on his side. It was a question of now or never.

Sarajevo: Wednesday 15th November 1967: In the freezing snow at the Kosevo stadium, with 45,000 fanatical home supporters screaming for their blood, Manchester United finally realised they had returned to the fire and furore and sheer unrelenting drama of the European Cup. A facile first round victory over the friendly locals of Hibernians of Malta had seen United feted from start to finish against amateurs managed by a local priest. Now, in the ancient, historic city of Sarajevo, high in the Balkan mountains, United faced a true test against a team that was technically superb and tough as nails.

Sarajevo was such an arduous place to reach by scheduled flight, as the United manager had discovered to his cost having undertaken a lone spying mission, with the result that for the first time since Munich the club flew by special chartered flight. Expensive at just over £3000 for the return journey, the *BAC*

111 bus stop jet would ease greatly a terribly difficult journey. Yet still 200 miles had to be travelled overland; a seven hour trek starting in Dubrovnik on the Adriatic coast, then onwards through the breathtaking, towering, Balkan peaks along winding roads carved into the mountainsides, some appearing more suited to goats than modern transport.

Sarajevo were a strong, skilful, no-nonsense combination; the pride of their city and region who, after decades of Serb and Croat dominance in the Yugoslav league, had wrestled the title away. Fighting a rearguard action from the off, United came under incessant pressure. A fierce Sarajevo side came out determined to take no prisoners. Only great composure from the visitors prevented what could easily have become a full-scale battle. Busby preached to his players beforehand the importance of not losing their heads, but as the tackles flew in dangerously, even the most patient of characters would have had his temperament severely tested.

Their captain, Mirsad Fazlagic, appeared single-handedly determined to put United players on stretchers. A savage series of assaults continued on Brian Kidd, Francis Burns and the biggest prize of all George Best. All Europe now knew that *Georgie Boy* held the key to United's success or failure. Not that it bothered him in the slightest but Best had become a marked man.

Fazlagic was finally cautioned by exasperated Italian referee Franchesini who would have needed eyes in the back of his head as United players went down at regular intervals. Yet somehow United's hotheads kept their composure. Paddy Crerand, whose dismissal against Yugoslav opposition had characterised United's last European exit, bit his lip and adhered to his manager's orders to keep calm despite fierce provocation. Crerand would later comment on that bruising encounter in the Balkans, "*Our trainer Jack Crompton was on the field so often treating our injured players, I bet the crowd thought he was playing!*"

Once they settled down to concentrate on playing, Sarajevo excelled. Their football was swift and skilful and at times cut apart United's defence. They looked to have taken the lead on the half hour when Yugoslav international striker Vahidin Musemic's shot appeared to have crossed the line before Stepney scooped it out but the referee declared no goal. Yet overall this slice of luck for United was deserved and a goalless draw well earned.

The final whistle saw the unusual scene of an angry Busby confronting the home team and letting them know exactly what he thought of their behaviour. *"Their tackles were disgraceful,"* Busby claimed later, *"I was pleased with the result and even more with the way the team reacted under extreme provocation"'* It was a relieved and somewhat content Manchester United squad that flew home, convinced that in fourteen days' time they would see off the Yugoslav champions on Mancunian soil. Little did they know events in Sarajevo had been a mere spat compared to what was set to unfurl at Old Trafford.

Manchester: Wednesday 29th November 1967: With feuds simmering and scores to settle, plus the small matter of a place in the quarter-finals at stake, the battle of Old Trafford began. A roaring crowd of 62,801 were ready to play their part with the gates having to be shut an hour before kick off. With memories of the Sarajevo tactics from the first leg still fresh, Matt Busby again urged calm. His message pre-match to both team and fans alike read *"Keep cool and stay steady, both on and off the field."*

United dictated the opening stages with Paddy Crerand's astute passing finding holes in a Sarajevo defence when there appeared none visible. Also impressive was eighteen-year old, Collyhurst born Brian Kidd. A promising forward from United's youth side, Kidd had been given his chance by Busby and Murphy and took it with a vengeance; his early twenty-five yard strike hitting the post and causing howls of frustration from the Stretford End. Moments later the electric youngster from North Manchester was foiled again, this time by a brave stop from goalkeeper Muftic.

Soon it was George Best's turn to test Yugoslav resolve. Picking up possession midway inside Sarajevo's half, Best slalomed past three Yugoslavs with alarming ease. Alongside him Bobby Charlton implored his young team-mate for a pass, but lost in the moment and deafened by the sound of invisible trumpets, George instead chose to shoot for glory and the ball rolled harmlessly wide, much to Charlton's chagrin who screamed at the Irishman in frustration.

Nevertheless United swarmed forward and the Yugoslav defence, marshalled superbly in the first leg by their impressive centre-half Svetozar Vujovic, began to weaken. As the noise level rose, on fourteen minutes a breakthrough occurred. Once more it was Paddy Crerand, who linked with Charlton, before releasing a flying Kidd to cross dangerously for a lurking Francis Burns. A thumping Burns' header was parried superbly by Muftic, only to fall towards United's number eleven John Aston to lash home from point blank range. Another Manchester boy, Aston had regularly suffered in comparison to the holy trio of Best, Law and Charlton and was frequently the subject of the United Road boo-boys. Now, as he took the plaudits, he was a hero for the night.

Half-time came with United in front but Sarajevo were very much alive in the tie and a Yugoslav goal would knock them out on the away goal rule. The second half began with the visitors pushing forward, only to be caught on the counter by the inestimable talent of George Best. Reacting first to a long throw out from Alex Stepney, the lightning winger picked up the ball and swept across the halfway line. Old Trafford roared as their favourite son blew away two Sarajevo defenders before letting fly a shot at goal. A wicked deflection off the unfortunate Vujovic left Muftic in no man's land and the goalkeeper watched first in horror, then relief as his post saved him and Sarajevo. They were still alive.

Seeking a killer second, United came again. Once more it was Paddy Crerand who began the move feeding Bobby

Charlton, who found Kidd with a glorious pass off the outside of his left foot. Taking on and beating a flustered Blazevic, Kidd crossed dangerously – George Best out-jumped two Yugoslav defenders but saw his brave header saved at full stretch by Muftic. As the ball was cleared Muftic went to help the fallen Best off the turf, only for the Irishman to react violently and appear to punch the goalkeeper in the face. Suddenly the battle of Old Trafford exploded! Muftic cut a sorry sight holding his nose, whilst team-mates surrounded the squat, balding French referee Monsieur Machin, demanding he send off United's young Irish talisman.

In reality Muftic's apparently friendly gesture had disguised the fact that he had dug his fingers into Best's armpits whilst picking him up, thus sparking the retaliation. Two minutes later George Best was almost cut in two when Sarajevo centre-forward Fahrudin Prijaca sliced him down on the edge of the box. The visitors' remonstrations that the referee had failed to act on Best's alleged assault cut little ice with the French official who sent off Prijaca to ignite the tinder box atmosphere further.

Pushed, shoulder charged, knocked and abused by the outraged Yugoslavs, Machin somehow stayed calm. He refused to be intimidated, remaining firm. Pointing to the touchline he finally asked for assistance from the Manchester constabulary to help calm the situation. Finally, onto the field came Sarajevo's coaching staff who pushed and pulled their hot-headed footballers away from the referee. The Sarajevo players had crossed the line and it did not sit well with a club that had intended to leave good impressions on their first sortie in the European cup. Sarajevo did not wish to be remembered as a team that had shamed itself at one of Europe's showpiece venues and Yugoslav officials were disgusted knowing that a place in the quarter-finals could still be won provided their players calm down. Prijaca finally left the field and the match resumed.

Within moments it was all but settled when, from the resulting free kick, the ball was hoisted high into the area; Foulkes hit the bar and the rebound was kept in by Francis Burns near the goal line for a recovered George Best to almost break the back of the net with a vicious volley. It was a wonderful way to repay Prijaca's scandalous assault, but again the Sarajevo players felt aggrieved as they claimed the linesman had flagged that the ball had gone out before Burns pulled it back. Not surprisingly this was waved away by Machin, who surely would not have been in any mood to do the Yugoslavs any favours. He instead pointed to the centre-circle and United were 2-0 up.

A crazed mob of white shirts sprinted across to the touchline and confronted the besieged linesman, who appeared in serious danger of getting beaten up. Mauled, sworn at and pushed backwards, it was only the timely intervention of police and Sarajevo's coaches who literally threw their men back onto the field that prevented the game being abandoned. Finally play resumed and a dazzling run by Best was met spectacularly by a John Aston overhead kick that flew straight at Muftic. A dramatic night at Old Trafford went on and three minutes from time, with Sarajevo now concentrating fully on playing football, they pulled a goal back; a deep cross was met by Delalic whose looping header this time deceived an out-rushing Stepney. At 2-1 the Yugoslavs still had time to score one more and level. In years gone by Matt Busby's Manchester United might well have charged for a third, but experience and a hardening of attitudes meant this match would not be thrown away.

Instead they kept possession and wound down the clock to waste precious seconds. It might not have been the United way but Busby had come too far and suffered too much to risk anything. Monsieur Machin's final whistle, when maybe a bell might have been more appropriate, was greeted with huge joy and even greater relief from a home crowd whose nerves lay shattered. A long, painful and eventful evening in Manchester had ended.

And yet the battle had not yet finished for in the players tunnel Muftic raced to get even with George Best, only to run into Paddy Crerand's right hook. This time Muftic hit the floor with good reason as Crerand later recalled, *"I gave him such a clout I nearly broke my hand!"* At witnessing the fray and knowing justice had been served, Busby simply pulled the fiery Scot away from the stricken Yugoslav and into the sanctity of the home dressing room. The quarter-finals had been reached and Manchester United could continue to dream.

SNOW FALLS IN KATOWICE

The closer they got, the more nerves threatened to derail Manchester United's attempt to win the most exalted of prizes. A hard earned victory over FK Sarajevo handed Matt Busby's side yet another ominous trip beyond the Iron curtain, this time they journeyed to Poland and the proud, exciting, and extremely tough Gornik Zabrze. Flowery talk of "written in the stars" and a "rainbow's end" were once more penned by scribes who appeared convinced United's name was already carved upon the trophy. The final was set to be fought out at Wembley a decade after Munich - a script writer could not have come up with a more appropriate ending. Yet this road to redemption remained littered with pitfalls. Human frailties and ill luck could still conspire to further the heartache. The brilliant, hard-bitten Poles of Gornik did not believe in fairytales; as snow fell in Katowice, Manchester United would find themselves once more dancing on the precipice of footballing disaster...

Manchester: Wednesday 2nd February 1968: Not since the great sides of Real Madrid and Benfica had a team come to Old Trafford and so thrilled a Mancunian audience. Thousands of Poles who resided in the city turned up in force to welcome their fellow countrymen and they draped a huge Polish flag over the United Road Paddock. Gornik had created shockwaves across the continent by eliminating crack Soviet side Dynamo Kiev, who themselves had caused one of the tournament's great upsets by knocking out European champions Celtic.

Before the match began, Spanish referee Ortiz de Mendibil

called the captains together and through an interpreter told them how he worked and what was expected in terms of behaviour towards him and the linesmen. This referee was fully aware of what occurred the last time an Eastern European team came to Old Trafford in FK Sarajevo and was determined the same scenario would not occur under his control. Senor Mendibil's worries were to be unfounded for the Poles were to prove a credit to themselves and their country.

Yet another huge capacity crowd of 63,458 watched with rising nerves as a determined and explosive Gornik side played on the counter attack, whilst defending resolutely and with great skill. Their star player, twenty-year old prodigy Wlodek Lubanski, had been a Polish international at just sixteen years of age. Time and again his wonderful sleight of foot, power and fearsome pace threatened the home team. But it was goalkeeper Hubert Kostka who took on the Manchester United forwards single-handedly and was for Gornik the undisputed star performer on the night. A succession of saves defied the eye; one close-range stop from Paddy Crerand appeared impossible, only for Kostka to then better it by somehow tipping a John Aston thunderbolt from six yards over his crossbar. At this even the United players applauded. Whatever the angle or distance Kostka remained defiant. A punch off Bobby Charlton's head, a courageous dive at the hypnotic, dancing feet of George Best – they all came the same to the custodian who kept United's stars at bay.

In front of him his defence was organised magnificently by giant defender Zyfgfryd Szoltysik, coping admirably with the intelligent prompting of Crerand and the ferocious long shooting of Charlton. Another in particular deserved special praise among the Polish defenders; twenty-four year old Henryk Latocha. Handed the unenviable task of shackling George Best, Latocha played hard but fair against his opponent, matching him for speed and awareness throughout.

The battle raged, every time United lost possession the Poles would swarm on the attack. Old Trafford watched in horror, an away goal their ultimate nightmare. Shortly before half-time Lubanski, set up superbly by the skilful Olék, raced away with just Alex Stepney to beat. As disaster loomed for the home team the youngster inexplicably miscontrolled, allowing Stepney vital seconds to clear. It was a chance that would return to haunt the Poles.

The second half saw United increase the pressure and it came as no surprise when on the hour courageous Gornik finally cracked. Paddy Crerand threaded an astute pass to Best who wriggled free of Latocha. Best's snapshot took a wicked deflection off the unlucky centre-half Florenski that took the ball past a raging goalkeeper into the net. A furious Kostka looked close to tears, such was his frustration. Old Trafford celebrated a vital breakthrough, lucky maybe but deserved. United continued to press for another that would be so essential for the second leg, but as if taking being beaten as a personal insult, Kostka produced yet more saves that caused gasps around the ground. There also existed the frightful scenario that the Poles would strike out on the break. A worry that almost became reality when Lubanski left three United players in his blistering wake before firing in a shot that Stepney did well to save. Nerves were fraying.

The minutes ticked down and with time almost up, Brian Kidd, a bus driver's son from North Manchester, cut inside the Gornik penalty area and hit a low drive that by some miracle evaded a host of legs and more importantly Kostka's despairing reach to limp embarrassingly into the far corner. Busby's team had pulled off a mighty win against a formidable outfit that were by far the best they had faced in years.

It was a fact much appreciated by both home players and fans for, as the supporters handed the Poles a standing ovation at the end, the United team formed a guard of honour to clap them off. Matt Busby himself was full of praise for the hugely impressive visitors, "*It was a fine sporting match - and this is something that has not always happened in the European Cup.*" There remained much work to be done for Gornik Zabrze, on home soil, unleashed and committed to attack, promised to be a deadly threat. One that Busby was fully aware of and intended to nullify, *"Away from home we have to try and contain the opposition. This is now what the European Cup is all about."* These were words that once the United manager would never have dreamed of uttering, now a stark reality if the holy grail was to be achieved.

With his star striker Denis Law suffering intolerably from a wretched niggling knee injury and looking increasingly unlikely to feature much that season, Matt Busby made a sensational record-breaking secret bid for West Ham centre-forward Geoff Hurst. Busby knew that without a recognised world class striker his chances of winning the European Cup were reduced. United needed more goals. Hurst's courage and finishing power, so evident with his legendary hat trick in the World Cup final, had made him amongst the most sought after footballers, and the United manager sent a telegram with the following words penned: *"£200,000 for Geoff Hurst? Yes or no?"* On reading it West Ham manager Ron Greenwood went apoplectic and considered Busby's impersonal approach insulting. An annoyed Greenwood's reply was even shorter and to the point; a terse *"No"*. For Busby, a gambler at heart, it had been a punt and nothing more.

Manchester United travelled to Poland ready to defend a lead that was decent but by no means impregnable. Again, as in Sarajevo, the Mancunians chartered a special flight. However they could never have dreamt of the conditions awaiting them beyond the Iron Curtain. Over 200,000 applications for tickets had been made for the second leg in the massive bowl of Katowice's *Stadion Slaski*. Temperatures well below zero and blinding snowstorms greeted United's arrival on Polish soil. Twenty-four hours before kick off Matt Busby and Jimmy Murphy went to inspect the pitch and came away horrified: Busby could not believe his eyes, *"There are three inches of snow on top and patches of ice underneath. It is dangerous and if the snow is removed players could easily break their legs."*

Determined that United would not become involved in a farce, he was ready to contemplate a postponement. *"I shall make representations to the referee, Mr Lo Bello, as soon as he arrives. This match is far too important for Manchester United. We have come all this way to play football and after the first great game at Old Trafford, I do not want a shambles of a pitch to spoil it."*

Even the Poles, who were accustomed to such conditions, admitted that it was hardly ideal. Promises by Gornik officials that they would lay plenty of salt on the playing surface hardly filled the United management duo with confidence and it appeared that United hopes would literally be left skating on thin ice. Come the morning of the game Italian referee Concerto Lo Bello arrived on the overnight sleeper train from Vienna; pompous, full of self-importance and not wanting to hang around in the frozen coalfields of Silesia. He was a man in a hurry who had no intention of calling off the quarter-final. His decision was met with shock from the United party but there was one who felt the Italian was correct. Bobby Charlton, now thirty years old and a European Cup veteran, felt it best to get matters over with, *"I feel two goals will be enough. Few teams can give us that lead and beat us. But I still shudder to think what would happen if we lose it now. These conditions are difficult but we can cope. It is the fierce cold that bothers me most. You almost have to run with your eyes shut."*

Katowice: Wednesday 16th February 1968: The game began and in the first minute Gornik winger Musialek went flying through, only to screw his shot wide of goal with Alex Stepney helpless. The massive 105,000 crowd groaned in disappointment, then roared once more in support for their heroes. Many were coal miners, Katowice born and bred. Hard men whom loved their football and drink with equal lust. Most had been in the stadium for hours before kick-off, warmed by copious amounts of vodka and the blowing of horns that could be heard for miles

As huge snowflakes continued to fall, pitch markings disappeared and visibility levels dropped to just a few yards, yet Lo Bello still refused to consider an abandonment. The crazy weather created yet another early chance for Gornik when Stepney's attempted throw out stuck in the snow and was intercepted by Lubanski. The young Pole took aim and fired a low drive inches wide. It was a second let-off for the visitors in what promised to a bitter struggle.

Despite the odd weather induced error, United defended with a sure footedness that belied their surroundings. It was a masterclass in terms of discipline and concentration, showing that at last they had grown up in the European arena. There were heroes aplenty, none more than Nobby Stiles and John Fitzpatrick. Unassuming, underrated and overshadowed by the galaxy of stars further forward, that day in Poland they were worth their weight in gold.

Like the tightening of a corkscrew, increased pressure came onto the visitor's defence. Their only release was to a wiry, dark-haired waif like figure from the *Cregagh* estate in Belfast. Hordes of white Polish shirts swarmed around George Best as his miraculous ability to keep possession handed team-mates valuable time to catch their breath. Best was remarkable as he purposefully went looking for trouble, teasing and taunting home defenders who were driven to distraction in their attempts to relieve him of the ball. This Irish kid, priceless to Busby, displayed all his grace and beauty on a surface that was rock hard and covered in frozen jagged potholes. Best staggered and bewitched a crowd that at times, despite their frustration with him, could not believe the skill and courage he displayed.

To an outsider it must have appeared a dour game; two sides struggling to cope in such dire Arctic conditions but giving every last ounce of energy. It wasn't until twenty minutes from time that Lubanski broke through for the home side – smashing home from close range via the crossbar to scrape one back for Gornik. It was the first away goal conceded by United in the competition and a furious last assault on Stepney's goal was launched, yet the Mancunians held firm. By full time they just about deserved to go through.

The match ended with similar scenes to the first leg – this time round it was the desolate Gornik players forming a guard of honour to applaud their opponents off the pitch. An ecstatic Matt Busby almost burst with pride at his team's performance, *"This is a prize we have been fighting for for years. And it would have been terrible if a two goal lead had been lost under conditions such as these, but I feel things are running for us this time, and I think it could be our year."*

For the fourth time Busby led a team to within touching distance of the European Cup final, and all at Old Trafford eagerly awaited the semi-final draw – would they face Juventus, Benfica or Real Madrid? As breaths were held across the continent out popped the Spaniards – they would meet again. Screenplay writers around Europe blushed.

STRICTLY BUSINESS

It was a beautiful, gentle spring evening in Manchester when thirty-four year old Francisco Gento stepped out at the head of his team into the Old Trafford sun. The dazzling all white strip still made the heart race faster for Manchester's football romantics, despite the dose of 1960s pragmatism that saw Real arrive with a five-man defensive plan intended to ensnare and strangulate United's attacking flair. It was the modern way. They, like United, knew it was essential to avoid defeat. A draw in Manchester would all but finish off Busby's men and leave them indefensible in the torrid cauldron of Estadio Bernabéu. Then you would see the Real Madrid.

The romantics with fond memories of Di Stefano, Puskás, Gento, Edwards, and Taylor would have to wait until the second leg, for now the Madrileños came bearing gifts; flowers and goodwill off the pitch but on it, it was strictly business. For this was the European Cup. The absent heroes would have understood...

Real Madrid were in rude health. Miguel Muñoz's team arrived in Manchester as newly crowned Spanish champions after a 2-1 home victory the previous weekend over Las Palmas. Goals from Velásquez and Pirri ensured an astonishing seventh consecutive league title as the *Madrileño's* dominance on home soil continued unabated.

To counteract United's forwards Muñoz had opted for a well-drilled, swift and ruthless defensive rearguard; Gonzalez, Zunzunegui, Sanchis, Zoco and Luis. A white cloak, orchestrated, pushed, pulled and ordered into position by the magnificent sweeper Pirri. The full-back Manuel Sanchis was handed the unenviable task of man-marking George Best. The cunning Muñoz had chosen well for this was an electric-heeled player, blessed with great concentration and tactical awareness. He was perfectly suited to his task.

Though denied the skill, pace and deadly prowess of Amaro Amancio through suspension, Muñoz remained supremely confident that with Velásquez, Grosso and the ageless Gento to counter-attack, they could return to Madrid with a favourable result. For after all was this not their tournament? The white knights of the *Bernabéu* were set once more to win back a trophy for a seventh time. But first Manchester United, a dear old friend, had to be dealt with.

Only the jarring pain of a cortisone injection and sheer courage allowed Matt Busby to name Denis Law in his line-up, but in all reality a serious knee injury had curtailed Law's genius to the point where he was a mere shadow of his true self. Busby knew a win was essential, he needed at least one goal to take to the *Bernabéu*. Anything less and United would require a miracle in Madrid to get through and Busby no longer believed in them.

A watching world-wide audience of 150 million and a capacity 63,500 Old Trafford crowd held their breath as the two teams came out to do battle. At first glimpse the all white strip still possessed the charisma to send a cold chill down the spine. However any feelings of nostalgia and goodwill towards the *Madrileños* would be temporarily shelved for ninety minutes, as the home crowd concentrated on helping their team topple the Spaniards from their imperial perch.

The songs from the Stretford End both amused and deafened. Chants of *"Hands off Gibraltar"* and *"Franco out, Busby in"* resonated loud. A few hundred Madrid followers lay scattered loud and proud in the cantilever stand, happy to make themselves seen and heard with an impressive array of banners and the traditional mass of white handkerchiefs.

United opened brightly when, from a superb George Best

cross, John Aston powered in a header which was brilliantly turned away by the goalkeeper Betancourt. From the ensuing corner Denis Law set up Paddy Crerand to smash in an effort which crashed against the Madrid post – it was a storming start from the home team but one which soon ran out of steam. Madrid took control, their ball artistry delightful and dangerous. None more than captain Francisco Gento, no longer flying but still capable of wreaking chaos as he showed with a deft defence-splitting pass that sent his *compadre* Miguel Angel Perez clear on goal. With just Alex Stepney to beat the recently signed Argentine took aim and beat the goalkeeper, only for the infamous Russian referee Tofik Bakhramov, forever to be remembered as the linesman who controversially allowed England's third goal by Geoff Hurst in the 1966 World Cup final, to blow for offside. It was an act the Spanish took great exception to but it was also a disturbing reminder for Busby's team. A timely example of what awaited if they dared to switch off. Despite United's two early opportunities, Real retained a strict defensive discipline. There was no air of panic amongst the white shirts despite the wall of noise that emanated from all four corners of the stadium. None were more supreme than Pirri, looking calm and assured. Sublime technique, he was the epitome of a true *Madrileño,* football's equivalent of a Hollywood superstar.

With Denis Law's injury reducing him to a forlorn straggler, the Old Trafford faithful looked elsewhere for inspiration to break the deadlock. On thirty-six minutes they got their wish when a sweeping United move ended with Aston jinking past Gonzalez on the left before squaring for George Best to fire a snapshot past Betancourt into the top corner. It was a stunning finish by Best, hit first time with his left foot showing wonderful technique and with an ease only great players possess. As the terraces erupted a black cat raced the length of the Old Trafford pitch – an omen perhaps? Comrade Bakhramov's whistle blew for half-time and Manchester United had edged in front.

But a first half resembling a chess match had shown beyond

doubt there was hardly a needle's thread between the two sides. The second half saw little change with United having the bulk of possession but few opportunities. Muñoz's team were proving exceptional at snuffing out any dangers posed. George Best met his match that evening in the form of the limpet-like Manuel Sanchis, who tracked and second guessed the Irish genius's every move. It was a remarkable performance by the twenty-five year old Valencia born defender and one always remembered by Best who would recall "*Sanchis was amongst the hardest opponents I ever faced.*"

With United's front four shackled and firmly under lock and key, Real Madrid looked to press forward. An equaliser looked certain when once more Perez went careering through, only for the deputising centre-half, the versatile David Sadler in for the injured Bill Foulkes, to catch him at the last. Sadler was yet another unsung hero but one destined to play a huge part as this epic clash ran its full course over two legs.

The game finished 1-0 with neither side particularly pleased or disappointed. The final whistle was greeted with muted applause from a knowledgeable Old Trafford crowd who knew United now faced an awesome task in Madrid to make the final. Matt Busby hid any doubts regarding what was to come in the second leg and remained bullish in post-match interviews. "*I think we will win through because I am convinced we are the better side.*" However many supporters feared the worst for Real had already shown in brief attacking spurts that they possessed enough flair to deeply trouble the Red Devils' defence.

In Madrid the war drums had already begun to beat loudly as they waited impatiently to end United's torment. For although they wished them well, the *Ye* ye like their forefathers before them, stood ready once more to turn out the light on Manchester United.

There would be warm embraces for their friends from Manchester. They would speak well of times past. Shed tears at those "*Champions of Honour*" who had been taken so cruelly. But once the last toast had been drunk and the *Bernabéu* crowds had gathered baying for blood, the *Madrileños* would have no choice but to obey – it was nothing personal, this was strictly business.

A TALE OF TWO CITIES

For the Madrileños an age of unsurpassed glory, for Manchester United an age of unrelenting pain. In Madrid summers of light, in Manchester winters of despair. As Real Madrid swept everything before them United's Babes lost everything. Now they would clash again. The footballing gods, determined to milk the last bit of emotion out of a journey that had left Manchester United all but spent. A loss in Madrid would have meant more than simple elimination from the European cup. For the Mancunians would surely have thrown in the towel. They would have one last chance - there would be ghosts present in the Bernabéu. Red ghosts. This tale of two cities was almost over...

On Saturday 11th May 1968, Manchester was divided as never before. Come the final day of the domestic season both the city's clubs were level at the top of the table but with City slightly ahead on goal difference. With United at home to Sunderland and the Blues facing a tough away trip to Newcastle, it was generally regarded that come full time the Reds would be smiling having won another league championship. However a shocking 2-1 loss at Old Trafford blew a hole in such wishful thinking and cast dark shadows over Manchester's red half, whilst causing untold joy on the blue side. United's defeat and City's dramatic 4-3 victory two hundred miles north meant the First Division title was on its way to Maine Road for the first time since 1937. Already two goals down to the visitors, a lone George Best strike from twenty-yards on the stroke of half-time proved insufficient.

This football mad metropolis would find itself for once

resonating to chants of *"Champions"* from those of a blue persuasion. A capacity Old Trafford crowd were stunned. The pubs and bars of Manchester promised to be a painful place for United supporters that evening. Hiding his bitter disappointment, a gracious Matt Busby went straight to the Granada Television studios after the game to offer his congratulations to City manager and close friend Joe Mercer.

Then Busby disregarded events on the home front and all thoughts turned to four days' time and a date with destiny in Madrid. No matter how painful it was, they could ill-afford to be scarred by losing out to City. Such disappointments had to be put away in a box and forgotten. For a much bigger prize lay at stake.

The Wednesday before Matt Busby had flown over to Lisbon to watch the other European Cup semi-final between Benfica and Juventus. Despite the home side winning 2-0 and almost certainly booking a place in the final, the Portuguese were, in Busby's opinion *"eminently beatable."* Though Eusebio remained a thunderous talent and showed few signs of waning, elsewhere in the *Eagles* ranks the United manager sensed they no longer soared to past heights. Now a little slower and susceptible to pace, he felt if Real Madrid could be overcome then Benfica's wings on Wembley's wide open spaces could well be clipped. He even admitted as much publicly, *"If only we can survive in Madrid then I feel that we have an excellent chance of winning the European Cup."*

On the Mancunians' arrival in the Spanish capital, Real President, seventy-two year old Santiago Bernabéu, welcomed them with a courtesy and charm typical of the man and the football club he proudly represented. *"I want Manchester United greeted and treated as the greatest football club in the world. And as our friends for many years nothing must go wrong. If we are beaten by United in the European Cup on Wednesday then we shall have lost to a great team. We have met them on many occasions and it is about time their luck changed."* They were kind and generous words by Don Santiago, but come the time when battle was most intense, when stakes were raised and tackles flew high and fierce, it was highly unlikely Bernabéu would be so magnanimous.

In a concerted effort to remain isolated from the prevailing madness consuming Madrid, the visitors stayed in a mountain retreat thirteen miles outside the city. On the morning of the match the Catholics in the United team went to a local church. There Nobby Stiles placed a 400 Peseta note into the collection box. Accompanying Stiles was Paddy Crerand who immediately blurted out, *"Bloody hell Nobby that's bribery!"*

The *Estadio Bernabéu* was host to 125,000 fanatical supporters. Paying £20 for a return flight from Manchester, United also had unparalleled backing for a European away match, around 5000. But though loud, the vastly outnumbered Mancunians would sound like a whisper in a thunderstorm compared to the noise set to erupt from an expectant home crowd.

Like gunshots fired across the massed terraces that towered up to the heavens, thousands of firecrackers ignited. The two teams led by captains Bobby Charlton and Francisco Gento looked pensive, the tension etched on the players' faces. Experienced Italian referee Antonio Sbardella led them to the centre-circle; there they broke and gave a quick dramatic wave to the crowds before posing for a final team photo. Real would kick off, their goal scoring superstar Amaro Amancio, back from suspension, appearing like a man rushing to make up for lost time. The Estadio burned like days of old, Madrid so expectant and demanding.

Yet any sentiment that may have resonated from their president's welcoming speech was disregarded as Real Madrid began with a determination to blow their Mancunians *compadres* into kingdom come. A Real line-up containing six of the Spanish national side pressed and probed. A Gonzales corner was headed against the bar by Amancio with Stepney well beaten and lashed clear by Tony Dunne. United employed their normal defence abroad with a five man rearguard. Bill Foulkes was back from injury to line up alongside the versatile David Sadler with Nobby Stiles close by. This left Brian Kidd and George Best to forage for scraps up front. They swiftly became isolated as the Spaniards dominated playing in a manner so different from the white shirts seen in Manchester.

Back on home soil and with the arrogance of a bullfighter biding his time, it was surely a matter of when not if. Real were superb; Zoco and Grosso were highly impressive but it was the darting Amancio who truly stood out. Quick and aggressive, he was forever looking to run in behind United defenders. He and Nobby Stiles were involved in a ferocious tussle both on and off the ball. Stiles had been handed the task of shackling *El Brujo* but the *Witch* was proving hard to lock down as his Mancunian jailer attempted to stem Amancio's deadly threat. Stiles snapped and snarled at the Spaniard's heels, always just within the laws but irritating him no end. Amancio raged and implored the referee to intervene. Theirs would be a battle vital to the game's outcome, one set to become increasingly taut, if at times not downright scandalous.

On the half hour the *Madrileños* took a deserved lead when Amancio's precise free kick found an unmarked Pirri, who soared above the United defence to head fiercely past Stepney from twelve yards. Matt Busby had warned his team in the dressing room only moments before they took the field, "*If they do get an early goal to equalise on aggregate watch yourselves, because for a spell you will think they have gone mad!*" Well not only their footballers but an entire city went crazy, for now it was advantage Madrid – their patch, their crowd and for most of the first half, their ball. Real came again, a whirlwind, the confidence now flowing, their football freewheeling and incise, every loose ball picked up by a white shirt. Two minutes before half-time a Bobby Charlton free kick was cleared and picked up by an exuberant Velásquez, who immediately fed Amancio on the right wing. However it was defender Shay Brennan who moved swiftly to intercept, only to miskick horribly allowing Francisco Gento to sweep behind him with a clear run on goal. As one of their favourite sons took aim the *Bernabéu* held its breath. The years and the yards melted away as Gento sprinted

into the penalty area and smashed a low drive past Stepney to put
Madrid ahead on aggregate. The stadium went into meltdown,
they had them. Manchester United were on the floor. As for
Brennan, the boy who became a man during the unforgettable
ninety minutes of that strange night against Sheffield Wednesday
10 years before, he was disconsolate but this was no time for self
doubt as United re-started looking to survive until half-time
without conceding further.

Yet the fates once more teased the senses, delivering yet
another twist in this tale of two cities. Straight from the restart a
long, hopeful ball hoisted into the Real box from defender Tony
Dunne found unexpected reward. To the home crowd's horror,
Ignacio Zoco, who had been arguably Real's best player until
that moment, inexplicably sliced an easy clearance spectacularly
past Betancourt into the net. The tall, blond haired defender cut
a forlorn figure. At 2-2 this semi-final was once more even and
despite being hugely outplayed, Manchester United remained
in the European Cup.

As Sbardella prepared to blow for the interval, Real swarmed
forward one last time. An astute left wing cross from the ever
impressive defender Sanchis was met with astonishing technique
by Amancio and a magnificent drive past Stepney's smoking
fingers sent the home crowd into more raptures. The *Bernabéu*
was a scene of utter chaos! An ecstatic Amancio took the salute
of an adoring support. His had been daunting shoes to fill and
yet as Madrid bowed in awe, Amancio appeared destined to fit
the bill of the legendary *Blond Arrow*. It was a cacophony of joy,
noise and relief not heard since Enrique Mateos signed off a 3-1
victory over the Mancunians eleven years before.

Cornered and on the ropes, United's hopes had waned
just when they appeared to have regained a fortunate foothold
back in the contest. One more blow and it was surely *Adiós*.
As in 1957 to use Matt Busby's dramatic phrase, "*The world
came tumbling down.*" The European albatross that hung around
Busby's neck weighed heavily once again. The nightmare
looked set to go on.

At half-time the visitors' dressing room was silent. In an attempt to lift his best friend's broken spirits, Bobby Charlton offered a kind word, only to be silenced by Shay Brennan, who angrily shot back there could be no excuses. He had erred badly and knew it. No words could ease his pain. The sorry sight of the United players with heads down and sick with disappointment as yet another European campaign (perhaps the final campaign) looked set to end in failure. So badly hurt was Nobby Stiles after a kick out from Amancio that he sat pouring whisky onto an open leg wound. The thought of not carrying on never entered Nobby's head.

Matt Busby had to literally scrape them off the floor. He spoke up, telling the players to forget the scoreline. Even at 3-1 down they remained just a goal behind. All was not lost. As he later recalled, "*I told them they were only 3-2 down on aggregate and to go out and play*" Paddy Crerand remembers listening on with incredulity, "*It could have been five or six in the first half and here was the boss telling us to go out and have a go at them! Well some of the lads were smiling by then. Here we were, having been totally outplayed and this man was telling us to go out and attack them!*"

To receive such a mauling and remain in with a chance meant anything could yet happen. Real Madrid had played well, brilliantly even but the mindset could now change. It was a dangerous ploy to torture the bull when it still possessed life to lash out; United had been wounded but not finished off. Busby's last words as his team left the dressing room: "*Come on boys, remember we are Manchester United. Let's have a go at them.*"

As the United players headed off up the tunnel it was obvious by the demeanour of many of their opponents that they already considered the game won. It was a cockiness that riled those in red. Sensing a simmering fuse, the referee pulled aside Nobby Stiles and Amaro Amancio. Smashing his fists down, Sbardella intimated to the two that there were to be no more antics. Both nodded in agreement then rejoined their team-mates with the official's warning already forgotten. So began the second half with Amancio wasting no time getting his retaliation in first. Knowing Stiles was all but playing on one leg, he went to finish him off. Only then to suffer the irate Mancunian's wrath when behind Sbardella's back, he was knocked out cold by a right hook. The punch caused howls of derision to sweep down from the terraces. Only to be met by a gentle shrug of the shoulders from the man christened with great irony *"Happy"* by long suffering team-mates. It was a marker laid down by the United man that left his Spanish opponent felled and in great pain on the turf.

From that moment Amancio's influence waned and he disappeared as a threat. To further infuriate the masses, Stiles gently tapped the referee on the shoulder and pointed out the distraught Amancio *"He's injured ref."* For his troubles the Mancunian was hit with a ripe tomato hurled from the crowd and a shoe that missed by an inch! Nobby Stiles would forever be known in these parts as the *"Assassin of Madrid."*

Real had begun to strut, their *Olé* football not appreciated by Manchester United midfielders Stiles and Crerand who ripped into challenges to upset the Spaniards' rhythm. The pace and momentum which had blown away the visitors in that blistering first half was no more. Suddenly it was United who posed the more potent threat, as a well-struck effort from Paddy Crerand flew narrowly over Betancourt's bar. Then Charlton robbed Perez in midfield before moving forward to unleash a similar effort that the Madrid goalkeeper was happy to see fly inches wide. A nervous air engulfed the *Bernabéu*. All was not yet over. Brian Kidd raced to the goal-line and crossed dangerously, only for Betancourt to save at his near post. On the bench Busby and Jimmy Murphy urged United to keep going forward, for it was clear the sheer enormity of the occasion was affecting their opponents. United pushed on, all was rushed as the clock ticked down. For the Mancunians the hands of time raced wretchedly fast, while for the Spaniards it appeared to stop. Oh for a Di Stefano, to tear a strip off those *Madrileños* who appeared more intent on blaming team-mates rather than ensuring their opponents did not dominate the ball.

The stadium was aghast, fraught with nervous exhaustion. For the first time the away supporters could be heard. With twenty minutes remaining Paddy Crerand urged Bobby Charlton further up field as he raced to take a free kick. Crerand's lofted chip into the Real penalty area found George Best, who flicked on dangerously to the far post. Arriving late came David Sadler, unmarked from six yards he forced the ball into the goal and set off in celebration around the back of Madrid's goal much to the fury of the seething locals. He cared little, for at 3-3 as the game entered its final stage all was set to win or lose. Told to abandon his defensive duties and play upfront by Busby, the twenty-two year old boy from Kent had levelled the tie.

With the thought of losing everything at such a late stage simply overwhelming, both teams became pensive in possession. All except one that is: thirteen minutes remained at the *Bernabéu* when Paddy Crerand's throw in found George Best wide on the right hand touchline. Faced by Zoco and his arch-nemesis Sanchis, the United winger turned and twisted to leave both trailing in his wake, before tearing into the Real penalty area. On reaching the goal-line Best glanced up to deliver a cut back, only then having to look again when he noticed who stood waiting for his pass. The same man who had staggered out of that inferno at the end of a Munich runway, thirty-six year old Bill Foulkes had arrived in the penalty area as if urged on by his long lost pals…

Best's glorious pass was as close to perfection as possible but the unlikely figure of Foulkes finishing low past Betancourt with a precise side-foot effort that would have done credit to Denis Law, was out of this world. A despairing Betancourt pounded the turf as Madrid's hearts lay broken. Bill Foulkes, a no nonsense former miner from St. Helens, plucked by Busby to play for United, relates the grand tale as if it was yesterday, *"The atmosphere was so strange: they were not really playing and we were holding on to what we'd got. Then I shouted to Pat and could see the shock on his face because it was me. I kept running and Pat threw the ball to George. He went past one, then two and I kept moving up.*

I was only jogging but I can tell you I was the only red shirt in the box. George feinted to drive it to the near post then flipped a perfect pass for me. I just hit it in the opposite corner."

Normally used to the sight of Foulkes ballooning the ball over the crossbar or screwing a shot haplessly wide, United players watched astonished as the granite man of their defence kept his cool and scored arguably the most important goal in the history of Manchester United Football Club. Paddy Crerand remembers thinking, *"What's that big idiot doing up there?"* Bobby Charlton's first reaction was, *"Oh no not Bill!"* Yet their worries proved unfounded as Foulkes kept his nerve and finished off the *Madrileños*. Buried in red shirts, Foulkes appeared determined to shrug off the compliments and return to his centre-half position, for there remained sufficient time for it all still to go horribly awry.

But Real had gone in mind and spirit, their confidence and belief wiped away in the emotional slipstream of United's dramatic comeback. Yet still they found enough to go to the last. Seconds remained when Velásquez went flying down the United left and fired in a low shot that was deflected and safely cleared. By now few could watch, the tension unbearable. The visitors broke with Brian Kidd setting up George Best to shoot straight at Betancourt.

Again Real swept forward only for Zoco's pass to be picked up by the referee who called proceedings to a halt on an unforgettable night of drama in Madrid. Across the field United players fell to the turf. Exhausted and filled with emotion. None more than Bobby Charlton as the memories of lost friends vividly returned amid the feelings of ecstasy evoked in the Spanish capital.

Onto the pitch streamed hundreds of jubilant United supporters to embrace their heroes. The Madrid police were too stunned and dazed to care. The United players embraced Matt Busby as they left the field. His smile was wide enough to light the *Bernabéu* as he waited for the team near to the tunnel. For Real Madrid it was a monumental loss and one it would take a generation to recover from.

Thirty-one years would pass before Real won the European cup again. A sporting Miguel Muñoz sought out the victorious United manager to shake his hand and wish Busby all the best for the forthcoming final against Benfica. Meanwhile, high in the Presidential box Don Santiago Bernabéu applauded the Mancunians' moment of triumph. Though sick with defeat, Bernabéu would later admit, *"If it had to be anyone, then I am glad it was them."*

The Manchester United dressing room, whilst hectic and joyful, was also awash with tears of relief and sadness. Matt Busby sat quietly. He was crying. Despite all attempts to console him Busby was heartbroken. *"I can't help it,"* he sobbed, *"I just can't help it."* He was embraced by a similarly distraught Bobby Charlton and Bill Foulkes; three survivors together, now so close to a journey's end that at times had been too painful to bear. The next day, on arriving back in Manchester, Busby was mobbed by the press within moments of disembarking and asked his thoughts on finally reaching the European Cup final. A still emotional United manger, his feelings in turmoil but knowing he was expected to deliver a triumphal victory line, declared with a beaming smile, *"In the immortal words of the great Satchmo, (Louis Armstrong), it's a wonderful world!"*

THE BOYS OF '68

It was the morning of Wednesday 29th May 1968 and across Manchester special masses were being prepared. The countless Mancunian priests who received free season tickets from Matt Busby, were having favours called in as they were expected to play their part in United's attempt to overcome Benfica. Their task; to call on an ever higher force to create a deflection, a gust of wind or in desperate needs maybe even a bolt of lightning to bring the cup home.

Candles were lit, prayers whispered and rosary beads clasped tight. A ten year odyssey in which they had staggered and stumbled, only to always get back on their feet, finally neared its end. A footballing redemption set to deliver them from the living nightmare of Munich. In the name of the father and of the son and of the holy…Please, please let Manchester United beat the hell out of the Portuguese and win the European Cup.

Lord graciously hear us…

Two weeks after the second leg in Madrid, United headed south by train to deepest Surrey. They stayed at *Great Fosters*, a historical country Manor hidden away in Egham where it was alleged Queen Elizabeth I was said to meet her secret lovers. The United players joked that it was lucky for her that George Best was not around at the time!

The team were heartened to receive news that a win bonus of £1000 per man would be paid to beat Benfica. Confidence was high; surely after coming so far, they would not blow it now? *"Their hearts are ready that is the most important thing,"* Busby commented on the eve of the final. He appeared completely at ease and ready for whatever fate and Benfica had ready to throw at his football club. There was much talk that the real final for United had been the second leg against Real but such chatter was quickly dismissed by Busby, for he knew Benfica were not just coming to Wembley as extras in the bigger picture of a glorious Manchester United victory. There was no script, no guarantee. They were in London to win. The Portuguese had never beaten United in European competition and the 5-1 thrashing in the *Stadium of Light* still cut deep.

What finer place to bury the demons of that infamous night for the *Eagles* two years before when they suffered such humiliation in front of their own supporters, than to return the medicine at the grand old home of English football. In the intense build up to the final, legendary Benfica captain Mario Coluna made it his personal mission to remind team-mates of the indignation and criticism following the aftermath of that debacle. Revenge was in the air.

Though not the ferocious force of past campaigns, Benfica remained a potent threat and capable on their day of taking apart the very best. Among their ranks were some of the finest players in Europe: the class and finishing ability of the huge centre-forward Jose Torres, the fast and explosive Antonio Simões and Jose Augusto on the flanks and the guile and sheer presence of the inspirational Mario Coluna. Then there was the player United fans feared more than any. Ready to be unleashed again upon Busby's team was the truly magnificent talent of the *Panther,* the kid born under the Mozambique stars was coming to get them. Given an inch, Eusebio could destroy United on his own and the job of suppressing this phenomenon fell once more to twenty-eight year old Norbert Peter Stiles. Collyhurst's finest, he was an unlikely looking hitman yet upon his slim shoulders rested United's hopes.

Stiles had enjoyed considerable success against Eusebio for England in the World Cup semi-final with his streetwise concoction of Mancunian nous and superb defensive awareness. By fair means and the odd foul he kept the lid on the great Portuguese superstar. Stiles was not adverse to bending the rules and occasionally breaking them completely. Yet despite the public perception of Stiles as being nothing more than a short sighted, toothless hatchet-man with limited talent, the specialist man-marking was a job requiring intelligence, tenacity, speed, tactical awareness and no little skill. It was testament to Stiles that both England manager Sir Alf Ramsey and Matt Busby viewed him as an integral part of their successful teams. Moreover, Nobby Stiles previous battles with Eusebio were memorable for the sporting manner in which both went about trying to outwit the other.

During training Matt Busby and Jimmy Murphy would pull Stiles aside many times to drill into him the importance of not letting Eusebio get a shot off on his dynamite right foot. Keep him on his left, shackle and harass, cut off his supply. To quote Murphy: *"Don't let that bastard breathe!"* Nobby had form for this particular task and Busby was supremely confident Eusebio would be snared. Nobby was no longer the broken hearted young apprentice who had cleaned out the playing skip when it returned from Munich with tears stinging his eyes; the Belgrade mud still fresh on the kit from those that perished. Stiles was given Eddie Colman's boots for a keep-sake – there was little doubt who would be in Nobby's mind when the final kicked off.

In the days leading up to Wembley, George Best was named English Football Writers' Player of the Year. He was the youngest ever recipient of the trophy. For Best, whose Northern Irish blood meant he was denied the opportunity to ply his remarkable talent at international level in the World Cup, the opportunity of playing in the European Cup final was the pinnacle. Feared hugely by Benfica after his masterful display in Lisbon, Best knew he would by targeted by Portuguese defenders intent on ensuring history was not repeated. But such was his self belief and desperation to be recognised as a world star: to ensure adoration on the beaches of Rio and across the planet, the *29th May 1968* had to be the day when George Best proved he was good enough to stand alongside the likes of Pele and Eusebio.

Sadly for another of the Old Trafford terrace idols, a much worse fate had conspired against him. After an endless onslaught of pain-killing injections, strappings and stitches, Denis Law's knee gave up and three days before the final he was admitted to St Joseph's Hospital in Whalley Range, Manchester for an operation. There the surgeon removed a one and a half inch piece of damaged cartilage and for the first time in three years Law was pain free. That season Denis contributed seven goals in twenty-three league appearances despite almost constant agony. He mustered a further two in three European matches. Though rushed back by Busby to play in the first leg of the semi against Real, it was a gamble that failed and come the return leg Law was taken to Madrid for purely psychological purposes. It was clear then that should United make the final, Law's chances of playing were minimal. Instead he would watch his team-mates' day of destiny in the relative comfort of a hospital bed, surrounded by close friends, sister-nuns and doctors, all wearing United rosettes. And with copious amounts of alcohol nearby should the need arise!

For one young man it was a birthday like no other. On the *29th May* Brian Kidd would be nineteen years old. Unlike other lads of his own age, Kidd would not be celebrating down the local pub with a few friends but in full view of 100,000 people singing *"Happy Birthday"* to a boy living just a short bus ride from Old Trafford. Kidd came from a family of reds and blues, his father was a City supporter whilst Brian's brother Jimmy was a United fanatic. Jimmy would be watching and praying on the terraces praying that *"Our Brian"* would have the night of his young life and help United finally lift the coveted trophy. From Saint Patrick's Livesy Street to Wembley's field of dreams, Brian Kidd was set to enter Manchester United folklore.

And then there were two. Bobby Charlton and Bill Foulkes

– ten seasons on from surviving the catastrophe of Munich – now stood ninety minutes away from finally honouring the lives and deaths of their lost pals. Never men to talk about such feelings, instead they spoke through their actions in a red shirt. For Charlton and Foulkes, defeat to Benfica was simply not an option as they prepared to give everything they had left and more. Too much pain and sorrow had passed. The Portuguese would be respected, but they would also be beaten. The best of times, the worst of times. It was time to come full circle.

From Manchester they came by train, car and coach in their tens of thousands. An estimated 80,000 of the 100,000 capacity crowd were said to have travelled south. A religious pilgrimage with the motto, *"Thou shalt not fail!"* Matt Busby's red and white army would ensure their team received rapturous support. London was daubed red, the sounds and colour of the expectant Mancunians filling every watering hole near Wembley stadium. The club had also invited the families of the Munich victims as honoured guests. There to witness with their own eyes an appropriate end to what their boys had begun. Twenty four parents, wives and team-mates from the crash including Harry Gregg, Jackie Blanchflower, Johnny Berry and Albert Scanlon. No doubt *Roger Byrne, Geoff Bent, Mark Jones, Eddie Colman, David Pegg, Liam Whelan, Tommy Taylor and Duncan Edwards* would also be there, cheering louder than any if Benfica were overcome.

It was the end of a ten year journey in which the club had stumbled so many times, but always kept going. Ever onwards; driven, incessant, never daring to look back to the image of the stricken fuselage and the bodies of the fallen. The 1968 European cup final would not be played for glory, fame or prestige but for the memory of the *Busby Babes* and the only proper memorial to their passing.

The boys of '68 daren't let them down.

BEYOND MUNICH

A decade had passed before Matt Busby had managed to lead Manchester United to within touching distance of the European Cup. But with the score at 1-1 and only three minutes remaining those emotions were lost on the Portuguese champions. Sensing a sensational victory they went for United's wilting defence with a vengeance. Convinced fellow defender Bill Foulkes was covering behind him, Eusebio's man-marker Nobby Stiles moved to intercept Benfica winger Antonio Simões pass, only to realise with horror that Foulkes was out of position and the Panther had sprung free! A wonderful pass by Simões left Eusebio in the clear – he only had to pick his spot from twelve yards to win a third European cup for Benfica. Always one for the spectacular he took aim and prepared to break Manchester United hearts...

The 1968 European Cup final:
Manchester United v Benfica:
Wednesday 29th May 1968:

The Teams:
Manchester United: *Stepney: Brennan: Dunne: Crerand: Foulkes: Stiles: Best: Kidd: Charlton: Sadler and Aston*
Benfica: *Henrique: Adolfo: Humberto: Jacinto: Cruz: Graca: Coluna: Augusto: Torres: Eusebio and Simões*

Wembley stadium had witnessed so many magnificent dramas and there had been none more dramatic or tense than the 1966 World Cup final. But as

Manchester United and Benfica prepared to do battle in the 1968 European Cup final, this grand old stadium threatened to explode with emotion and excitement. The teams came into view to be greeted by a raging sea of red and white flags and banners. The welcome that thundered out from the terraces produced a cacophony of noise; a symphony for the fallen. A deafening, throaty, lustful scream, almost primeval in its longing for the night to go well. A defiant roar to tell the world we are still here.

Led by captains Bobby Charlton and Mario Coluna, the teams made their way onto the field. United, resplendent in white tracksuit tops with an away change of all blue strip beneath, Benfica in white. The referee was the flamboyant, well-known Sicilian, Concerto Lo Bello. Smiling for the watching world-wide audience, Lo Bello strode imperiously before the teams, basking in his moment of glory. An estimated 250 million people around the globe were tuning in.

Suddenly the crowd broke into a wonderful rendition of *"Happy Birthday"* for Brian Kidd. It was a magical moment for the youngster, one he could happily take to the grave. Lo Bello called the captains together in the centre-circle where they exchanged handshakes and pendants. Charlton and Coluna shared a quiet word. Idolised by the Benfica supporters, the thirty-three year old Coluna, nicknamed *O Monstro Sagrado (The Sacred Monster)* was playing his fiftieth game in the European Cup. A great respect had developed over the years between he and Charlton, men whose paths had crossed many times for club and country.

Seconds before United kicked off, Eusebio raced into the centre-circle to shake hands with Charlton. It was a gesture typical of Benfica's number ten. Then as Wembley held its breath, the game began. United opened brightly with left-winger John Aston taking on and beating Portuguese right full-back Adolfo Calisto. It was a taste of what was to follow from Aston who was to give the unfortunate Adolfo nightmares and an evening under the London stars he would never forget.

George Best was targeted early by Benfica when left-back Fernando Cruz and centre- half Jacinto Santos combined to bring the Irishman to ground. Best reacted with a few choice words in Cruz's direction when he went to catch him with a sly raised elbow. Portuguese intentions were clear – they did not intend to take prisoners.

The first chance for United came from a Paddy Crerand free kick that David Sadler failed by inches to control from six yards, though this apart it was cat and mouse. Neither dared risk all for fear of being caught on the break. Nerves took hold, only the direct running of the flying John Aston carried any real attacking intent on either side, as he took on and beat Adolfo at every attempt. The cries of "Johnny Aston" rang out from the United supporters, it was rare acclaim for someone who had been scapegoated all too often by United fans.

On ten minutes Nobby Stiles introduced himself once more to Eusebio with a double lunge. The first just below his waist, the second knee high. Lo Bello sprinted in with whistle in mouth warning Stiles no more. United's number six backed away with a comical look of remorse etched upon his face. From the resulting free kick the fuming Eusebio smashed the ball high over Alex Stepney's crossbar, much to the delight of the massed ranks of United fans behind the goal who goaded the great one. Two minutes later George Best carelessly lost possession and the ball fell at the feet of a still outraged Eusebio. Stiles again flew in with a cynical tackle but was this time left sprawling as on went the *Panther* in full flow towards the United penalty area. As if to prove a point he unleashed a vicious swerving shot that crashed violently against Stepney's bar and rebounded to safety. Thirty-six goals in thirty-eight European cup games meant it not wise to mock such genius.

United hit back, and should have taken the lead when Kidd's wonderfully timed through ball split Benfica's central defenders for David Sadler again to run onto and shoot, only to pull the ball horribly wide from just eight yards. The groans of disappointment from the terraces told their own story, for these were heaven-sent opportunities that United could ill afford to squander.

Overall the first half was a dour, drab affair, littered with mistakes and with defences well on top. Aston's personal duel with Adolfo was the exception, otherwise negativity ruled. The exquisite threat of George Best snuffed out by any number of Portuguese white shirts queuing to eagerly kick the Belfast Boy back across the Irish Sea at every given opportunity.

Meanwhile Nobby Stiles, with an impressive if grim enthusiasm and ruthless professionalism, had got on top of his charge and was winning his personal battle with the *Panther* hands down. The piercing shrill of Concerto Lo Bello's whistle for half- time brought proceedings to a temporary halt and rather surprisingly there were a few boos from a frustrated crowd. It had been a sparse contest, lacking the attacking football anticipated. However what it lacked in quality was made up for in drama. As a nervous applause accompanied both teams back down the Wembley tunnel, a knife could slice the tension-racked London air. Mancunian expectations were being re-assessed as the wildly optimistic had received a dose of reality. Benfica were not about to roll over.

Under orders from Matt Busby, United began after the interval at a much faster pace as crosses a-plenty flew with intent into Benfica's penalty area. Busby's pre-match belief that the Portuguese would struggle to cope with pace looked to be coming to fruition, as Aston continued to flourish and Best was now beginning to have an impact from wide positions. Suddenly the noise level lifted a notch and belief was restored among the red hordes.

Eight minutes into the second half it reached volcanic proportions when a menacing cross from David Sadler found a leaping Bobby Charlton who, with deadly intent, directed a stunning header past goalkeeper Henrique into the far corner. Charlton raced away with arms raised to be mobbed by a sea of blue shirts. United led and Wembley ignited with joy! Off the bench came Matt Busby and Jimmy Murphy as celebrations ran wild across the stadium.

Looking to kill the game off, Paddy Crerand stole possession straight from the re-start and played in George Best who ran through and flicked a sublime finish over a stranded Henrique only to be called offside by an eagle-eyed Lo Bello. Benfica were rocked, another for United would surely end the contest. Still the blue shirts came forward, the pressure relentless. On the hour an electrifying Best again latched onto a terrible error by Cruz to race through with just Henrique to beat. Knowing it was game over if he was beaten, the goalkeeper kept his calm and foiled the Irishman. Somehow Benfica were still alive as the 1968 European Cup final entered a dramatic final quarter. A renewed sense of urgency, or was it panic, surged through the Portuguese ranks. This night too bore historical references for Benfica. A third European triumph in eight years would be some achievement but it was Crerand and now more than ever Bobby Charlton controlling the tempo of the match. Always one eye on the clock, just see it home make no mistakes.

The Portuguese champions attacked, their passes aiming for the head of the giant Torres. His knockdowns were anticipated then cleared by Bill Foulkes who had marshalled the United rearguard superbly. Benfica came again; eleven minutes remained when the heavens crashed in on Manchester United. Jose Augustos' long cross was headed down with great precision by the 6'4 Torres, for the onrushing midfielder Jaime Graca to shoot low past Alex Stepney from eight yards and break Mancunian hearts. Wembley was shaken. The Portuguese contingent present let loose their emotions. Bobby Charlton remembers the sickening feeling in his stomach as the ball hit the net, *"It was my worse nightmare. I couldn't see him missing and he didn't."*

Written off from the start, Benfica now looked favourites. Matt Busby watched on as if sat waiting for the inevitable. His team looked shattered as the *Eagles* soared. Sensing a truly remarkable winner, Benfica went all out to bury this myth perceived by the English that all Manchester United had to do was turn up and win the final. Eusebio probed, looking for gaps where previously none had existed in a now porous United defence. He sprinted across the halfway line, leaving a weary Stiles in his wake, only for Tony Dunne to cover a relieved team-mate but the *Panther* was loose, uncaged. Then a rare foray forward from Mario Coluna who, belying his thirty-three years, sprinted past Shay Brennan and crossed for Jose Torres to leap high, but luckily for Manchester United and Stepney he headed over the bar. Again Eusebio threatened. Midway inside the United half and surrounded by four blue shirts, a swift thinking one-two with Torres saw him roar clear before running on and letting fly a tremendous drive straight into a grateful Alex Stepney's midriff.

The United supporters once more held their breath, they could not take much more and implored their team to simply play the ball forward rather than just keeping hold.

Finally the crowd's wish was granted as Paddy Crerand's long pass found Bobby Charlton on the edge of Benfica's penalty area. However a fine challenge from Humberto robbed Charlton and Antonio Simões sprinted away towards the halfway line. Convinced fellow defender Bill Foulkes stood covering behind him, Eusebio's jailer Nobby Stiles moved to intercept the Benfica winger, only to realise with horror that Foulkes was out of position and the *Panther* had gone. From a wonderful pass by Simões, Eusebio just had to pick a spot from twelve yards past Alex Stepney and win a magnificent third European cup for Benfica - Wembley watched aghast as Eusebio fired goal wards.

Matt Busby shut his eyes. The search for redemption was surely set to continue. Unbelievably he shot with his weaker left foot straight at Stepney, who held on to the ball and earned the gratitude of every Manchester United supporter forever more. Ever the sportsman, Eusebio attempted to congratulate the goalkeeper on his courageous save but Stepney gave him short shrift, waving away the Portuguese striker. "*I smothered the shot and felt the ball go soft. It either burst when he hit it or when it hit me, either way it took away some of the sting. But the marks are still there, and I've had Mitre written on my chest ever since!"*

Still Benfica looked for a killer goal as they massed with deadly intent and encamped around the United penalty area. From the wings came the *Eagles* as Augusto's cross was met superbly by Eusebio's header that flew within an angel's breath of winning the day for the Portuguese. With time almost up United broke out.

Best darted through Benfica's defence only to be run wide of goal before firing into a relieved Henrique's side-netting. Disappointment and anxiety etched with excitement engulfed Wembley stadium as Concerto Lo Bello blew for full time. It finished 1-1 and another thirty minutes on an unbelievably humid and sweltering Wembley evening awaited the two teams. All but out on their feet, Nobby Stiles later admitted *"we were spent and another ten minutes they would have beaten us."*

Busby and Murphy walked amongst their Players, urging and cajoling. Some of the United lads noticed that the Portuguese appeared more worse for wear than them. It was a point reinforced by their manager, *"They're finished,"* he said, *"You're throwing the game away. Keep possession, get the ball to George and Johnny and start attacking."* Now in the final straight with the finishing line so close Busby would trust his footballing principles and three minutes into extra time Manchester United were back in front.

A long clearance from Alex Stepney was flicked on by Brian Kidd into the Benfica half. Just when Cruz looked in control of the ball it was taken off him by George Best who raced twenty-five yards into the penalty area, dummied Jose Henrique and twisted left before rolling the ball home as a desperate goalkeeper dived in vain. Rehearsed on Belfast's cobbled streets then performed to a world-wide audience – now they knew his name! In a career that from this moment would start to diminish, Best's wonderful individual effort proved to be the defining image of arguably Manchester United's greatest ever player.

What should have been a glorious beginning later turned into George Best's epitaph. But on *29th May 1968,* as Wembley stadium exploded once more and a beaming Best fell into the arms of joyful team-mates, it felt like *Georgie Boy* would live forever.

Now United went for Benfica's throats. A revitalised Bobby Charlton fed the amazing John Aston who simply pushed the ball past the beleaguered Adolfo and ran the entire length of the Portuguese half before finally being brought to ground at the expense of a corner. The words unsung hero seemed to have been invented for the magnificent Aston.

Across ran Charlton to huge applause from the United supporters. His right foot delivery swung over toward a melee of bodies; reacting quickest Brian Kidd turned in a close range header that was bravely blocked by a flailing Henrique, before the birthday boy forced home the rebound, arcing his effort over the prone goalkeeper and into the goal. From the heaving, dancing terraces a torrent of noise greeted Kidd's goal. It was a joyful awe-inspiring crescendo. The red half of Manchester knew their team were almost there. As Wembley saluted the nineteen-year old Kidd, a brave but surely beaten Benfica looked dead on their feet. Charlton again, *"When that ball went in I had to fight back the tears because I knew it was all over. Benfica had gone. We just had to guard against stupidity and we had finally won this thing."*

Straight from the re-start Aston careered once more over the halfway line before finding George Best wide on the right. Racing into the Portuguese penalty area Best's astute clip bounced off the Portuguese crossbar and away. United were rampant! Playing to Busby's instructions Paddy Crerand and Bobby Charlton kept the ball. Teasing the exhausted Benfica players, their hearts and legs equally shattered.

On ninety-nine minutes United roared forward again as Bobby Charlton with socks down around his ankles fed a raiding Brian Kidd to sprint down the touchline. Off soared the long-legged youngster before placing a perfect cross onto the right foot of a waiting Charlton, the boy on whose slim shoulders the hopes and dreams of every United supporter had rested since Munich. Charlton swept a majestic effort past Henrique into the top corner. Years later an emotional Charlton related: *"That was for Dunc and the boys. My pals."*

With such grace and artistry the European cup was won.

First to congratulate Bobby Charlton was George Best who jumped into his arms. Both men were quickly joined by ecstatic team-mates. Up came a laughing Crerand to embrace Charlton who gestured to his Scottish colleague, *"That's it. It's over."* Lo Bello blew to end the first period of extra time and Manchester had simply blown away Benfica. Fifteen minutes of blistering attacking football had been dragged from who knows where when they appeared to have nothing left. The Wembley crowd were on their feet. A sense of wonder and disbelief filled the ranks.

Again Matt Busby and Jimmy Murphy implored their players to keep the ball. Murphy stood over Bobby Charlton massaging his legs. The shy young kid from the north east who arrived at Old Trafford and was meted out for special attention by Murphy, who knew that here was a truly, exceptional footballer. Murphy had knocked off the rough edges and polished up the rest and Charlton's two superb goals on that long gone Wembley evening epitomised everything 'The Preacher' believed.

"We shall not be moved," sang the crowd.

At the final whistle, amid a hub of well-wishers, a beaming Matt Busby strode onto the pitch. Trying desperately to fight away the tears and keep his composure, Busby headed towards the centre circle to sportingly shake hands with the forlorn Benfica players. However his path was cut short when a crying Bobby Charlton fell into his arms and the pair embraced. No words were necessary. This was the best of times.

Avoiding the mad huddle of cameras and flashlights exploding all around walked Jimmy Murphy. Never one for the spotlight, this proud Welshman stood content in the knowledge that it had really not all been for nothing. Munich would never go away but for one night the pain would ease, his boys could salute a job done well. It was a victory earned the Manchester United way. First you raise spirits, then you break hearts. Then you rise again and prevail. A wink to the stars and the fallen and Jimmy Murphy vacated the stage.

So the time came for the presentation and the United players, Paddy Crerand foremost amongst them, tried desperately to persuade Matt Busby to go and raise the famous trophy high. Two years had passed since Crerand had talked his manager out of retirement in the dressing room after the bitter defeat to Partizan Belgrade, it felt like a lifetime. However all efforts were in vain as Busby refused point-blank and instead insisted his captain Bobby Charlton be first up the Wembley steps to collect the Holy Grail.

On being handed the trophy a smiling Charlton lifted it into the air and Wembley erupted! Looking drained and close to collapse he made his weary way back down. It was to be a strange night for Bobby Charlton whose thoughts even today never appear to be far away from those dear friends he had lost in the crash.

To them went the glory and spoils of victory. A man who has dedicated almost his entire life to Manchester United, and for whom a piece of his heart will remain forever on a far off German runway.

In the celebrations that followed one of the first telegrams arriving to congratulate Matt Busby and United on finally winning the European Cup came from an old friend. It was post marked Madrid.

"To a wonderful football man and club. Real Madrid toast your great success. Don Santiago Bernabéu"

As for Busby it is only apt to end with a line from the novel on whose title this book has gratefully borrowed:

"I wish you to know that you have *been the last dream of my soul."*

INDEX